INCLUSION FOR ALL:
THE UN CONVENTION ON THE RIGHTS
OF PERSONS WITH DISABILITIES

INCLUSION FOR ALL:
THE UN CONVENTION ON THE RIGHTS
OF PERSONS WITH DISABILITIES

Deborah A. Ziegler, editor

international debate education association

New York & Amsterdam

Published by
The International Debate Education Association
400 West 59th Street
New York, NY 10019

Library of Congress Cataloging-in-Publication Data

Inclusion for ALL : the UN Convention on the Rights of Persons with Disabilities / Deborah A. Ziegler, editor.
    p. cm.
 ISBN 978-1-932716-79-5
1. People with disabilities--Government policy. 2. Human rights. I.
Ziegler, Deborah A. II. International Debate Education Association.
 HV1568.I56 2010
 323.3--dc22

                        2010014750

Design by Kathleen Hayes
Printed in the USA

 IDEBATE PRESS

Contents

Introduction   1

Chapter 1: Understanding Human Rights.   7

A Brief Introduction to Human Rights *by Save the Children*.   9

Disability Rights in the USA and Abroad *by Robert L. Burgdorf, Jr.*. . .   12

'Nothing About Us Without Us': Recognizing the Rights of
People With Disabilities *by United Nations Publications*   17

Chapter 2: Advocating for Inclusion.   23

Early Childhood Inclusion: A Joint Position Statement *by the
Division for Early Childhood of the Council for Exceptional
Children and the National Association for the Education of
Young Children*.   26

The Council for Exceptional Children Policy on Inclusive
Schools and Community Settings *by the Council for Exceptional
Children*   34

Children with Intellectual Disabilities and Their Families: A
Position Paper of Inclusion Europe *by Inclusion Europe*   37

Autism and Inclusion *by Autism Europe*.   43

Position Statement on Inclusion *by The Arc and the American
Association on Intellectual and Developmental Disabilities*.   46

Chapter 3: Understanding the United Nations Convention on the Rights of Persons with Disabilities 49

Lauding Disability Convention as 'Dawn of a New Era,' UN Urges Speedy Ratification *by UN News Centre* 51

Convention on the Rights of Persons with Disabilities: Questions and Answers *by United Nations Enable* 54

Finding the Gaps: A Comparative Analysis of Disability Laws in the United States to the United Nations Convention on the Rights of Persons with Disabilities (CRPD) *by the National Council on Disability* 74

Chapter 4: Honoring Family Cultures and Values 83

Responsiveness to Family, Culture, Values and Education *by the Division for Early Childhood, Council for Exceptional Children* 85

The Effects of Culture on Special Education Services: Evil Eyes, Prayer Meetings, and IEPs *by Suzanne Lamorey* 104

Chapter 5: Reducing Poverty and Social Exclusion 117

Including Persons with Disabilities in Development: Opportunities and Accessibility *by Iqbal Kaur* 119

Mainstreaming the Rights of Persons with Disabilities in National Development Frameworks *by Teresa Njoroge Mwendwa, Ambrose Murangira, and Raymond Lang* 126

Chapter 6: Guaranteeing Deinstitutionalization 147

Torment not Treatment: Serbia's Segregation and Abuse of Children and Adults with Disabilities *by Mental Disability Rights International* 149

Keeping Children Out of Harmful Institutions: Why We Should Be Investing in Family-Based Care *by Save the Children* 158

Supreme Court Upholds ADA 'Integration Mandate' in Olmstead Decision *by The Center for An Accessible Society* 162

Recommendation CM/Rec(2010)2 of the Committee of
Ministers to Member States on Deinstitutionalisation and
Community Living of Children with Disabilities *by the Council
of Europe* 168

Chapter 7: Advancing Education 185

A Context Ripe for Change: The 1980s *by James McLeskey* 187

Teacher Attitudes Toward Inclusion *by Nancy L. Waldron* 198

Reflecting on Teacher Attitudes *by Nancy L. Waldron* 201

Inclusive Education: Moving from Words to Deeds *by the
European Disability Forum*.. 209

Chapter 8: Supporting Independent Living 227

Deinstitutionalisation and Community Living—Outcomes and
Costs: Report of a European Study *by Jim Mansell, Martin
Knapp, Julie Beadle-Brown and Jeni Beecham*...................... 229

ENIL Research Paper on Community Living and the Support of
Independent Living for the Disabled Women, Men and
Children of Europe *by the European Network on Independent
Living* 252

The State of Housing in America in the 21st Century: A
Disability Perspective *by the National Council on Disability* 268

Chapter 9: Accessing Employment 281

The Difference a Job Makes: The Effects of Employment among
People with Disabilities *by Lisa Schur* 283

Overview—Supreme Court Ruling in *Alabama v. Garrett by the
National Association of Protection and Advocacy Systems* 296

The Applicability of the ADA to Personal Assistance Services in
the Workplace *by Robert Silverstein* 298

Chapter 10: Ensuring Self-Determination 309

Self-Determination: Position Statement *by The Arc and the
American Association of Intellectual and Developmental
Disabilities* 311

Self-Determination and the Education of Students with
Disabilities *by Michael Wehmeyer* 314

Promoting the Self-Determination of Students with Severe
Disabilities *by Michael Wehmeyer* 321

Leadership by People with Disabilities in Self-Determination
Systems Change *by Laurie E. Powers, Nancy Ward, Lisa Ferris,
Tia Nelis, Michael Ward, Colleen Wieck, and Tamar Heller* 328

Convention on the Rights of Persons with Disabilities 351

Introduction

For the 650 million people with disabilities worldwide, the adoption of the UN Convention on the Rights of Persons with Disabilities on December 13, 2006, was a landmark. People with disabilities are the world's largest minority; approximately 10 percent of the world's population has been identified as having a disability. This population has been discriminated against for centuries, often lives in poverty, and is the most disadvantaged among all minorities—experiencing the most extreme lack of access to education, opportunities for independent living, and employment.

According to UNESCO, 90 percent of children with disabilities in developing countries have no access to school; the International Labour Organization reports that in some countries the unemployment rate of adults with disabilities is as high as 80 percent. Although the exact number of people with disabilities living in institutions cannot be determined, evidence suggests that hundreds of thousands continue to experience substandard institutional conditions—without therapeutic and rehabilitative services, with threats of physical and sexual abuse, and sometimes coerced by physical restraints. Many residents are held against their will with no hope of due process or of being able to live freely as contributing members of society.

In the face of such conditions, the Convention is a vital, new treaty for the advancement of rights of and opportunities for people with disabilities. It represents the culmination of an unprecedented global exchange of ideas about the universal rights of people with disabilities and seeks to empower individuals with disabilities to achieve economic self-sufficiency, independent living, and integration and inclusion into all aspects of society. The Convention, which serves to advance an ideal vision of disability policy and practice, is a beacon to people around the world.

The Convention establishes international standards about the rights and freedoms of people with disabilities and a common basis for greater civic and political participation and self-sufficiency. It reflects certain core values and principles: dignity of the individual; access to justice; importance of family decision making; and access to education, independent living, and employment. These standards carry a moral authority that lends weight and credibility to efforts worldwide. This Convention creates an unprecedented vision for global democracy and human rights. States that sign and ratify the Convention are legally bound to provide services and supports to persons with disabilities and will no longer be able to discriminate against them in any manner. The UN News Centre described the important role the Convention plays in international human rights law:

> Filling a gap in international human rights law, the 50 article Convention elaborates in detail the rights of persons with disabilities. It covers, among others, civil and political rights, accessibility, participation and inclusion, the right to education, health, work and employment and social protection. Importantly, the Convention recognizes that a change of attitude in society is necessary if persons with disabilities are to achieve equal status. (UN News Centre, 2006)

Currently, 144 states have signed the Convention, and of these states, 84 have ratified the Convention. States that ratify the Convention must promulgate corresponding implementing legislation in order to meet their legal obligations. The United States, an international leader in disability policy and practice, is among those who have not ratified the Convention. However, legislation alone is insufficient to ensure effective implementation of the Convention;

to bring to fruition the real hope the Convention embodies, the attitudes of both the general public and government must change. The perception of people with disabilities as objects of assistance and intervention needs to change to the recognition that they are individuals with rights.

This book provides a historical perspective on human rights; the critical nature of inclusion; the Convention provisions; the necessity of honoring family culture and values; the need for reducing poverty and social exclusion; the imperative to deinstitutionalize; the importance of providing adequate education; and the importance of enabling independent living, employment, and self-determination. Although this book does not address all 50 articles of the Convention, it discusses those provisions of the Convention that are priority areas for implementation.

Whether programs for people with disabilities should be provided is not a research issue, it is a social and moral imperative. Uniformly, research demonstrates that early intervention programs improve the lives of individuals with disabilities. Even stronger is the social and moral obligation to foster the development of people with disabilities in the earliest years of life.

In his closing statement at a speech delivered at the National Early Childhood Conference on Children with Special Needs, in Denver, Colorado, on October 8, 1985, Nicholas J. Anastasiow, an early intervention researcher summarized this concept:

> I believe that these research data and the data from the efficacy studies are sufficient to pursue vigorously the continuation and expansion of service to all children. I recently read what Einstein wrote for the time capsule in the 1930's. "Dear Posterity, If you have not become more just, peaceful, and generally more rational than we are (or were)—why then, the devil take" (Seyen, 1985). If Einstein had been a special educator, he might have written: "Dear Posterity, If you have not continued and increased service of impaired infants, children, and their families and reduced the numbers of high-risk infants due to the intensity and poverty and not become more rational and loving than we are, then the

devil take you." I believe we should follow John Dewey's advice when he wrote: "What the best and wisest parent wants for his own child that must be what the community wants for all its children. Any other ideal for our society is narrow and unlovely; acted upon it destroys our democracy." (Grubb & Lazerson, 1982, 43)

Professionals and advocates serving people with disabilities must guard against defending the wrong question. They do not need to respond to the "should" question. They do not need to defend why persons with disabilities need to be served. The real research questions to be asked are: How do we deliver services better, with what materials, and in what setting?

The Convention offers great promise for people with disabilities and a significant challenge to states to answer these essential questions. To comply with the Convention, public resources must be directed toward programs and policies and legislation must establish the right to services for all people with disabilities. This will require states to provide programs and services consistently from year to year and ensure, through law, the right of these services to exist. Finally, states must provide fiscal resources and set high standards for the provision of services.

Well-articulated policy and legislation are required worldwide to ensure that people with disabilities are considered to be individuals with rights, to support family strengths, to ensure fairness in access to high-quality services, and to make wide use of limited resources. Legislation mandating services for people with disabilities is only the first step on the road to ensuring that all people with disabilities receive the help that will enable them to develop to their full capacity.

States are also responsible to assure meaningful inclusion in society of people with disabilities and to hold those who use public funds accountable for the quality and cost effectiveness of these programs. Policy and legislation that require states to establish appropriate administrative systems and enforce appropriate safeguards and standards are the only way to equal opportunity and inclusion. Indeed, only this will allow people with disabilities to become full citizens and contributing members of society.

To move this bold public policy agenda forward and meet the requirements of the Convention, the entire global community must embrace the inclusion of all people with disabilities and advocate on their behalf. As an important step in the right direction, nongovernmental organizations (NGOs), for the first time, actively participated in the formulation of a human rights instrument during the passage of the UN Convention on the Rights of Persons with Disabilities. Chapter 2 discusses the critical role of NGOs and associations in influencing policy and practice. Advocacy is one of the most powerful ways to ensure that the rights of people with disabilities are supported and strengthened. Advocacy efforts will need to continue to support or defend the cause and persuade other like-minded individuals, organizations, and coalitions to support the cause. Vigorous grassroots advocacy will be needed—focusing on creating, modifying, implementing, and enforcing specific public policies to meet the requirements in the Convention.

In some democratic societies, systems of law were created to protect the individual from the abuses of society, particularly from abuses of the government agencies established by society to serve its needs. In an attempt to provide what appear to be needed services, the rights of the individual may be overlooked. Consequently, constant vigilance on the part of all persons engaged in the provision of services to people with disabilities is necessary to assure that the rights of these individuals and their families are understood and honored. As civil societies we have the incredible opportunity and immense responsibility to share our experience and expertise to put disability law into practice, with the resulting positive effect on people's lives. Adopting the UN Convention on the Rights of Persons with Disabilities is a bold step toward the goal of including all people with disabilities in full participation in society and governance. It is hoped that the reader will embrace the goal of inclusion for all and join the advocacy movement to ensure the rights of people with disabilities.

REFERENCES

Grubb, W. Norton, and Marvin Lazerson. *Broken Promises: How Americans Fail Their Children.* New York: Basic Books, 1982.

Sayen, Jamie. *Einstein in America: The Scientist's Conscience in the Age of Hitler and Hiroshima.* New York: Crown, 1985.

UN News Centre. "Lauding Disability Convention as 'Dawn of a New Era,' UN Urges Speedy Ratification." Press release, December 13, 2006.

CHAPTER 1:

Understanding Human Rights

Chapter 1 focuses on the human rights of the disabled—the core of the UN Convention on the Rights of Persons with Disabilities (CRPD). Human rights are the basic rights and freedoms to which all humans are entitled, often held to include the right to life and liberty, freedom of thought and expression, and equality before the law. Freedom from arbitrary interference or restrictions by governments is basic to human rights.

The CRPD guarantees that persons with disability are equal before the law and are entitled to equal protection of the law; it also prohibits discrimination on the ground of disability. It requires states to both ensure effective protection against such discrimination and to ensure the provision of reasonable accommodation.

"A Brief Introduction to Human Rights," by Save the Children, identifies the central features of human rights, including universality and inalienability; indivisibility; interdependence and interrelatedness; and equality and nondiscrimination. The article outlines where human rights are documented and lists key human rights documents related to the CRPD.

"Disability Rights in the USA and Abroad" reviews the status of laws prohibiting discrimination on the basis of disability in the United States and several other countries. It discusses a range of country-specific historical, sociological, political, and cultural factors that influence policies and practices in serving individuals with disabilities that ultimately may result in disability discrimination. The disability nondiscrimination policy in the United States has been largely influenced by the earlier civil rights laws addressing African Americans, women, and other groups. Many other countries have not considered or adopted these guarantees of basic civil rights; accordingly, any implementation of disability nondiscrimination policy and practice will certainly be more difficult and may be impossible without such adoption.

The final article, "'Nothing About Us Without Us': Recognizing the Rights of People with Disabilities," discusses the need for a principle of participation and the integration of persons with disabilities into every aspect of political, social, economic, and cultural life. The article points out that a number of UN core treaties address human rights issues in general but none cover the rights of people with disabilities explicitly. The article assists the reader to understand some of the history of the thinking about disability and human rights that led to the argument for the need of a core treaty that would advance the rights of people with disabilities.

A Brief Introduction to Human Rights

*By Save the Children**

WHAT ARE HUMAN RIGHTS?

Human rights are rights a person has because he or she is a human being. Human rights can also be defined as those basic needs without which people cannot live in dignity. If you violate a person's human rights, you are treating them as less than a human being. Human rights recognise and affirm that the human dignity of all people—and that includes all children—must be respected.

THE CENTRAL FEATURES OF HUMAN RIGHTS

+ **Universality and inalienability**: All people everywhere in the world have human rights. An individual cannot voluntarily give them up. Nor can others take them away from him or her.
+ **Indivisibility**: Human rights are indivisible. Civil, cultural, economic, political and social rights are all fundamental to the dignity of every human being. Consequently, they all have equal status as rights, and cannot be ranked in a hierarchical order.
+ **Interdependence and interrelatedness**: The realisation of one right often depends, wholly or in part, upon the realisation of others. For example, the right to education for children with disabilities can only be fully achieved if other rights are also respected—non-discrimination, freedom from poverty, protection from violence.
+ **Equality and non-discrimination**: All individuals are equal as human beings and are entitled to their human rights without discrimination of any kind.

Where Are Human Rights Documented?

International Systems

Rights for every human being were elaborated in 1948 in the United Nations Universal Declaration of Human Rights (UDHR). Its 30 articles form a comprehensive statement covering economic, social, cultural, political and civil rights. It sets out the fundamental principle that "the inherent dignity and the equal and inalienable rights of all members of the human family are the foundation of freedom, justice, and peace in the world". However, the UDHR is a statement of intent or a set of principles; it is not a legally binding document. Since 1948, therefore, the United Nations (UN) has used the UDHR as the foundation from which to develop a number of human rights treaties (also called conventions or covenants), which translate its principles into legally binding obligations on the countries that ratify them.

The first two human rights treaties were the International Covenant on Civil and Political Rights (ICCPR) and the International Covenant on Economic, Social and Cultural Rights (ICESCR), which were adopted by the UN in 1966. Together with the UDHR, they make up what is known as the International Bill of Rights. Since then, a number of further treaties have been adopted to address the rights of specific groups of people, including women, children, migrant workers, racial minorities and people facing torture. The Convention on the Rights of Persons with Disabilities (CRPD) is the most recent treaty to be adopted.

Regional Systems

Some regions of the world have also developed systems for protecting human rights that serve to strengthen or complement the international system, for example:

+ European Convention for the Protection of Human Rights and Fundamental Freedoms, 1950
+ American Convention on Human Rights, 1978
+ African Charter of Human and People's Rights, 1981

♦ African Charter on the Rights and Welfare of the Child, 1990.

National Systems

Individual countries also have constitutions and laws that guarantee and protect the rights of citizens, including children. These frameworks can serve to introduce international human rights into domestic law, or to set higher standards than those provided in the international treaties. The difference between national laws and human rights treaties is that the latter are universal—they apply to all people everywhere, regardless of their citizenship or where they live.

KEY HUMAN RIGHTS DOCUMENTS

♦ Universal Declaration of Human Rights, 1948
♦ International Covenant on Civil and Political Rights, 1966
♦ International Covenant on Economic, Social and Cultural Rights, 1966
♦ International Convention on the Elimination of all Forms of Racial Discrimination, 1966
♦ Convention on the Elimination of all Forms of Discrimination against Women, 1979
♦ Convention against Torture and Other Cruel, Inhuman or Degrading Treatment or Punishment, 1984
♦ Convention on the Rights of the Child, 1989
♦ Convention on the Rights of Migrant Workers and the Members of their Families, 1990
♦ Convention on the Protection of All Persons from Enforced or Involuntary Disappearances, 2006
♦ Convention on the Rights of Persons with Disabilities, 2006

For full texts of the treaties, go to: http://www.ohchr.org/english/law/index.htm

---

*Save the Children is a nonprofit organization advocating for children's rights and helping children in need in the United States and around the world.

Disability Rights in the USA and Abroad

*By Robert L. Burgdorf, Jr.**

In signing the Americans with Disabilities Act (ADA) into law in 1990, President Bush heralded the new Act as an "historic new civil rights Act ... the world's first comprehensive declaration of equality for people with disabilities." He added that other countries, including Sweden, Japan, the Soviet Union, and each of the twelve member nations of the European Economic Community, had announced their desire to enact similar legislation. The picture of the United States as the accepted leader in guaranteeing civil rights for people with disabilities, with other countries poised to follow the U.S. example, turned out to be only partially accurate. President Bush's rosy predictions have not fully come to pass, and the reality is somewhat more complex than his comments suggested. A variety of historical, sociological, political, and cultural factors unique to each country have resulted in widely differing approaches to disability discrimination.

To be sure, a number of countries have passed laws prohibiting discrimination on the basis of disability since 1990, and the model of the ADA certainly influenced many of these laws. For example, Australia passed a Disability Discrimination Act in 1992, and Great Britain enacted its Disability Discrimination Act in 1995. Each of these laws was affected, to a greater or lesser extent, by the U.S. enactment of the ADA, and borrowed concepts and language from it. The British and Australian laws illustrate, however, that various nations have followed very different paths in passing laws that can be loosely considered "ADA-like."

The Australian Disability Discrimination Act is extremely comprehensive, forceful, and specific. With some accuracy one can describe it as having out-ADAed the ADA. As one concrete example, while the Bush Administration insisted on inserting into the ADA language from the Civil Rights Act of 1964 exempting private clubs, the Australian statute has a specific section prohibiting clubs and associations from discriminating on the grounds of disability.

The British version of a Disability Discrimination Act, in contrast, is much less broad, specific, and substantial than the ADA. Critics have contended that the 1995 statute is too narrow in the range of activities it covers, too restrictive in the scope of persons afforded protection from discrimination, and too watered down in prohibiting acts of discrimination. A prominent civil liberties lawyer, Lord Lester, reportedly described the British Act as "riddled with vague, slippery and elusive exceptions, making it so full of holes that it is more like a colander than a binding code." Whether or not such attacks are fully justified, even a cursory reading of Great Britain's law reveals that it is not nearly as extensive or definitive as its American counterpart.

A few countries had laws prohibiting discrimination on the basis of disability prior to the ADA. A 1982 amendment to the Canadian Charter of Rights and Freedoms made Canada one of the very few nations in which nondiscrimination on the basis of disability is a constitutional right. At the statutory level, the Canadian Human Rights Act has prohibited disability discrimination since 1985. The interpretation and implementation of the Canadian requirements were influenced to a limited degree by regulations and court decisions under a U.S. statute that was a partial predecessor to the ADA—Section 504 of the Rehabilitation Act of 1973. The Canadian courts have proven to be very receptive to the spirit of disability nondiscrimination laws, in contrast to the sometimes technical and wary reactions of some American courts.

In July of 1990, just weeks before the ADA became law in the U.S., France enacted an unusual statute that makes discrimination by an employer against a worker or applicant based on disability or state of health a criminal offense punishable by imprisonment for up to a year and a fine of up to 20,000 Francs. Many other countries, however, have never passed laws prohibiting discrimination on the basis of disability. Of the three countries mentioned explicitly in President Bush's address as having expressed a desire to enact ADA-like legislation—Sweden, Japan, and the Soviet Union—the first two have yet to act on this desire and the Soviet Union was dismantled without having done so.

The reasons for failing to adopt such legislation are many and often closely related to the structure, philosophy, and character of particular nations. Sweden, for example, does not have a law explicitly prohibiting discrimination on the basis of disability, although the government is presently considering and expected to propose a narrow measure that would prohibit some such discrimination in employment. As part of Sweden's overall character as a welfare state, however, its laws guarantee all its citizens the right to work and prohibit employers from discharging workers or reducing their pay for any reason other than certain specified grounds—essentially only documented downsizing or serious work misconduct. Disability discrimination is, therefore, prohibited *sub silentio*. This welfare state rationale has limitations, however. Such generic guarantees do not protect workers with disabilities from discriminatory practices other than discharge or pay inequities, and do not require any type of workplace accommodation for employees with disabilities, nor do they apply to persons who are merely applicants for employment. Outside of employment, Swedish laws do not prohibit disability discrimination in other aspects of society, such as access to transportation or public accommodations.

Japan's laws regarding people with disabilities rely mainly on encouraging rather than requiring nondiscrimination. Illustrative is an article of the Disabled Person's Fundamental Law, as revised in 1993, that establishes "Responsibilities of the Nation" as follows: "The nation shall, on the basis of social solidarity, endeavor to cooperate in promoting the welfare of disabled persons." Likewise, a

1994 law popularly known as the Heartful Building Law promotes accessibility in buildings used by the public by declaring that owners of such buildings "are encouraged to modify designs" to incorporate accessibility. Local governments are authorized to give advice about accessibility, and may, if they wish, order modifications to construction plans. Such laws highlight the overriding importance of politeness and cooperation in Japanese society in contrast to the enforceable legal mandate approach prevalent in American legislation.

In the post-Soviet era, Russia has passed legislation that provides some protection against disability discrimination. President Boris Yeltsin twice vetoed earlier renditions of such legislation, but a compromise version was finally signed in December of 1995. Other countries that have enacted laws prohibiting discrimination on the basis of disability include New Zealand and Kuwait. South Africa included a prohibition against disability discrimination in its new constitution that took effect in 1996 and is considering legislation to implement it. Various other countries are continuing to consider such legislation.

The laws of Sweden, Japan, Russia, and many other countries, particularly including European countries, contain a major feature not found in U.S. law—employment quota requirements Arguably, such systems invoke a "special protection" model at odds with the equality mandate upon which the ADA is based. Britain repealed its quota law when it passed its Disability Discrimination Act. The laws of some countries, however, include both quota requirements and antidiscrimination measures. A more complete discussion of quota systems is beyond the scope of this article.

Historically, the development of the ADA and similar laws rested upon the legacy of the earlier civil rights struggles and methodologies of African Americans, women, and other groups in achieving legal guarantees of equality under the law in the United States. In part, differences between U.S. laws and those of other countries can be explained by the fact that many of those countries have not had a similar civil rights tradition. The lack of a civil rights mentality among the public, politicians, and even the disability community itself makes the successful enactment of disability nondiscrimination laws quite an uphill battle in such countries.

***Robert L. Burgdorf, Jr.** is a professor at the University of the District of Colombia, David A. Clarke School of Law. While working at the National Council on Disability, he wrote the original draft of the Americans with Disabilities Act that was introduced in Congress in 1988.

Burgdorf, Robert L., Jr. "Disability Rights in the USA and Abroad." *Journal of Civil Rights*, vol. 3, no. 1. (1998): 3–5.

'Nothing About Us Without Us': Recognizing the Rights of People With Disabilities

By United Nations Publications*

Some 10 per cent of the global population is disabled as a result of mental, physical or sensory impairment, with approximately 80 per cent living in developing countries. The global disabled population is increasing, according to the World Health Organization (WHO). Population growth, medical advances that prolong life, war injuries, landmines, HIV/AIDS, malnutrition, substance abuse, accidents and environmental damage all contribute to this increase. It has become increasingly clear that persons with disabilities should be viewed as people who enjoy the full spectrum of political, civil, economic, social and cultural rights. Physical or social barriers limit their lives, often denying them access to essential services. This affects not only the disabled and their families but also the economic and social development of entire societies, where a significant reservoir of human potential goes untapped.

Considering that disabilities are frequently caused by human activities or a lack of care, assistance from the entire international community is needed to put an end to this "silent emergency". Recognition has been slow, but it is steadily taking place in all parts of the world. The growth of the international disability movement, with its motto "Nothing About Us Without Us", encapsulates this fundamental shift in perspective towards a principle of participation and the integration of persons with disabilities in every aspect of political, social, economic and cultural life. Commemorating the 2004 International Day of Disabled Persons, observed every year on 3 December, Secretary-General Kofi Annan stressed that "no society can claim to be based on justice and equality without persons with disabilities taking decisions as full-fledged members".

There is no universally agreed definition of disability. It is now considered a socially created problem and not an attribute of an individual. The social perspective is reflected in the WHO International Classification of Functioning, Disability and Health, which defines disability as a universal human experience and not the concern of a minority; every human being can suffer from a health loss and thus experience some disability. The old "medical model" of disability has been replaced by a human rights model, in recognition of the fact that it is society that is "disabling" people with disabilities by making it difficult for them to exercise their human rights. The changing nature of disability and the realization that it was an inevitable part of the life of any individual or society require that the concept of disability be related to the issue of human dignity.

There is still no global treaty to protect the rights of people with disabilities, who are only implicitly covered by existing human rights treaties. Among the eight UN core treaties, only the Convention on the Rights of the Child makes explicit reference to children with disabilities. Declarations and principles that address the rights of the disabled are legally non-binding and are considered inadequate by many disability advocates, reflecting a change in the way societies view themselves and promote integration of the disabled. As the world ages, the number of people with disabilities is expected to increase, underscoring the importance of a new treaty.

In 2001, President Vicente Fox of Mexico proposed to the UN General Assembly the drafting of the first-ever convention on the rights of people with disabilities. The Assembly established an Ad Hoc Committee to prepare "a comprehensive and integral international convention to protect and promote the rights and dignity of people with disabilities". Like all international conventions elaborated through the United Nations, the 191 Member States are the main drafters of the treaty, which will have the force of law for those countries that ratify it. Chaired by Ambassador Luis Gallegos of

Ecuador, the Ad Hoc Committee recently completed its fourth session and issued its report to the General Assembly.

Mr. Gallegos said that the challenge of the convention was to articulate a human rights framework and accompanying practices that would translate disability-specific needs into the legal provisions of a treaty. He said that the broad consultative process among all stakeholders, as well as the working partnership between Governments and disabled persons' organizations, were essential to the success of the convention. Mr. Gallegos emphasized that despite the complex nature of the issue, negotiations had created a momentum that, he hoped, might make it possible for the treaty to be ready for adoption by the General Assembly in September 2005, in time for the review of the implementation of the Millennium Development Goals. "If we miss that mark", he said, the dynamics of the process would be lost and "it will take us much more time". The Ad Hoc Committee's next session is scheduled for 24 January to 4 February 2005.

When adopted, the draft Comprehensive and Integral International Convention on Protection and Promotion of the Rights and Dignity of Persons with Disabilities would create a legally binding framework within a single universal instrument, establishing persons with disabilities as "rights holders" and "subjects of law", with full participation in formulating and implementing plans and policies affecting them. It would also promote an understanding of "disability", changing the way societies view people with disabilities.

DISCRIMINATION AGAINST PEOPLE WITH DISABILITIES

Persons with disabilities often are excluded from the mainstream of society and denied their human rights. Discrimination against them takes various forms, ranging from the denial of opportunities to segregation and isolation, because of the imposition of physical and social barriers. Effects of disability-based discrimination have been particularly severe in such fields as education, employment, housing, transport, cultural life and access to public places and services. This may result from distinction, exclusion, restriction or preference, and denial of reasonable accommodation on the basis of disablement, which effectively nullifies or impairs the recognition, enjoyment or exercise of the rights of persons with disabilities.

The consequences of disability are particularly serious for women, because they are discriminated against on the double grounds of gender and disability. Women are more exposed to the risk of becoming disabled because of neglect and certain forms of abuse and harmful traditional practices directed against them. They have less access to essential services, such as health care, education and vocational rehabilitation. They are also specially affected because they are often entrusted with the responsibility of caring for disabled persons in the community.

Despite some progress over the past decade, the human rights of persons with disabilities have not been systematically addressed in society. Most disability legislation and policies are based on the assumption that persons with disabilities simply are not able to exercise the same rights as non-disabled persons. Consequently, the situation of persons with disabilities is often addressed in terms of rehabilitation and social services. More comprehensive legislation is needed to ensure their rights in all aspects on an equal basis with persons without disabilities. Appropriate measures are required to address existing discrimination and to promote opportunities for the disabled to participate on an equal basis in social life and development.

There also are certain cultural and social barriers that have served to deter full participation of persons with disabilities. Discriminatory practices against them may be the result of social and cultural norms that have been institutionalized by law. Changes in the perception and concepts of disability will involve both changes in values and increased understanding at all levels of society, as well as a focus on those social and cultural norms that can perpetuate erroneous and inappropriate myths about disability.

*United Nations Publications is the source for over 5,300 titles that articulates the UN's aspirations and is produced by the Organization and its key agencies.

"'Nothing about Us without Us': Recognizing the Rights of People with Disabilities." UN Chronicle 41, no. 4 (December 2004): 10–11.

Used by permission.

DISCUSSION QUESTIONS

1. The article by Save the Children talks about interdependence and interrelatedness. Discuss the realization that one right often depends, wholly or in part, upon the realization of other rights for individuals with disabilities.

2. The picture of the United States as the respected leader in guaranteeing civil rights for people with disabilities turned out to be only partially accurate. What may be potential issues in the implementation of the Americans with Disabilities Act?

3. Discuss the reasons for nations failing to adopt discrimination legislation, with particular attention to the structure, philosophy, and character of each nation.

4. Why has the old "medical model" of disability been replaced by a human rights model?

CHAPTER 2:

Advocating for Inclusion

Chapter 2 introduces the policy and position statements on inclusion of five major disability associations and NGOs. These statements cover the entire lifespan of an individual—beginning with infants through adulthood—and may be the most prominent and, in some cases, the only policy or position statement the organization has promulgated. All five organizations emphasize the importance of inclusion.

The terminology used to describe the education of students with disabilities in general education classrooms has changed. These terms reflect how the concepts are defined. "Mainstreaming" was used generally in reference to children with mild disabilities and suggested that a child with a disability had to fit into the general education classroom with little accommodations for his or her needs. Contrast such assumption with the situation today where "inclusion" is viewed as a right of all children with disabilities—the assumption being that general education will change to meet the child's needs.

The first article, "Early Childhood Inclusion," a joint position statement of the Division for Early Childhood (DEC) of the Council for Exceptional Children (CEC) and the National Association for the Education of Young Children (NAEYC), advocates that infants and young children with and without disabilities play, develop, and learn together in a variety of places. These two professional associations—one focused on children with disabilities and the other primarily on children without disabilities—have identified the defining features of inclusion as access, participation, and supports. The DEC–NAEYC statement was designed to be a blueprint for identifying the key components of high-quality, inclusive programs.

In the second article, the Council for Exceptional Children presents the organization's policy on inclusion. The CEC believes that access to an inclusive education leads to positive outcomes for individuals with disabilities, including satisfying relationships with others, ability to live independently, productively engage with their community, and participation in society at large. The outcomes are consistent with those espoused by the UN Convention on the Rights of Persons with Disabilities (CRPD). The CEC identifies key policy implications for schools, communities, and professional development.

The third statement, "Children with Intellectual Disabilities and Their Families: A Position Paper of Inclusion Europe," argues that state parties that have ratified the CRPD must implement broad-based actions to be in compliance in certain areas. These include respect for the home and family; access to health care; rehabilitation and habilitation; access to inclusive education; protection from violence, harassment, bullying, or sexual abuse; participation in political and public life; full participation in cultural life, leisure, recreation, and sports; and living within rather than excluded from the community.

"Autism and Inclusion," a position statement of Autism Europe, advocates for full, inclusive opportunities for individuals with disabilities throughout their lives regardless of the specific disability or its severity in order to maximize their potential. The position of Autism Europe highlights six key provisions of inclusive practices, including: individualization of program; entitlement to services and supports; quality and relevance of services and supports; assessments provided by skilled professionals which are inclusive of parents; provision of services and supports in a more protected environment if needed by the individual; and recognition that autism is a spectrum condition that requires services and supports ranging from most inclusive to least inclusive. The Council for Exceptional Children also recognizes the necessity of having available a continuum of services for a small number of children.

The concluding piece, The Arc and the American Association on Intellectual and Developmental Disabilities "Position Statement on Inclusion," reiterates that all people with intellectual and/or developmental disabilities benefit when fully included in community life. The groups note that, in the past, the focus on individuals with intellectual and/or developmental disabilities was on their deficits rather than on their strengths and lifestyle choices; they emphasize that this thinking must change. *All* children and adults must be treated equally in our society.

Early Childhood Inclusion: A Joint Position Statement

By the Division for Early Childhood of the Council for Exceptional Children and the National Association for the Education of Young Children*

Today an ever-increasing number of infants and young children with and without disabilities play, develop, and learn together in a variety of places—homes, early childhood programs, neighborhoods, and other community-based settings. The notion that young children with disabilities[1] and their families are full members of the community reflects societal values about promoting opportunities for development and learning, and a sense of belonging for every child. It also reflects a reaction against previous educational practices of separating and isolating children with disabilities. Over time, in combination with certain regulations and protections under the law, these values and societal views regarding children birth to 8 with disabilities and their families have come to be known as early childhood inclusion.[2] The most far-reaching effect of federal legislation on inclusion enacted over the past three decades has been to fundamentally change the way in which early childhood services ideally can be organized and delivered.[3] However, because inclusion takes many different forms and implementation is influenced by a wide variety of factors, questions persist about the precise meaning of inclusion and its implications for policy, practice, and potential outcomes for children and families.

The lack of a shared national definition has contributed to misunderstandings about inclusion. DEC and NAEYC recognize that having a common understanding of what inclusion means is fundamentally important for determining what types of practices and supports are necessary to achieve high quality inclusion. This

DEC/NAEYC joint position statement offers a definition of early childhood inclusion. The definition was designed not as a litmus test for determining whether a program can be considered inclusive, but rather, as a blueprint for identifying the key components of high quality inclusive programs. In addition, this document offers recommendations for how the position statement should be used by families, practitioners, administrators, policy makers, and others to improve early childhood services.

DEFINITION OF EARLY CHILDHOOD INCLUSION

Early childhood inclusion embodies the values, policies, and practices that support the right of every infant and young child and his or her family, regardless of ability, to participate in a broad range of activities and contexts as full members of families, communities, and society. The desired results of inclusive experiences for children with and without disabilities and their families include a sense of belonging and membership, positive social relationships and friendships, and development and learning to reach their full potential. The defining features of inclusion that can be used to identify high quality early childhood programs and services are access, participation, and supports.

What Is Meant by Access, Participation, and Supports?

Access. Providing access to a wide range of learning opportunities, activities, settings, and environments is a defining feature of high quality early childhood inclusion. Inclusion can take many different forms and can occur in various organizational and community contexts, such as homes, Head Start, child care, faith-based programs, recreational programs, preschool, public and private pre-kindergarten through early elementary education, and blended early childhood education/early childhood special education programs. In many cases, simple modifications can facilitate access for individual children. Universal design is a concept that can be used to support access to environments in many different types of settings through the removal of physical and structural barriers. Universal Design for Learning (UDL) reflects practices that provide multiple and varied formats for instruction and learning. UDL principles and practices help to ensure that *every* young child has access to learning environments, to typical home or educational routines and activities, and to the general education curriculum. Technology can enable children with a range of functional abilities to participate in activities and experiences in inclusive settings.

Participation. Even if environments and programs are designed to facilitate access, some children will need additional individualized accommodations and supports to participate fully in play and learning activities with peers and adults. Adults promote belonging, participation, and engagement of children with and without disabilities in inclusive settings in a variety of intentional ways. Tiered models in early childhood hold promise for helping adults organize assessments and interventions by level of intensity. Depending on the individual needs and priorities of young children and families, implementing inclusion involves a range of approaches—from embedded, routines-based teaching to more explicit interventions—to scaffold learning and participation for all children. Social-emotional development and behaviors that facilitate participation are critical goals of high quality early childhood inclusion, along with learning and development in all other domains.

Supports. In addition to provisions addressing access and participation, an infrastructure of systems-level supports must be in place to undergird the efforts of individuals and organizations providing inclusive services to children and families. For example, family members, practitioners, specialists, and administrators should have access to ongoing professional development and support to acquire the knowledge, skills, and dispositions required to implement effective inclusive practices. Because collaboration among key stakeholders (e.g., families, practitioners, specialists, and administrators) is a cornerstone for implementing high quality early childhood inclusion, resources and program policies are needed to promote multiple opportunities for communication and collaboration among these groups. Specialized services and therapies must be implemented in a coordinated fashion and integrated with general early care and education services. Blended early childhood education/early childhood special education programs offer one example of how this might be achieved.[4] Funding policies should promote the pooling of resources and the use of incentives to increase access to high quality inclusive opportunities. Quality frameworks (e.g., program quality standards, early learning standards and guidelines, and professional competencies and standards) should reflect and guide inclusive practices to ensure that all early childhood practitioners and programs are prepared to address the needs and priorities of infants and young children with disabilities and their families.

RECOMMENDATIONS FOR USING THIS POSITION STATEMENT TO IMPROVE EARLY CHILDHOOD SERVICES

Reaching consensus on the meaning of early childhood inclusion is a necessary first step in articulating the field's collective wisdom and values on this critically important issue. In addition, an agreed-upon definition of inclusion should be used to create high expectations for infants and young children with disabilities and to shape educational policies and practices that support high quality inclusion in a wide range of early childhood programs and settings. Recommendations for using this position statement to accomplish these goals include:

1. *Create high expectations for every child to reach his or her full potential.* A definition of early childhood inclusion should help

create high expectations for every child, regardless of ability, to reach his or her full potential. Shared expectations can, in turn, lead to the selection of appropriate goals and support the efforts of families, practitioners, individuals, and organizations to advocate for high quality inclusion.

2. *Develop a program philosophy on inclusion.* An agreed-upon definition of inclusion should be used by a wide variety of early childhood programs to develop their own philosophy on inclusion. Programs need a philosophy on inclusion as a part of their broader program mission statement to ensure that practitioners and staff operate under a similar set of assumptions, values, and beliefs about the most effective ways to support infants and young children with disabilities and their families. A program philosophy on inclusion should be used to shape practices aimed at ensuring that infants and young children with disabilities and their families are full members of the early childhood community and that children have multiple opportunities to learn, develop, and form positive relationships.

3. *Establish a system of services and supports.* Shared understandings about the meaning of inclusion should be the starting point for creating a system of services and supports for children with disabilities and their families. Such a system must reflect a continuum of services and supports that respond to the needs and characteristics of children with varying types of disabilities and levels of severity, including children who are at risk for disabilities. However, the designers of these systems should not lose sight of inclusion as a driving principle and the foundation for the range of services and supports they provide to young children and families. Throughout the service and support system, the goal should be to ensure access, participation, and the infrastructure of supports needed to achieve the desired results

related to inclusion. Ideally, the principle of natural proportions should guide the design of inclusive early childhood programs. The principle of natural proportions means the inclusion of children with disabilities in proportion to their presence in the general population. A system of supports and services should include incentives for inclusion, such as child care subsidies, and adjustments to staff-child ratios to ensure that program staff can adequately address the needs of every child.

4. *Revise program and professional standards.* A definition of inclusion could be used as the basis for revising program and professional standards to incorporate high quality inclusive practices. Because existing early childhood program standards primarily reflect the needs of the general population of young children, improving the overall quality of an early childhood classroom is necessary, but might not be sufficient, to address the individual needs of every child. A shared definition of inclusion could be used as the foundation for identifying dimensions of high quality inclusive programs and the professional standards and competencies of practitioners who work in these settings.

5. *Achieve an integrated professional development system.* An agreed-upon definition of inclusion should be used by states to promote an integrated system of high quality professional development to support the inclusion of young children with and without disabilities and their families. The development of such a system would require strategic planning and commitment on the part of families and other key stakeholders across various early childhood sectors (e.g., higher education, child care, Head Start, public pre-kindergarten, preschool, early intervention, health care, mental health). Shared assumptions about the meaning of inclusion are critical for determining who would

benefit from professional development, what practitioners need to know and be able to do, and how learning opportunities are organized and facilitated as part of an integrated professional development system.

6. *Influence federal and state accountability systems.* Consensus on the meaning of inclusion could influence federal and state accountability standards related to increasing the number of children with disabilities enrolled in inclusive programs. Currently, states are required to report annually to the U.S. Department of Education the number of children with disabilities who are participating in inclusive early childhood programs. But the emphasis on the prevalence of children who receive inclusive services ignores the quality and the anticipated outcomes of the services that children experience. Furthermore, the emphasis on prevalence data raises questions about which types of programs and experiences can be considered inclusive in terms of the intensity of inclusion and the proportion of children with and without disabilities within these settings and activities. A shared definition of inclusion could be used to revise accountability systems to address both the need to increase the number of children with disabilities who receive inclusive services and the goal of improving the quality and outcomes associated with inclusion.

ENDNOTES

1. Phrases such as "children with special needs" and "children with exceptionalities" are sometimes used in place of "children with disabilities."

2. The term "inclusion" can be used in a broader context relative to opportunities and access for children from culturally and linguistically diverse groups, a critically important topic in early childhood requiring further discussion and inquiry. It is now widely acknowledged, for example, that culture has a profound influence on early development and learning, and that early care and education practices must reflect this influence. Although this position statement is more

narrowly focused on inclusion as it relates to disability, it is understood that children with disabilities and their families vary widely with respect to their racial/ethnic, cultural, economic, and linguistic backgrounds.

3. In accordance with the Individuals with Disabilities Education Act (IDEA), children ages 3-21 are entitled to a free, appropriate public education (FAPE) in the least restrictive environment (LRE). LRE requires that, to the extent possible, children with disabilities should have access to the general education curriculum, along with learning activities and settings that are available to their peers without disabilities. Corresponding federal legislation applied to infants and toddlers (children birth to 3) and their families specifies that early intervention services and supports must be provided in "natural environments," generally interpreted to mean a broad range of contexts and activities that generally occur for typically developing infants and toddlers in homes and communities. Although this document focuses on the broader meaning and implications of early childhood inclusion for children birth to eight, it is recognized that the basic ideas and values reflected in the term "inclusion" are congruent with those reflected in the term "natural environments." Furthermore, it is acknowledged that fundamental concepts related to both inclusion and natural environments extend well beyond the early childhood period to include older elementary school students and beyond.

4. Blended programs integrate key components (e.g., funding, eligibility criteria, curricula) of two or more different types of early childhood programs (e.g., the federally funded program for preschoolers with disabilities [Part B-619] in combination with Head Start, public pre-k, and/or child care) with the goal of serving a broader group of children and families within a single program.

---

*Division for Early Childhood of the Council for Exceptional Children promotes policies and practices that support families and enhance the development of young children who have or are at risk for developmental delays and disabilities.

National Association for the Education of Young Children (NAYEC) is a professional organization that promotes educational and developmental services for all children from birth through age eight.

Division for Early Childhood of the Council for Exceptional Children, and the National Association for the Education of Young Children. "Early Childhood Inclusion: A Joint Position Statement of the Division for Early Childhood (DEC) and the National Association for the Education of Young Children (NAEYC)." April 2009, http://www.dec-sped.org/uploads/docs/about_dec/position_concept_papers/PositionStatement_Inclusion_Joint_updated_May2009.pdf.

The Council for Exceptional Children Policy on Inclusive Schools and Community Settings

By the Council for Exceptional Children*

Inclusive Schools and Community Settings

The Council for Exceptional Children believes all children, youth, and young adults with disabilities are entitled to a free and appropriate education and/or services that lead to an adult life characterized by satisfying relations with others, independent living, productive engagement in the community, and participation in society at large. To achieve such outcomes, there must exist for all children, youth, and young adults a rich variety of early intervention, educational, and vocational program options and experiences. Access to these programs and experiences should be based on individual educational need and desired outcomes. Furthermore, students and their families or guardians, as members of the planning team, may recommend the placement, curriculum option, and the exit document to be pursued.

CEC believes that a continuum of services must be available for all children, youth, and young adults. CEC also believes that the concept of inclusion is a meaningful goal to be pursued in our schools and communities. In addition, CEC believes children, youth, and young adults with disabilities should be served whenever possible in general education classrooms in inclusive neighborhood schools and community settings. Such settings should be strengthened and supported by an infusion of specially trained personnel and other appropriate supportive practices according to the individual needs of the child.

Policy Implications

Schools

In inclusive schools, the building administrator and staff with assistance from the special education administration should be primarily responsible for the education of children, youth, and young adults with disabilities. The administrator(s) and other school personnel must have available to them appropriate support and technical assistance to enable them to fulfill their responsibilities. Leaders in state/provincial and local governments must redefine rules and regulations as necessary, and grant school personnel greater authority to make decisions regarding curriculum, materials, instructional practice, and staffing patterns. In return for greater autonomy, the school administrator and staff should establish high standards for each child, youth, and young adult, and should be held accountable for his or her progress toward outcomes.

Communities

Inclusive schools must be located in inclusive communities; therefore, CEC invites all educators, other professionals, and family members to work together to create early intervention, educational, and vocational programs and experiences that are collegial, inclusive, and responsive to the diversity of children, youth, and young adults. Policy makers at the highest levels of state/provincial and local government, as well as school administration, also must support inclusion in the educational reforms they espouse.

Further, the policy makers should fund programs in nutrition, early intervention, health care, parent education, and other social support programs that prepare all children, youth, and young adults to do well in school. There can be no meaningful school reform, nor inclusive schools, without funding of these key prerequisites. As important, there must be interagency agreements and collaboration with local governments and business to help prepare students to assume a constructive role in an inclusive community.

Professional Development. And finally, state/provincial departments of education, local educational districts, and colleges and universities must provide high-quality preservice and continuing professional development experiences that prepare all general educators to work effectively with children, youth, and young adults representing a wide range of abilities and disabilities, experiences, cultural and linguistic backgrounds, attitudes, and expectations. Moreover, special educators should be trained with an emphasis on their roles in inclusive schools and community settings. They also must learn the importance of establishing ambitious goals for their students and of using appropriate means of monitoring the progress of children, youth, and young adults.

---

*Council for Exceptional Children is the largest international professional organization dedicated to improving the educational success of individuals with disabilities and/or gifts and talents.

Council for Exceptional Children. CEC Policy Manual, 1997. Section 3, Part 1, Chapter 3, "Special Education in the Schools," para. 6. http://www.cec.sped.org/AM/Template.cfm?Section=CEC_Policy_Resources1&Template=/CM/ContentDisplay.cfm&ContentID=1449.

Used by permission.

Children with Intellectual Disabilities and Their Families: A Position Paper of Inclusion Europe

*By Inclusion Europe**

Children with intellectual disabilities have the same needs and wishes as any other children: they want to interact with their peers, play and laugh, learn and develop into a respected adult member of society. As with other children, this development process can be challenging for the child and its family, but is an intrinsic part of growing up.

Even more than for other children, the development phase of a child with intellectual disability determines its abilities and capacities later in life. Support, teaching and therapies can reduce the impact of a disability and contacts with other children in all areas of life create necessary friendships and abilities for a life fully included in society.

However, children with disabilities in all European countries are more likely than other children to be denied equal opportunities for their development. They are more often abandoned by their families and put in institutional care. They are more often victims of violence, harassment, bullying or sexual abuse than other children. They are denied education on an equal level to others, and have less access to healthy living conditions and health care. They are also often excluded from leisure, cultural or sports activities, which are crucial for their personal development and for finding their place in the society. Due to their need for additional support, poverty of their families has a very negative effect on the development chances of children with intellectual disabilities.

Article 7 of the UN Convention on the Rights of Persons with Disabilities addresses these situations by placing a clear obligation on governments:

> States Parties shall take all necessary measures to ensure the full enjoyment by children with disabilities of all human rights and fundamental freedoms on an equal basis with other children.

It also stipulates that in all actions the best interests of the child shall be a primary consideration and that the views of the child shall be given due weight in accordance with their age and maturity. These core principles, also enshrined and monitored by the Convention on the Rights of the Child, constitute an important heritage for the fulfillment of the rights of children with intellectual disabilities and their full participation in society.

For children with intellectual disabilities, the following rights are of paramount importance as a precondition to make the most of their lives on an equal basis with other children:

+ Respect for the home and the family
+ Access to health care, rehabilitation and habilitation
+ Access to inclusive mainstream education with the necessary support
+ Protection from violence, harassment, bullying or sexual abuse
+ Participation in political and public life
+ Full participation in the cultural life, leisure, recreation and sports
+ Living included in the community

Inclusion Europe and its members demand from all States Parties that have ratified the UN Convention clear and decisive action in the following priority areas:

Respect for the Home and the Family

The Preamble of the UN Convention on the Rights of Persons with Disabilities states that "the family is the natural and fundamental group unit of society" and therefore the Convention recognizes the family as a primary place for a child and underlines the importance of growing up in a family setting. Families include not only the traditional family model, but all existing forms of family life.

The birth of a child with an intellectual disability changes the plans that families have for their lives and places additional demands on all family members. To maintain the capacity of families to meet these additional demands, governments should develop and implement comprehensive policies for supporting all families with disabled children. The policies should not only ensure respite for the parents when this is required, but also consider the support necessary to brothers and sisters, ways of enhancing employment opportunities for the primary caretaker (most often the mother), and the financial situation of the family as a whole. The Convention clearly stipulates that where the immediate family is unable to care for a child with disabilities, governments should undertake every effort to provide alternative care in the wider family and failing that, within the community in a family setting. The family continues also to be an important resource of help and support for adult persons with intellectual disabilities.

Children with intellectual disabilities should be effectively protected against discrimination in all areas of life, as stated in the Convention. Families of children with disabilities should also be protected from discrimination by association. States Parties should include in their legislation specific provisions for the prohibition of discrimination by association.

Access to Health Care, Rehabilitation and Habilitation[1]

Children with intellectual disabilities benefit much from early intervention services that start at birth and aim at minimizing the impact of an intellectual impairment. Governments should ensure access to free and comprehensive early identification and early intervention services for all children at risk of intellectual disability. These services should be available, accessible and affordable for all families in the whole territory of a country and should be delivered in an inclusive way without requiring the child to be placed in an institution.

Equal access to mainstream health care and dental care is a prerequisite for a good development of a child. Governments should ensure that medical professionals are able and willing to care for children with disabilities without discrimination. Medical professionals should inform all children by appropriate means about planned medical interventions.

Some disabled children need specialized rehabilitation services. Governments should ensure that this need for special services never leads to the exclusion of children from their families and from their social environment. Especially, it should be recognized as discrimination if the need for specific rehabilitation services leads to the placement of children in residential institutions.

Access to Inclusive Education[2]

It is important for children with intellectual disabilities to have equal access to all types of mainstream pre-school and school education as well as to vocational training and informal learning opportunities. Governments should ensure that all existing mainstream pre-school services and schools cater for all children of appropriate age from their catchment area, including those with different levels of intellectual disabilities. Governments should provide a range of support that meets the needs of all students to the greatest possible extent.

Protection from Violence, Harassment, Bullying or Sexual Abuse

Children with intellectual disabilities are vulnerable to abuse and harassment from other children, family members, professional carers, teachers and other people. Governments should ensure that adequate and effective reporting and control mechanisms exist, that all children know about them and that children can report easily any incidents. Governments should provide professional support to victims.

A specific issue is the protection of the personal integrity of a child with disabilities from medical interventions that have no positive effect on the health status of a child. Governments should ensure that children with disabilities retain their fertility on an equal basis with others and that children are not subjected to inhuman medical interventions that serve the interests of carers rather than of the child.

Participation in Political and Public Life

Children with intellectual disabilities are equal citizens of their country and will have all associated public rights once they come of age. Furthermore, the UN Convention stipulates that the views of children shall be taken into account in all decisions that affect their lives. Therefore, Governments should promote and support the movement of self-advocacy of people with intellectual disabilities and provide relevant information to their citizens in a format accessible to children with intellectual disabilities.

Full Participation in Cultural Life, Leisure, Recreation and Sports

Cultural and leisure time activities have an enormous potential for inclusive activities with nondisabled children and adults.

Governments should ensure that all those activities are accessible and affordable for children with intellectual disabilities.

LIVING INCLUDED IN THE COMMUNITY

In many European countries, children with intellectual disabilities are still forced to live in residential institutions instead of in family-type settings. Governments should ensure that families with disabled children receive all necessary support and that disabled children who are not cared for by their original families have priority access to foster family care. To prevent concealment, abandonment, neglect and segregation of children with disabilities, governments should undertake to provide early and comprehensive information, services and support to children with disabilities and their families.

ENDNOTES

1. "**Habilitation**" refers to a process aimed at helping people gain certain new skills, abilities, and knowledge. "**Rehabilitation**" refers to re-gaining skills, abilities or knowledge that may have been lost or compromised as a result of acquiring a disability, or due to a change in one's disability or circumstances. The goals of habilitation and rehabilitation as defined in the Convention on the Rights of Persons with Disabilities (CRPD) are to "enable persons with disabilities to attain and maintain maximum independence, full physical, mental, social and vocational ability, and full inclusion and participation in all aspects of life."

2. See also Inclusion Europe's Position Paper on "Education for all: Diversity as an opportunity for school education"

***Inclusion Europe** is a non-profit organization that campaigns for the rights and interests of people with intellectual disabilities and their families throughout Europe.

Inclusion Europe. *Children with Intellectual Disabilities and Their Families: A Position Paper of Inclusion Europe.* 2008. http://www.inclusion-europe.org/documents/ChildrenfamiliesEN.pdf.

Used by permission.

Autism and Inclusion

*By Autism Europe**

BACKGROUND

1. The term inclusion is used to describe an entitlement to education and support for all individuals with a disability within the mainstream of provision. It is a major plank of government policy at European level.

2. Inclusion differs from 'mainstreaming' or 'integration' in that the latter terms describe participation of disabled individuals when it is able to be demonstrated that they are able to benefit and that the mainstream setting will not be adversely affected by their presence within it.

3. Advocates of inclusion argue that segregation, either by disability, diagnosis or other factor or that having to 'earn' the right to be included is not in the interests of the child or adult. Over the past two decades, the impact of ideas; primarily from the USA and from Scandinavia around 'normalisation' have emphasized the importance of promoting valued social roles for those at risk of devaluation by reason of disability or other factors.

4. The development of policy around these ideas has largely reflected ideology rather than individual need. Segregation in large institutions has largely ceased and there has largely been an opening of the way for greater community presence and participation. There are however concerns that some individuals and their families have been seriously disadvantaged as a result of poorly resourced alternatives or the dilution of specialized expertise. In short, services have been based more on dogma than the needs of the disabled person.

5. Autism-Europe has been involved with advocacy on behalf of children and adults with autism and their families since 1985. It promotes good practice in the fields of education and

educational approaches, in medical treatment and provision for the residential, support and vocational needs of adults.

6. Autism-Europe strongly advocates experiences for individuals with autism which will maximize their opportunities as citizens regardless of the nature and degree of their disability. These include an entitlement to education, support and freedom from abuse or exploitation. Autism-Europe believes that each individual with autism should receive such services and support within the mainstream of public provision unless this conflicts with their individual needs and requirements.

THE POSITION OF AUTISM-EUROPE

1. Autism-Europe believes that the cornerstone of effective provision is individualisation to ensure that each person receives appropriate education and support in order to achieve and sustain successful functioning as independently as possible and to exercise choice.

2. Inclusion in the mainstream should be based on entitlement, not privilege and reflect the best interests and individual need of each person. Reasonable adjustments should be expected within educational or other facilities to provide better access and sustainable participation and benefit. The Policy of Inclusion should never be used to deny any service to any individual or to provide symbolic or token services which may give the illusion of provision whilst in reality denying opportunity.

3. The policy of inclusion must essentially ensure that appropriate learning or other positive experiences take place. It is not simply about 'where' an individual is educated or receives services or support; it is about quality and relevance.

4. Autism-Europe emphasizes the importance of skilled diagnosis and ongoing specialised assessment and a partnership between parents and professionals in order to determine appropriate

educational or other programmes. Autism-Europe advocates that all such programmes be supported by professionals or other persons with acknowledged expertise in autism who can provide all the necessary practical guidance and assistance, and can evaluate the effects of such provision.

5. The policy of inclusion does not replace the need for sensitive, individual planning. This is particularly so in the case of complex individuals whose needs are especially difficult to accommodate in mainstream settings or who find such settings distressing.

6. Autism is a spectrum condition requiring a range of individual sophisticated responses. It is hoped that increasingly these will occur within the mainstream of provision, for all or most of the time. There are however those individuals whose lifelong interests are best served by appropriately specialised services that provide the most appropriate and meaningful education and support.

***Autism Europe** is an international association whose main objective is to advance the rights of persons with autism and their families and to help them improve their quality of life.

Autism Europe. *Autism Europe Adopts the Position Held by the National Autistic Society*. 2003, http://www.autismeurope.org/portal/Portals/0/AE_EYPD_INCLUSION_FINAL_ENG.pdf.

Used by permission.

Position Statement on Inclusion

By The Arc and the American Association on Intellectual and Developmental Disabilities*

All people with intellectual and/or developmental disabilities[1] benefit when fully included in community life.

Issue

Individuals with intellectual and/or developmental disabilities often are not treated equally. They have been labeled by their disability and separated from the community. For many years they were relegated to sterile, dehumanizing institutions. Even as they have begun living in the community, they have experienced exclusion from its schools, jobs, and social life. Moreover, the services they receive frequently segregate, isolate, and focus on an individual's deficits rather than their strengths and lifestyle choices.

Position

All people benefit when persons with intellectual and/or developmental disabilities are included in community life. People with disabilities should be welcomed and included in all aspects of our society. This includes public activities, programs and settings, and private establishments which are open and accessible to members of the general public. People with disabilities should receive the supports they need to participate actively in community life without having to wait.

Children should have the opportunity to:
- Live in a family home;
- Have access to the supports that they need;

- Grow up enjoying nurturing adult relationships both inside and outside a family home;
- Enjoy typical childhood relationships and friendships;
- Learn in their neighborhood school in a general education classroom that contains children of the same age without disabilities;
- Participate in the same activities as children without disabilities;
- Play and participate with all children in community recreation; and
- Participate fully in the religious observances, practices, events, and ceremonies of the family's choice.

Adults should have the opportunity to:
- Have relationships of their own choosing with individuals in the community, in addition to paid staff and/or immediate family;
- Live in a home where and with whom they choose;
- Have access to the supports that they need;
- Engage in meaningful work in an inclusive setting;
- Enjoy the same recreation and other leisure activities that are available to the general public; and
- Participate fully in the religious observances, practices, events, and ceremonies of the individual's choice.

NOTE

1. "People with intellectual and/or developmental disabilities" refers to those defined by AAIDD classification and DSM IV. In everyday language they are frequently referred to as people with cognitive, intellectual and/or developmental disabilities although the professional and legal definitions of those terms both include others and exclude some defined by DSM IV.

---

*The Arc is the world's largest community-based organization devoted to promoting and improving supports and services for all people with intellectual and developmental disabilities.

American Association on Intellectual and Developmental Disabilities is the oldest and largest interdisciplinary organization of professionals and citizens concerned about intellectual and developmental disabilities.

The Arc and American Association on Intellectual and Developmental Disabilities. *Position Paper on Inclusion.* 2009. http://www.thearc.org/NetCommunity/Page.aspx?pid=1359.

Used by permission.

Discussion Questions

1. How does the concept of mainstreaming differ from, and resemble, the concept of inclusion?

2. What recommendations would you have for a better policy on inclusion for persons with disabilities in your local schools and communities?

3. What are the advantages and the disadvantages of inclusive schools and communities for individuals with disabilities?

4. Think of a relative, friend, or neighbor who has a disability. How is that individual included in society? How is that individual affected by inclusion?

CHAPTER 3:

Understanding the United Nations Convention on the Rights of Persons with Disabilities

Chapter 3 describes the basic structure of the Convention on the Rights of Persons with Disabilities (CRPD) and presents an analysis of U.S. law and its consistency with the CRPD. The first article, a press release from the UN News Service, "Lauding Disability Convention as 'Dawn of a New Era,' UN Urges Speedy Ratification," reports on the landmark disability convention. Quotations by world leaders celebrating and welcoming the Convention and urging governments to ratify and implement the Convention are prominent throughout.

The second article, a United Nations Enable Web document, "Convention on the Rights of Persons with Disabilities: Questions and Answers," helps the reader understand the content, principles, definitions, and rights set out in the CRPD. This document addresses important considerations around becoming a party to the Convention and optional protocols, including signing, ratification, and accession. The article also describes how the Convention was negotiated and outlines the involvement of civil society and national human rights institutions.

The chapter concludes with an article from the National Council on Disability, "Finding the Gaps: A Comparative Analysis of Disability Laws in the United States to the United Nations Convention on the Rights of Persons with Disabilities (CRPD)." This article compares existing U.S. law with the CRPD and finds, in general, that the two are consistent. This analysis, however, also identifies several CRPD provisions that differ significantly from U.S. disability law. The comparison of U.S. laws with the provisions of the Convention was made because many consider U.S. policy and practice around serving people with disabilities to be the most advanced in the world. This comparison highlights the far-reaching nature of the CRPD, as it points out discrepancies with U.S. policy. The Convention will, indeed, be challenging to implement across the globe.

Lauding Disability Convention as 'Dawn of a New Era,' UN Urges Speedy Ratification

*By UN News Centre**

13 December 2006—The General Assembly today adopted a landmark disability convention, the first human rights treaty of the twenty-first century and one that United Nations Secretary-General Kofi Annan said represents the "dawn of a new era" for around 650 million people worldwide living with disabilities.

Mr. Annan, along with Assembly President Sheikha Haya Rashed Al Khalifa and other UN officials, as well as members of civil society that lobbied for the pact, urged all 192 Member States to quickly ratify the convention, which covers rights to education, health, work and a raft of other protective measures for people with disabilities.

"Today promises to be the dawn of a new era—an era in which disabled people will no longer have to endure the discriminatory practices and attitudes that have been permitted to prevail for all too long. This Convention is a remarkable and forward-looking document," Mr. Annan said in a speech read out by Deputy Secretary-General Mark Malloch Brown.

The Assembly adopted the Convention on the Protection and Promotion of the Rights and Dignity of Persons with Disabilities in a vote by consensus.

"In three short years, the Convention became a landmark several times over: it is the first human rights treaty to be adopted in the twenty-first century; the most rapidly negotiated human rights treaty in the history of international law; and the first to emerge from lobbying conducted extensively through the Internet. . . I urge all governments to start by ratifying, and then implementing it, without delay."

Sheikha Haya echoed this call, adding that by adopting the Convention, Member States were sending a "clear message of solidarity" by reaffirming the dignity of all humankind and recognizing that "all societies stand to benefit from empowering this important community."

"I look forward to the full implementation of the convention by Member States, with the involvement of all concerned parties. In particular, the NGOs (non-governmental organizations) and civil society groups whose energy, compassion and willingness to work in the spirit of cooperation greatly contributed to the final agreement."

High Commissioner for Human Rights Louise Arbour added her voice to calls for ratification, with her office (OHCHR) noting that the agreement—which comprises 50 articles—fills a major gap in international human rights law.

"The convention... marks a historic step in ensuring that persons with disabilities enjoy full participation in society and can contribute to the community to their full potential. Speedy ratification... will end the protection vacuum that has, in practice, affected persons with disabilities," Ms. Arbour said.

The convention provides that States which ratify it should enact laws and other measures to improve disability rights, and also abolish legislation, customs and practices that discriminate against persons with disabilities. It will be open for signature and ratification on 30 March 2007, and will enter into force after it has been ratified by 20 countries, the OHCHR said.

Speaking at a press conference after the Assembly session, Ambassador Don MacKay of New Zealand, chairman of the committee that negotiated the convention, described today's adoption as "an historic event," adding that those involved in the process "can I think be pleased with the convention that we have. It is in effect an extraordinarily far-reaching convention."

Representatives from the International Disability Caucus (IDC) also welcomed the document, stressing its all-inclusive nature, while at the same time urging states to urgently ratify the deal and also raising several concerns.

"We... celebrate and welcome the convention on the rights of persons with disabilities... which recognizes that disability is a human rights issue," Pamela Molina Toledo, one of the IDC leaders, told reporters, speaking in Spanish and also using sign language.

"This convention is an example of unity and cooperation...for the benefit of all," she said, while urging its speedy ratification, a point also made by Tina Minkowitz, another of the IDC leaders.

"The International Disability Caucus urges governments to ratify and implement the convention within national legislation policies and legal structures and to change those legislation and policies when that is necessary," she said, adding that a particular concern was the need for governments to recognize sign language and other alternative methods of communication in all situations of information, education and employment.

---

*UN News Centre is a daily reporting service of UN news, UN documents and publications, UN overview information, and other UN-related news stories.

UN News Centre. "Lauding Disability Convention as 'Dawn of a New Era,' UN Urges Speedy Ratification." Press release, December 13, 2006.http://www.un.org/apps/news/story.asp?NewsID=20975&Cr=disab.

Used by permission.

Convention on the Rights of Persons with Disabilities: Questions and Answers

*By United Nations Enable**

Introductory Questions

What Are the Human Rights of Persons with Disabilities?

All members of society have the same human rights—they include civil, cultural, economic, political and social rights. Examples of these rights include the following:

+ equality before the law without discrimination
+ right to life, liberty and security of the person
+ equal recognition before the law and legal capacity
+ freedom from torture
+ freedom from exploitation, violence and abuse
+ right to respect physical and mental integrity
+ freedom of movement and nationality
+ right to live in the community
+ freedom of expression and opinion
+ respect for privacy
+ respect for home and the family
+ right to education
+ right to health
+ right to work
+ right to an adequate standard of living
+ right to participate in political and public life
+ right to participate in cultural life

All persons with disabilities have the right to be free from discrimination in the enjoyment of their rights. This includes the right to be free from discrimination on the basis of disability, but also on any other basis such as race, colour, sex, language, religion, political or other opinion, national or social origin, property, birth or other status.

What Is the Convention on the Rights of Persons with Disabilities?

The Convention on the Rights of Persons with Disabilities is an international treaty that identifies the rights of persons with disabilities as well as the obligations on States parties to the Convention to promote, protect and ensure those rights. The Convention also establishes two implementation mechanisms: the Committee on the Rights of Persons with Disabilities, established to monitor implementation, and the Conference of States Parties, established to consider matters regarding implementation.

States negotiated the Convention with the participation of civil society organizations, national human rights institutions and inter-governmental organizations. The United Nations General Assembly adopted the Convention on 13 December 2006 and it was opened for signature on 30 March 2007. States that ratify the Convention are legally bound to respect the standards in the Convention. For other States, the Convention represents an international standard that they should endeavour to respect.

What Is the Optional Protocol to the Convention?

The Optional Protocol is also an international treaty. The Optional Protocol establishes two procedures aimed at strengthening the implementation and monitoring of the Convention. The first is an individual communications procedure allowing individuals to bring petitions to the Committee claiming breaches of their rights; the second is an inquiry procedure giving the Committee authority to undertake inquiries of grave or systematic violations of the Convention.

What Other International Instruments Recognize the Rights of Persons with Disabilities?

States have adopted specific instruments to protect and promote the rights of persons with disabilities over the last decades. Important milestones include:

+ the Declaration on the Rights of Disabled Persons (1995);
+ the World Programme of Action concerning Disabled Persons (1981);
+ the Principles for the Protection of Persons with Mental Illness and the Improvement of Mental Health Care (1991);
+ the Standard Rules on the Equalization of Opportunities for Persons with Disabilities (1993).

Although guidelines, declarations, principles, resolutions and other documents are not legally biding, they express a moral and political commitment by States, and can be used as guidelines to enact legislation or to formulate policies concerning persons with disabilities. It is important to note that some provisions of the Principles for the Protection of Persons with Mental Illness and the Improvement of Mental Health Care have been criticized and the Convention on the Rights of Persons with Disabilities now supersedes these standards to the extent that there is any conflict between the two instruments.

In Addition to the Convention on the Rights of Persons with Disabilities, What Other Human Rights Conventions Are Relevant?

All human rights conventions relate to everyone, including persons with disabilities. The International Covenant on Economic, Social and Cultural Rights and the International Covenant on Civil and Political Rights protect against discrimination on any basis. There are also human rights conventions dealing with discrimination, such as discrimination against women and specific issues or groups of people, such as children or migrant workers. The core human rights treaties are as follows:

* The International Covenant on Economic, Social and Cultural Rights
* The International Covenant on Civil and Political Rights
* The International Convention on the Elimination of All Forms of Racial Discrimination
* The Convention against Torture
* The Convention on the Elimination of All forms of Discrimination against Women
* The Convention on the Rights of the Child
* The International Convention on the Protection of the Rights of All Migrant Workers and Members of Their Families
* The International Convention for the Protection of All Persons from Enforced Disappearance
* The Convention on the Rights of Persons with Disabilities.

All human rights conventions include a provision protecting against discrimination. However, only one of these Conventions, the Convention on the Rights of the Child, specifically recognizes the need to protect against discrimination on the grounds of disability.

Nevertheless, all Conventions are understood to refer to "disability" implicitly as a ground of discrimination. This makes it clear that persons with disabilities should not be discriminated against when these conventions are applied. Thus, the Convention on the Elimination of All Forms of Discrimination against Women, for example, applies to all women, including women with disabilities.

Why Is It Necessary to Have a Convention on the Rights of Persons with Disabilities?

The Convention is necessary in order to have a clear reaffirmation that the rights of persons with disabilities are human rights and to strengthen respect for these rights. Although existing human rights conventions offer considerable potential to promote and protect the rights of persons with disabilities, it became clear that this potential was not being tapped. Indeed, persons with disabilities continued being denied their human rights and were kept on the margins of society in all parts of the world. This continued discrimination against persons with disabilities highlighted the need to adopt a legally binding instrument which set out the legal obligations on States to promote and protect the rights of persons with disabilities.

Why Is the Convention Unique?

The Convention is the first human rights convention of the 21st century and the first legally binding instrument with comprehensive protection of the rights of persons with disabilities. While the Convention does not establish new human rights, it does set out with much greater clarity the obligations on States to promote, protect and ensure the rights of persons with disabilities. Thus, the Convention not only clarifies that States should not discriminate against persons with disabilities, it also sets out the many steps that States must take to create an enabling environment so that persons with disabilities can enjoy real equality in society. For example, the Convention requires States to take measures to ensure accessibility of the physical environment and information and communications technology. Similarly, States have obligations in relation to raising awareness, promoting access to justice, ensuring personal mobility, and collecting disaggregated data relevant to the Convention. In this way, the Convention goes into much greater depth than other human rights treaties in setting out the steps that States should take to prohibit discrimination and achieve equality for all.

The Convention incorporates a social development perspective. The Convention recognizes the importance of international cooperation and its promotion to support national implementation efforts. An innovation in this regard concerns specific references to actions the international community could take to promote international cooperation such as:

+ ensuring that international development programmes are inclusive of and accessible to persons with disabilities;
+ facilitating and supporting capacity-building;
+ facilitating cooperation in research and access to scientific and technical knowledge;
+ providing technical and economic assistance as appropriate.

SPECIFIC QUESTIONS ON THE CONVENTION

What Is the Content of the Convention on the Rights of Persons with Disabilities?

The Convention sets out the human rights of persons with disabilities and the obligations on States to promote, protect and ensure those rights as well as mechanisms to support implementation and monitoring. The content can be broken down in the following way:

+ Preamble—gives general context to the Convention and identifies important background issues
+ Purpose—sets out the goal of the Convention which is to promote, protect and ensure the full and equal enjoyment of all human rights and fundamental freedoms of all persons with disabilities, and to promote respect for their inherent dignity
+ Definitions—define key terms in the Convention, namely: communication, language, discrimination on the basis of disability, reasonable accommodation and universal design

- General principles—identify the standards or imperatives that apply to the enjoyment of all rights in the Convention, such as the principle of non-discrimination and the principle of equality
- Obligations—clarify the steps that States must take to promote, protect and ensure the rights in the Convention
- Specific rights—identify the existing civil, cultural, economic, political and social human rights, affirming that persons with disabilities also hold those rights
- Enabling measures—identify specific steps that States must take to ensure an enabling environment for the enjoyment of human rights, namely: awareness-raising, ensuring accessibility, ensuring protection and safety in situations of risk and humanitarian emergencies, promoting access to justice, ensuring personal mobility, enabling habilitation and rehabilitation, and collecting statistics and data
- International cooperation—recognizes the importance of the international community working together to ensure the full enjoyment of the rights of persons with disability
- Implementation and monitoring—requires States to establish national frameworks for monitoring and implementing the Convention and establishes a Conference of States Parties to consider any matter in relation to implementation of the Convention and a Committee on the Rights of Persons with Disabilities to monitor the Convention
- Final clauses—set out the procedures for signature, ratification, entering into force, and other procedural requirements relevant to the Convention.

What Are the Principles of the Convention?

Article 3 sets out the General Principles that apply to the enjoyment of the rights of persons with disabilities. These are:

- Respect for inherent dignity, individual autonomy, including the freedom to make one's own choices and independence of persons

- Non-discrimination
- Full and effective participation and inclusion in society
- Respect for difference and acceptance of persons with disabilities as part of human diversity and humanity
- Equality of opportunity
- Accessibility
- Equality between men and women
- Respect for the evolving capacities of children with disabilities and respect for the right of children with disabilities to preserve their identities.

Are the Terms "Disability" and "Persons with Disabilities" Defined in the Convention?

The Convention does not include a definition of "disability" or "persons with disabilities" as such. However, elements of the preamble and article 1 provide guidance to clarify the application of the Convention.

- "Disability"—The preamble recognizes that "disability is an evolving concept and that disability results from the interaction between persons with impairments and attitudinal and environmental barriers that hinders their full and effective participation in society on an equal basis with others".
- "Persons with disabilities"—Article 1 states that "(p)ersons with disabilities include those who have long-term physical, mental, intellectual or sensory impairments which in interaction with various barriers may hinder their full and effective participation in society on an equal basis with others".

Several elements of these provisions are relevant to highlight. First, there is recognition that "disability" is an evolving concept resulting from attitudinal and environmental barriers hindering the participation of persons with disabilities in society. Consequently, the notion of "disability" is not fixed and can alter, depending on the prevailing environment from society to society.

Second, disability is not considered as a medical condition, but rather as a result of the interaction between negative attitudes or an unwelcoming environment with the condition of particular persons. By dismantling attitudinal and environmental barriers—as opposed to treating persons with disabilities as problems to be fixed—those persons can participate as active members of society and enjoy the full range of their rights.

Third, the Convention does not restrict coverage to particular persons; rather, the Convention identifies persons with long-term physical, mental, intellectual and sensory disabilities as beneficiaries under the Convention. The reference to "includes" assures that this need not restrict the application of the Convention and States parties could also ensure protection to others, for example, persons with short-term disabilities or who are perceived to be part of such groups.

What Are the Specific Rights in the Convention?

The Convention reaffirms that persons with disabilities enjoy the same human rights as everyone. The specific rights recognized in the Convention are:

+ equality before the law without discrimination
+ right to life, liberty and security of the person
+ equal recognition before the law and legal capacity
+ freedom from torture
+ freedom from exploitation, violence and abuse
+ right to respect physical and mental integrity
+ freedom of movement and nationality
+ right to live in the community
+ freedom of expression and opinion
+ respect for privacy
+ respect for home and the family
+ right to education

- right to health
- right to work
- right to an adequate standard of living
- right to participate in political and public life
- right to participate in cultural life

What Are the Obligations on States Parties to the Convention?

The Convention identifies general and specific obligations on States parties in relation to the rights of persons with disabilities. In terms of general obligations, States have to:

- adopt legislation and administrative measures to promote the human rights of persons with disabilities;
- adopt legislative and other measures to abolish discrimination;
- protect and promote the rights of persons with disabilities in all policies and programmes;
- stop any practice that breaches the rights of persons with disabilities;
- ensure that the public sector respects the rights of persons with disabilities;
- ensure that the private sector and individuals respect the rights of persons with disabilities;
- undertake research and development of accessible goods, services and technology for persons with disabilities and encourage others to undertake such research;
- provide accessible information about assistive technology to persons with disabilities;
- promote training on the rights of the Convention to professionals and staff who work with persons with disabilities;
- consult with and involve persons with disabilities in developing and implementing legislation and policies and in decision-making processes that concern them.

How Is the Convention Monitored?

The Convention requires monitoring at both the national and international level. Nationally, the Convention requires States, in accordance with their legal and administrative systems, to maintain, strengthen, designate or establish a framework to promote, protect and monitor implementation of the Convention.

Internationally, the Convention establishes a Committee on the Rights of Persons with Disabilities which has the role of reviewing periodic reports submitted by States on the steps they have taken to implement the Convention. The Committee also has authority to examine individual communications and conduct inquiries in relation to those States that have recognized the Committee's authority to do so by ratifying the Optional Protocol.

What Are National Frameworks to Promote, Protect and Monitor Implementation of the Convention?

The notion of a national framework to promote, protect and monitor the Convention is relatively open. The Convention recognizes that such frameworks might differ from country to country by allowing flexibility to establish the frameworks in accordance with each State's legal and administrative system. However, the Convention also requires that whatever body is established must be independent. Normally, national frameworks will include at least establishing some form of independent national human rights institution such as a Human Rights Commission or Ombudsman's Office. However, a framework could contain other elements such as courts.

What Is the Committee on the Rights of Persons with Disabilities?

The Committee on the Rights of Persons with Disabilities is a body of independent experts tasked with reviewing States' implementation of the Convention. These experts will serve in their personal capacity. Initially, the Committee comprises twelve independent experts which will rise to 18 members after an additional 60 ratifications or accessions to the Convention. States parties will chose experts on the basis of their competence and experience in the field of human rights and disability, and also in consideration of equitable geographic representation, representation of different forms of civilization and legal systems, gender balance, and participation of experts with disabilities.

The Committee periodically examines reports, prepared by States, on the steps they have taken to implement the Convention. For those States that are party to the Optional Protocol, the Committee also has authority to receive complaints from individuals of alleged breaches of their rights and to undertake inquiries in the event of grave or systematic violations of the Convention.

What Is the Conference of States Parties?

The Convention also establishes a Conference of States Parties that meets regularly in order to consider any matter with regard to the implementation of the Convention. The Convention leaves open the exact nature of the role of the Conference of States Parties, although responsibilities include electing the members of the Committee on the Rights of Persons with Disabilities and debating and adopting proposed amendments to the Convention.

What Is Periodic Reporting?

Each State party to the Convention must submit to the Committee on the Rights of Persons with Disabilities an initial comprehensive report on measures taken to implement the Convention. Each State must submit its initial report within two years after the Convention enters into force for that State. The initial report should:

+ establish the constitutional, legal and administrative framework for the implementation of the Convention;

- explain the policies and programmes adopted to implement each of the Convention's provisions;
- identify any progress made in the realization of the rights of persons with disabilities as a result of the ratification and implementation of the Convention.

Each State must submit subsequent reports at least every four years or whenever the Committee requests one. Subsequent reports should:

- respond to the concerns and other issues highlighted by the Committee in its concluding observations to previous reports;
- indicate progress made in the realization of the rights of persons with disabilities over the reporting period;
- highlight any obstacles that the Government and other actors might have faced in implementing the Convention over the reporting period.

Is It Possible to Complain to the Committee if Rights Have Been Breached?

Yes. The Optional Protocol to the Convention establishes an individual communications procedure that permits individuals and groups in a State party to the Protocol to complain to the Committee on the Rights of Persons with Disabilities that the State has breached one of its obligations under the Convention. The complaint is known as a "communication". The Committee examines the complaint and the observations of the State, and on this basis formulates its views and recommendations, if any, forwards them to the State, and makes them public.

Can the Committee Undertake Inquires?

Yes. The Optional Protocol establishes an inquiry procedure. If the Committee receives reliable information indicating grave or systematic violations by a State party to the Optional Protocol of any of the provisions of the Convention, the Committee may invite the

State in question to respond to such information. After considering the State party's observations and any other reliable information, the Committee may designate one or more of its members to conduct an inquiry and issue a report urgently. If the State agrees, the Committee may visit the country in question. After undertaking the inquiry, the Committee transmits its findings to the State which has six months to submit further observations. The Committee eventually summarizes its findings which it makes public. A State ratifying the Optional Protocol may "opt out" of the inquiry procedure.

What Is the Role of Civil Society in the Monitoring Process?

Civil society has an important role to play in the monitoring process, both nationally and internationally. In relation to national monitoring, the Convention expressly stipulates that civil society, in particular persons with disabilities and their representative organizations, shall be involved and participate fully in the monitoring process (see Convention article 33.3). In relation to international monitoring, States parties are invited to give due consideration to consulting with and actively involving persons with disabilities and their representative organizations when nominating experts for the treaty body (see Convention article 34.3). Further, experience from other international human rights treaty monitoring bodies highlights the critical role that civil society can play in the periodic reporting process, in supporting individuals in bringing individual communications, and in providing reliable information to the Committee on grave or systematic human rights violations as a basis for an inquiry.

Becoming a Party to the Convention and Optional Protocol

What Is the Signature of the Convention?

The first step in becoming a party to the Convention is signing the treaty. States and regional integration organizations (RIO) may sign the Convention or Optional Protocol. A State or RIO may sign the Convention at any time. By signing the Convention or Optional Protocol, States or RIOs indicate their intention to take steps to be bound by the treaty at a later date. Signing also creates an obligation, in the period between signing and ratification, to refrain from acts that would defeat the object and purpose of the treaty.

What Is Ratification?

The next step in becoming a party to the Convention or Optional Protocol is ratification. Ratification is a concrete action taken by States which signals the intention to undertake legal rights and obligations contained in the Convention or the Optional Protocol. Regional integration organizations express their consent to be bound by the Convention or Optional Protocol through "formal confirmation"—an act which has the same effect as ratification.

What Is Accession?

A State or regional integration organization may also express its consent to be bound by the Convention or Optional Protocol through the act of accession. Accession has the same legal effect as ratification; however, unlike ratification, which must be preceded by signing to create binding legal obligations under international law, accession requires only one step—depositing the instrument of accession.

When Does the Convention Come into Force?

The Convention comes into force on the 30th day after the deposit of the 20th instrument of ratification or accession. The Optional Protocol comes into force on the 30th day after the deposit of the 10th instrument of ratification or accession. It is likely that the two instruments will enter into force on two distinct dates. At the moment each enters into force, the Convention and Optional Protocol become legally binding on States parties.

What Will Be the Role of the United Nations Secretariat with Regard to the Convention?

The United Nations has established a joint secretariat for the Convention, consisting of staff of both the United Nations Department of Economic and Social Affairs (DESA), based in New York, and the Office of the High Commissioner for Human Rights (OHCHR) in Geneva. The Department for Economic and Social Affairs (DESA) supports the Conference of State Parties and the Office of the High Commissioner for Human Rights (OHCHR) supports the Committee on the Rights of Persons with Disabilities. DESA and OHCHR work together to support States, civil society and national human rights institutions to implement and monitor the Convention.

What Will Be the Role of the Special Rapporteur on Disability?

The Special Rapporteur on Disability is tasked with monitoring the implementation of the Standard Rules on Equalization of Opportunities for Persons with Disabilities, and reports to the United Nations Commission for Social Development, which is a functional commission of the Economic and Social Council (ECOSOC) of the United Nations. Though the mandate of the Special Rapporteur is specific to the Standard Rules, not the Convention, the work of the Special Rapporteur will have direct significance to the implementation of the Convention due to the degree of overlap between the content of the Standard Rules and the Convention. The Standard Rules, however, is not a legally binding instrument.

THE NEGOTIATION PROCESS

How Was the Convention Negotiated?

The Convention was drafted by the Ad Hoc Committee on a Comprehensive and Integral International Convention on the Protection and Promotion of the Rights and Dignity of Persons with Disabilities (Ad Hoc Committee), which was a committee of the United Nations General Assembly. Its membership was open to all United Nations Member States and observers. During its first session, the Ad Hoc Committee decided that representatives from non-governmental organizations (NGOs) accredited to the Ad Hoc Committee could also participate in meetings and make statements in accordance with United Nations practice.

The Ad Hoc Committee held eight sessions. At its first two sessions, in 2002 and 2003, the Committee considered the possibility of drafting an international instrument on the rights of persons with disabilities, and discussed the type of instrument and possible elements to be included. At its second session, the Ad Hoc Committee established a working group to prepare a draft text of a convention. The Working Group, composed of government and NGO representatives, met in January 2004 and drafted a text for negotiation. At its third, fourth, fifth, sixth, seventh and eighth sessions, the Ad Hoc Committee continued its negotiations. The Convention text was finalized by the Ad Hoc Committee on 26 August 2006.

A drafting group tasked with ensuring uniformity of terminology throughout the text of the draft convention and harmonizing the versions in the official languages of the United Nations reviewed the text from September to November 2006.

The United Nations General Assembly adopted the text of the Convention on the Rights of Persons with Disabilities and its Optional Protocol on 13 December 2006.

Did Civil Society Participate in the Convention Negotiation?

During its first session, the Ad Hoc Committee decided that representatives from non-governmental organizations (NGOs) accredited to the Ad Hoc Committee could also participate in meetings and make statements in accordance with United Nations practice. Thereafter, the General Assembly repeatedly urged that efforts be made to actively involve disability organizations in the work of the Ad Hoc Committee.

Throughout the process, organizations of persons with disabilities and other NGOs were very active in providing comments and information from a disability perspective.

Did National Human Rights Institutions Participate in the Negotiations?

National human rights institutions (NHRI) were also active in the negotiations. Partly as a result of the efforts of representatives of NHRIs, States agreed to a dedicated article on national implementation and monitoring which requires States to have some form of national human rights institution that protects, promotes and monitors the Convention.

Were Consultations Held at the Regional Level during the Negotiation of the Convention?

Regional consultative meetings were held in many regions and in some sub-regions from 2003 to 2006. Consultative meetings comprised of both training on the Convention process and content, as well as dialogue on regional priorities and implications. The meetings' outcome documents provided suggestions and recommendations reflecting the national, sub-regional and regional priorities which contributed to the work of the Ad Hoc Committee.

What Was the Role of the United Nations Voluntary Fund on Disability in the Negotiation of the Convention?

During the negotiation process the United Nations Voluntary Fund on Disability supported the participation of representatives of organizations of persons with disabilities from developing countries—and in particular from the least developed countries—in the Ad Hoc Committee sessions. Grants from the Voluntary Fund are targeted to support pilot and innovative action around the Convention promotion and implementation.

How Was Accessibility of the Negotiation Documentation Ensured?

The methods to ensure accessibility during the negotiation process increased in sophistication over time. Methods progressed from diskettes and documents in Braille, to email and website facilitated communication. A website was created to be accessible to conformance level A according to the standards set by the Web Content Accessibility Guidelines version 1.0 (WCAG 1.0). Among other features, this level of accessibility allowed users of assistive technology such as screen readers to access the website effectively, and allowed for the resizing of text for those who needed to view enlarged text. Working documents of negotiation of Convention text were posted to the website as soon as they were discussed during a session of the Ad Hoc Committee, an innovative practice for United Nations convention negotiations. The website thus provided instant worldwide access to the rapidly changing progress of the discussions, giving the opportunity for groups around the world to feed into the process in a timely manner and on precise issues. In addition, the conference room at United Nations headquarters in New York where negotiations were held was made WiFi-accessible midway through the negotiation process. The WiFi allowed persons in the room to electronically access and read the documents being discussed using assistive devices as necessary. All Ad Hoc Committee meetings were held in a wheel-chair accessible conference room, and neck loops were provided upon request for persons with hearing impairments.

FURTHER INFORMATION

Where Can I Find All the Documents Related to the Convention Negotiation?

Department of Economic and Social Affairs—*http://www.un.org/disabilities.*

Office of the High Commissioner for Human Rights—*http://www.ohchr.org.*

---

*United Nations Enable** is the central site for news regarding the United Nations Department of Economic and Social Affairs and the Convention on the Rights of Persons with Disabilities and its Optional Protocol.

United Nations Enable. "Convention on the Rights of Persons with Disabilities: Questions and Answers," 2008–09 UN Enable. http://www.un.org/disabilities/default.asp?navid=23&pid=151.

Used by permission.

Finding the Gaps: A Comparative Analysis of Disability Laws in the United States to the United Nations Convention on the Rights of Persons with Disabilities (CRPD)

By the National Council on Disability

EXECUTIVE SUMMARY

This paper is geared toward understanding the degree to which U.S. law (in form, spirit, and practice) is consistent with the CRPD. Because any comparison is of necessity at times between "apples and oranges," the paper endeavors to analyze the issue in the way a treaty monitoring body would—to see if any area within federal law contravenes the Convention and/or whether there are gaps where legislation or practice might be introduced or reformed to ensure compliance. The paper finds that, as a general matter, the aims of the CRPD are consistent with U.S. disability law. For the majority of articles, U.S. law can be viewed as either being of a level with the mandates of the Convention or capable of reaching those levels either through more rigorous implementation and/or additional actions by Congress. However, this paper also identifies several CRPD Articles that illustrate significant gaps between United States disability laws and the Convention.

Purpose

Bearing in mind that United States domestic civil rights laws and international human rights laws operate from distinct, although not necessarily mutually exclusive perspectives, this paper provides an initial comparison of the articles comprising the United Nations Convention on the Rights of Persons with Disabilities (CRPD), adopted by the General Assembly on December 13, 2006, and opened for signature on March 30, 2007, with relevant United States federal laws relating to persons with disabilities.

Current U.S. disability laws run the gamut. The Americans with Disabilities Act, the Individuals with Disabilities Education Act, § 504 of the Rehabilitation Act, and the Fair Housing Act are the most well known. But disability laws can be found sprinkled throughout other statutes as well, such as the Voting Rights Act and Vocational Rehabilitation Act. These laws collectively aim to protect Americans with disabilities from discrimination.

This paper is geared toward understanding the degree to which U.S. law (in form, spirit, and practice) is consistent with the CRPD. Because any comparison is of necessity at times between "apples and oranges," this paper endeavors to analyze the issue in the way a treaty monitoring body would—to see if any area within federal law contravenes the Convention and/or whether there are gaps where legislation or practice might be introduced or reformed to ensure compliance. At this juncture, the CRPD has not been subjected to the scrutiny and interpretation of an international monitoring body. The CRPD creates a Committee tasked with reviewing regular reports of States Parties. It will ultimately be up to that Committee to fill in the gaps and choose between competing interpretations. Having said that, it is possible to set forth a plausible estimate of the CRPD's reach against which to analyze U.S. law.

Synopsis of Analysis

This paper identifies areas in which U.S. law is harmonious to that of the CRPD's requirements, as well as existing gaps in U.S. law when compared to each Article in the CRPD. It also highlights potential areas within the body of U.S. disability laws that would require examination if the U.S. either signed and ratified the CRPD, or desired to have its domestic disability laws and policies be of a level with the Convention's coverage.

This comparative analysis is an extremely important tool if our nation is to consider joining the global community as part of this historic Convention, or simply to reevaluate domestic laws and policies in a manner that would respond to current shortcomings and thereby maintain America's precedence in the field. This paper can therefore serve as background for an informed decision on the issue of signing and ratifying the CRPD, as well as an introspection of currently prevailing laws, policies, and practices more generally. Although the current U.S. administration does not lean towards signing or ratifying the Convention, this may be influenced by a lack of crucial information towards making that decision. Alternatively, future administrations may take a different approach to international treaties generally, and the CRPD specifically.

Several points bear mentioning. The U.S. legal system is a federalist one, meaning that both state and federal constitutions, statutes, and common law impact the rights of persons with disabilities. This paper focuses nearly exclusively on federal law, and specifically on the primary statutes. It is not intended, nor can it be within its mandate, absolutely comprehensive in scope. Thus, while constitutional law and federal statutes rest at the top of the federal disability policy pyramid, there are multiple and various programs within the Executive branch that impact the lives of people with disabilities, although they will vary greatly in terms of longevity, sustainability, and actual impact. The paper discusses these programs to the extent that they have generally been noted by experts in the field to have been sustained and effective.

Explanation of Key Findings

As a general matter, the aims of the CRPD are consistent with U.S. disability law, in respect of which significant segments of the CRPD drew inspiration. For the majority of articles, U.S. law can be viewed as either being of a level with the mandates of the Convention or capable of reaching those levels either through more rigorous implementation and/or additional actions by Congress. In addition to highlighting areas of harmonious thresholds of legal protection, this paper also identifies several CRPD Articles that illustrate gaps between United States disability laws and the Convention. The Articles identified as currently having the most significant gaps between U.S. law and policy and the CRPD are as follows:

Article 5—Equality and Non-Discrimination. Current U.S. law and policy lacks equality measures such as vocational training, affirmative action, quotas, and job set-asides.

Article 6—Women with Disabilities. Current U.S. law and policy lacks positive measures sufficient to ensure the full and equal enjoyment of all human rights.

Article 7—Children with Disabilities. In the main, State rather than U.S. law, governs the rights of children.

Article 8—Awareness raising. Current U.S. law and policy has no affirmative mandate to alter social stereotypes.

Article 9—Accessibility. Current under-enforcement of federal laws creates a gap between legal requirements and reality.

Article 11—Situations of risk and humanitarian emergencies. Current U.S. laws and policies prohibiting discrimination in the provision of services relating to emergency services have not been implemented.

Article 12—Equal recognition before the law. Legal capacity is governed primarily by State-level law.

Article 13—Access to Justice. U.S. courts have interpreted physical access to court services to be limited by a fundamental alteration defense, and have not sufficiently ensured other access to justice.

Article 16—Freedom from Exploitation, Violence, and Abuse. Current U.S. law and policy does not provide for proactive education and training to prevent exploitation, violence, and abuse.

Article 18—Liberty of movement and nationality. Current U.S. immigration policy restricts potential residents and certain visitors with disabilities.

Article 19—Living independently and being included in the community. Current U.S. law and policy limits the right to live in the community to services that do not cause fundamental alterations.

Article 20—Personal mobility. Current U.S. law and policy does not recognize a right to the provision of medical and assistive devices in the manner required by the CRPD.

Article 23—Respect for Home and the Family. State, rather than U.S. law, mainly governs these rights.

Article 24—Education. Current U.S. law does not seek to develop children's full potential but instead requires an adequate education.

Article 25—Health. State, rather than U.S. law, mainly governs this right.

Article 27—Work and Employment. Current U.S. law and policy does not provide equality measures, such as vocational training, affirmative action, or job set-asides.

Article 28—Adequate standard of living and social protection. Current U.S. law does not recognize economic or social protections as rights.

Article 29—Participation in Political and Public Life. Current U.S. law explicitly protects most of what the CRPD envisions, yet has been laxly implemented in the field of voting rights.

Article 30—Participation in Cultural Life, Recreation, Leisure, and Sport. Current U.S. law does not recognize cultural, recreational, leisure or sport participation as an affirmative right.

Article 32—International cooperation. Current U.S. law does not mandate inclusive-development practices abroad.

It is important to emphasize, however, that these gaps are capable of being narrowed or eradicated through either more rigorous implementation of existing U.S. laws and policies, and/or through Congressional action.

Conclusion and Recommendations

The ultimate conclusion of this paper is that there is no legal impediment to U.S. signature and ratification on the basis that, in large measure, the legal standards articulated in the CRPD align with U.S. disability law.

The U.S. disability rights agenda, premised on a social model of disability, has exerted a powerful international influence in revising legal regimes affecting disabled persons. But the U.S. scheme, which is primarily an antidiscrimination one, has limits that are reflected in the gaps discussed above. Specifically, it has proven difficult to transform society's institutional structures and attitudes towards marginalized individuals. Further complicating the U.S. disability antidiscrimination project have been cramped judicial interpretations on threshold definition of disability issues,[1] as well as uneven implementation of existing federal law.[2]

An example of all of these factors involves employment levels for people with disabilities. Observers have alternatively blamed restrictive Supreme Court decisions and noted the abysmal success rates of ADA Title I plaintiffs. Just as importantly, however, are the missing pieces in the U.S. disability policy scheme, including health insurance gaps and lack of training and rehabilitation services, which can actually create disincentives and barriers to work.

The overall U.S. disability employment policy has been criticized as non-integrated and lacking in extra-statutory support.[3]

These gaps are capable of being narrowed or eradicated through either more rigorous implementation of existing U.S. laws and policies, and/or through Congressional action. To the extent that this paper identifies gaps or potential inconsistencies between U.S. disability law and the CRPD, the tools of law reform and ratification processes could serve to address and facilitate ratification by the United States.

Signature by the United States of the CRPD would be a realistic aim, insofar as signature implies taking no steps that would undermine the principles of the treaty in question but does not render the treaty legally binding on the United States unless and until ratification is undertaken. Any subsequent ratification process would, as with any human rights convention ratification, entail a careful review of existing law and could be coupled with law reform in targeted areas where appropriate, as well as the use of other tools of ratification, including the attachment of reservations, declarations and understandings that have facilitated U.S. accession to human rights conventions.[4] To provide one illustration, when the U.S. ratified the Convention on the Elimination of All Forms of Racial Discrimination, it attached a reservation in respect of provisions that could have the effect of restricting American constitutional and federal laws according extensive protections on individual freedom of speech. This reservation served to facilitate U.S. ratification of that Convention, and the mechanism of reservations, declarations and understandings would be a tool available to the United States in the case of CRPD ratification.[5]

ENDNOTES

1. *See* National Council on Disability, *The Americans with Disabilities Act Policy Brief Series: Righting the ADA, No. 6: Defining "Disability" in a Civil Rights Context: The Courts' Focus on Extent of Limitations as Opposed to Fair Treatment and Equal Opportunity* (Feb. 2003), available at <http://www.ncd.gov/newsroom/publications/2003/extentoflimitations.html>.

2. *See* National Council on Disability, *Implementation of the ADA: Challenges, Best Practices, and New Opportunities for Success* (July 2007), available at <http://www.ncd.gov/newsroom/publications/2007/implementation_07-26-07.html>.

3. *See infra* discussion of Article 27 (employment).

4. For a clearly articulated explanation on US policy in respect of the ratification of human rights conventions, *see* THOMAS BUERGENTHAL, DINAH SHELTON, & DAVID STEWART, INTERNATIONAL HUMAN RIGHTS 359–377 (2002).

5. See David Stewart, *U.S. Ratification of the Covenant on Civil and Political Rights: The Significance of the Reservations, Understandings and Declarations*, 14 HUM. RTS. L. J. 77 (1993).

---

*National Council on Disability is an independent U.S. federal agency that promotes policies and programs, that guarantee equal opportunity for all individuals with disabilities, with the ultimate goal of enabling them to lead independent lives.

National Council on Disability. *Finding the Gaps: A Comparative Analysis of Disability Laws in the United States to the United Nations Convention on the Rights of Persons with Disabilities (CRPD).* Washington, DC: National Council on Disability, 2008: 1–7. http://www.ncd.gov/newsroom/publications/2008/pdf/ncd_crpd_analysis.pdf.

Discussion Questions

1. How is the Convention on the Rights of Persons with Disabilities (CRPD) an example of embracing unity and cooperation?

2. What should the role of civil society be in implementing the convention?

3. All people with disabilities have the right to be free from discrimination in enjoying their rights. Do you believe the CRPD is comprehensive in its inclusion of selected rights? If yes, why? If no, why not?

4. How will the CRPD interface with other core human rights treaties?

5. Since the CRPD is so far reaching and the United States has identified some gaps in compliance, what will be the challenges for developing countries in its implementation?

CHAPTER 4:

Honoring Family Cultures and Values

This chapter explores the need for individuals who work with people with disabilities to respect and support the culture, values, and languages of each home and promote the active participation of all families in society. The research surrounding the collaboration of school personnel with culturally and linguistically diverse families is also described, with recommendations for improvement of the collaboration.

The first article, "Responsiveness to Family, Culture, Values and Education," a position statement from the Division of Early Childhood of the Council for Exceptional Children, discusses the six characteristics of responsive organizations in regard to family cultures and values. These characteristics are:

1. respecting the values and practices of all members,
2. encouraging multiple viewpoints,
3. extending the competence of families, governance, and practitioners,

4. implementing policies that ensure leaders at all levels of service are representative of individuals from different cultural, ethnic, and language backgrounds,
5. developing and disseminating products, and
6. encouraging professional development that incorporates the concept and reality of family diversity.

The second article, "The Effects of Culture on Special Education Services: Evil Eyes, Prayer Meetings, and IEPs," by Suzanne Lamorey, focuses on how culture affects the way educators provide special education services. This is a global issue that challenges educators as providers of an array of services to diverse populations of children with disabilities and to their families.

In implementing the articles of the Convention on the Rights of Persons with Disabilities, all personnel at all levels of the service and support system must honor family cultures and values. Honoring family cultures and values is the cornerstone of the provision of services and supports in deinstitutionalization, employment, education, and community living, ensuring an adequate standard of living, and social protection.

Responsiveness to Family, Culture, Values and Education

By the Division for Early Childhood, Council for Exceptional Children*

For optimal development and learning of all children, DEC believes that individuals who work with children must respect and support the culture, values and languages of each home and promote the active participation of all families. Legislation and recommended practices call for individualized approaches to serving infants, toddlers and young children with special needs and their families (Harbin & Salisbury, 2000; Sandall, McLean, & Smith, 2000). Individualized services begin with acceptance of both similarities and differences in race, ethnicity, culture, language, ability, religion, education, income, family configuration, geographic location and other characteristics that contribute to human uniqueness. For example, Turnbull and Stowe (2001) suggest that individuals with disabilities have different perspectives compared to parents of individuals with disabilities, and individuals from various disciplines (e.g., law, policy, medicine). According to Turnbull and Stowe, differing perspectives are reflected in how one views and reacts to core concepts, including disability, which in turn impacts disability policies.

Responsiveness grows from interpersonal relationships that reflect a mutual respect and appreciation for diversity among individuals within and across groups. DEC defines diversity "as a highly inclusive construct, embracing all aspects of individuals and groups that make them different [from each other], which includes, but is not limited to, language, race, ethnicity, gender, ability, geographic location, class, and lifestyle" (Division for Early Childhood, 2004). Barrera, Corso and Macpherson (2003) suggest that diversity is a construct that is both dynamic and relative in any given context.

"No single person can be said to be diverse, culturally or otherwise, except in reference to other persons or environments. Diversity . . . cannot exist independently of its context. Recognizing this point is essential to responding respectfully to cultural diversity and honoring those who are diverse from us" (pp. 6–7). Responsive early childhood professionals and programs honor the beliefs and practices of the families being served as well as the people providing the services.

We believe that there are many sources of diversity. We also recognize that cultural diversity in the United States is distinct from cross-cultural international diversity. This concept paper addresses diversity in the U.S. stemming from cultural and linguistic variables. This paper includes a description of the beliefs held by DEC regarding family cultures, values and languages and how each may impact the activities and policies of organizations and service programs that cater to children with disabilities, their families, and professionals who work with them.

The six beliefs of a responsive organization listed in DEC's position statement on family cultures, values and languages (2002) and discussed in this paper are:

1. Respecting the values and practices of all members.
2. Encouraging multiple viewpoints to enrich the whole organization.
3. Seeking ways to extend the competence of the leadership (e.g., families, governance and practitioners), with regard to understanding similarities and differences in family cultures, values and languages.
4. Developing, implementing and reviewing of policies and procedures in recruitment and leadership at all levels of service to ensure meaningful local, state, national and international representation and participation of people from different cultures, values and languages.

5. Encouraging and supporting the development and dissemination of products that address family cultures, values and languages.
6. Incorporating in training and dissemination activities (e.g., meetings, events, conferences and publications) the impact of family cultures, values and languages.

In an effort to provide the field with a common understanding of concepts, including culture, cultural and linguistic diversity, inclusiveness, multiculturalism, and values, a glossary of selected terms follows the discussion. Readers may wish to review the definitions to familiarize themselves with this terminology prior to reading this paper.

DEC strongly believes in respecting the values and practices of all members. Respecting diverse values and practices is an ongoing commitment of DEC. This commitment is made explicit in DEC's code of ethics: "Demonstrate our respect and concern for children and families, colleagues and others with whom we work, honoring their beliefs, values, customs and culture" (Sandall, McLean, & Smith, 2000, p. 163). Respect, however, can be difficult to communicate across diverse cultural parameters. What is considered respectful within one culture may not be perceived as such within other cultures (Barrera 2000; Lynch & Hanson, 1998). Often, underlying differences in cultural beliefs and practices contribute to ineffective or disrespectful interactions between individuals (Harry, Kalyanpur, & Day, 1999).

Barrera, Corso and Macpherson identify two qualities essential to effectively communicating respect: reciprocity and responsiveness. These two qualities give insight into how to increase the probability that actions are perceived as respectful, even across diverse cultural parameters (Kalyanpur & Harry, 1999; Villegas & Lucas, 2000).

Reciprocity involves making space for equal voice or "power" in all interactions (Barrera, Corso, & Macpherson, 2003; Harry,

Kalyanpur & Day, 1999). This can be accomplished by highlighting the range of values and practices existing within one's organization or program, and the positive contributions of these diverse values and practices. For example, DEC should use both active (e.g., keynote addresses; procedures used to develop policy) and passive (e.g., in DEC literature and posters; demographic membership "pie charts"; or translated materials that are representative of the multiple languages of DEC members) methods for showcasing our high regard for diverse values and practices within the organization. The diversity of values and practices of organizations and service programs and the children and families they serve need to be consistently mirrored in all contexts (e.g., conferences, publications, policies and practices) and in ways that clearly acknowledge and show appreciation for its diverse membership. Such acknowledgment and appreciation will then lead to true responsiveness.

Responsiveness occurs when individuals "decenter" and create sufficient space to integrate the riches and power of diverse voices (Barrera, Corso, & Macpherson, 2003). The most challenging aspect of responsiveness is that one must become comfortable with limits and uncertainty.

Responsiveness requires moving away from preset or "this is the way it is" agendas and staying open to what might emerge as diverse voices converge on an equal level. Developing a variety of ways for members' voices to be heard may lead all to being truly responsive to what is heard. Some opportunities for responsiveness may already exist within organizations and service programs while others still need to be developed. By strengthening opportunities for reciprocity and responsiveness, one's commitment to respecting diverse values and practices will encourage the organization and its constituency to speak strongly and clearly.

DEC strongly encourages multiple viewpoints to enrich the whole organization. Many professional organizations seek to "move beyond merely valuing diversity to building an inclusive, high-performing organization. In the process, diversity ceases to be merely a human-resource initiative and becomes a fundamental competency: Diversity and inclusiveness become the responsibility of everyone in the organization" (Norris & Lofton, 1995, p. 2). Organizations and service programs should seek not to merely focus on differences but to build inclusiveness around a shared set of values articulated in the organization's mission statement, position statements, strategic plan and other documents. For example, the DEC Executive Board recently adopted a five-year strategic plan that includes goals and objectives that relate to planning, developing and implementing activities, products and outreach efforts that recognize and promote diversity (Division for Early Childhood, 2004).

Organizations are under increasing pressure to become more service- and customer-oriented in order to establish a competitive advantage in the marketplace (Bryant, 1991). Understanding the marketplace argument for diversity impacts all levels of the organization, in contrast to being delegated as a "special initiative" or assigned to a specific task force or committee (Norris & Lofton, 1995). In some cases, the membership takes the initiative before the leadership in making a full commitment to diversity-building efforts. Norris and Lofton note that in their case studies, a strong commitment from leaders was critical to the success of organization's initiatives related to diversity. In every organization's strategic plan, activities should emerge from its stakeholders and be incorporated across the goals set for given periods of time. Commitment across all levels facilitates the incorporation of diversity goals into every strategy, initiative and program.

DEC strongly believes in seeking ways to extend the competence of its leadership (e.g., families, governance and practitioners), as well as acknowledge different leadership styles with regard to understanding similarities and differences in family cultures, values and languages. DEC believes that leadership development is a key to creating quality EI/ECSE programs and that its members (e.g., service providers, family members, students, faculty and trainers, Subdivision members, etc.) do not have to be in formally appointed supervisory, administrative or organizational roles to be "leaders." DEC believes its membership can and should exercise leadership and become involved at the local, state and national levels.

As a professional organization, DEC provides vital leadership to its members as well as in the larger national political context. Given the diverse nature of global, national and local professional environments, it is critical to ensure that leadership in organizations and service programs is both culturally responsive and culturally informed. Three aspects emerge as critical in developing culturally responsive and culturally informed leadership at any level, whether as teachers in classrooms or as members in professional organizations. The first is exploring diverse paradigms; the second is supporting opportunities for diverse voices to be heard; and the third is finding avenues for integrating the diverse contributions those voices can make (Norris & Lofton, 1995; Wheatley & Kellner-Rogers, 1996).

Diverse paradigms. One of the characteristics of cultural diversity is the fact that there are multiple perspectives and multiple values around those perspectives. Culturally responsive and informed leadership respects this fact and explores individuals' diverse understanding of the concept of leadership. Exploration is a first step in building the competence we seek. Once diverse leadership paradigms are identified, it is important to develop a means of integrating them into policy and governance. As these differing perspectives become more visible, the diverse voices of individuals within organizations and service programs will emerge. For example, the literature on women's leadership styles is growing, and the focus on women's leadership from the center of the organization, rather than the top, is a paradigm shift in the traditional corporate world (Helgesen, 1990 and 1995). Organizational charts depict circular structures rather than a "top-down" approach typically found in the hierarchical model.

Diverse voices. Supporting opportunities for diverse voices to be heard requires a deep appreciation of the relevance of stakeholders and the gifts of pluralism. Individuals acquire "voice" as their views and opinions are acknowledged by colleagues and peers. Culturally responsive and informed leadership makes time to listen to and highlight the diverse voices of its constituents. Having the courage to initiate conversations with constituents is key. Wheatley (2002) notes that large-scale efforts often start small, with passion and not power.

"One of the most important results of creating opportunities for diverse voices to be heard is that individuals begin to define themselves as citizens of the organizations in which they participate" (Block, 2002, p. 81). Block goes on to elaborate that when individuals see themselves as citizens of an organization they choose to "vote with [their] feet, [their] hearts, [their] energy, [to express their] care or indifference toward how [their] institution fares in the world" (p. 84). In adapting Block's approach, it is critical that organizations and service programs provide opportunities for its diverse constituents and membership to do just that, to vote with their feet, their hearts, their energy, and to act with care toward how their organizations or programs fare in the world. As this happens, every individual has opportunities to participate in the organization's leadership—every member can offer his or her diverse contributions toward the whole. For example, Helgesen (1990 and 1995) refers to the "web of inclusion" in her discussion of women's leadership styles. This approach emphasizes accessibility and equality by ensuring that communication lines are "multiple, open and diffuse" (Helgesen, 1990, p. 266).

Diverse contributions. The distinct talents we each possess become visible as our voices are valued and acknowledged. Culturally responsive and informed leadership invites individuals to add their distinct talents to those of others so that the total community may benefit. Rather than ask for volunteers to participate in preassigned tasks and activities, we should collectively find avenues for each other's contributions, weaving a seamless tapestry for the whole. Culturally responsive and informed leadership recognizes that following is as critical as leading; that listening in silence is as valuable as speaking out; and that staying in the background is as important as standing out. Each contribution adds something to the whole. Through attending to diverse paradigms, diverse voices and diverse contributions, leadership competence will grow and become stronger in regard to similarities and differences in cultures, values and languages.

DEC strongly believes in the development, implementation and review of policies and procedures in recruitment and leadership at all levels of service to ensure meaningful local, state, national and international representation and participation of people from different cultures, values and languages. The meaningful participation of diverse individuals is critical if we are to effect change in services for all children and families (National Research Council, 2002). Thus, it is important that policies and procedures related to recruitment and leadership at all levels of service reflect a degree of commitment to achieve participation of diverse individuals. This includes local schools and programs, state and federal agencies, institutions of higher education, and national organizations such as DEC. This commitment could in turn, help to increase interest and membership of diverse individuals in the early intervention (EI) and early childhood special education (ECSE) profession.

There is a critical need in our field for leaders from different cultural and linguistic backgrounds who can serve as mentors to young professionals (Elliott et al. 1999a; Fenichel, 1992; Hood & Boyce, 1997). Issues of fragmented health, education and social service systems; low wages; lack of career paths; and limited access to formal training, higher education and professional development contribute to the lack of diverse personnel advancing into leadership positions (Elliott et al. 1999a; Kagan & Bowman, 1997). In a publication about creating a viable career development system for practitioners, Elliott and colleagues noted that to be able to better address the needs of children and families, professionals need to reflect and represent the communities they serve (Elliott et al. 1999b, p. 2).

The shortage of qualified personnel to work in EI, ECSE and special education continues (23rd Annual Report to Congress, 2001). This shortage is accentuated by the need for qualified personnel of different cultures, values and languages. Hanson (1998) found that even with the increasing number of nonwhite, non-Anglo-European children and their families being served in EI, there is still a disproportionately low representation of workers of non-Anglo-European cultures being trained to work with these children and families. Similarly, few higher education preparation programs are responsive to ethnic and language diversity (Gay, 2002; Isenberg, 2000; Kushner & Ortiz, 2000) or have diverse faculty (American Psychological Association, 1996a and 1996b; Isenberg, 2000).

Leadership development is essential to ensuring quality services and programs for all children and families (Elliott et al. 1996a). Through its policies and procedures, organizations and service programs can facilitate diversity in its leadership within EI and ECSE. A clearly defined mission statement and action plan convey a strong message to the field that creates opportunities that are available, appropriate and accessible for all. We as individuals and as an organization need to "[commit] resources, [exert] coordinated efforts to influence institutional policies and [make] internal policy and structural changes" (Hood & Boyce, 1997, pp. 152–153). For example, one way to examine policies and procedures is to adopt the premise that "work settings are language communities" and "all leaders are leading language communities" (Kegan & Lahey, 2001,

p. 8). Kegan and Lahey recommend three languages to transform customary organizational arrangement, and one of them is moving "from the language of rules and policies to the language of public agreement" (p. 9).

According to Elliott and colleagues, many who advance into early childhood leadership positions lack the necessary support and training to allow them to address the needs of the communities they serve. Often, disparities between the backgrounds of early childhood leaders and members of the communities they serve lead to policies and practices that are inconsistent and inappropriate with the values and needs of those communities. In addition, the diversity of professional preparation and professional roles is much greater in early childhood fields than in other areas of education (National Institute on Early Childhood Development and Education, 2000). Thus, the concept of "career lattice" seen in early childhood does not match the corporate models of "lock-step" promotions (Bredekamp & Willer, 1992; Jalongo & Isenberg, 2000; National Association for the Education of Young Children, 1994).

The American Council on Education identified four key issues for advancing leadership in higher education: (1) leadership development, (2) career advancement, (3) workplace and campus climate, and (4) mentoring (Brown, Ummersen, and Hill, 2002). In essence, these areas apply to all members of the EI/ECSE field (from various backgrounds, race/ethnicity, income levels, disciplines, skill levels, etc.). Organizations and service programs have the opportunity to establish a blueprint or guide for promoting the untapped potential for new and emerging leaders as well as supporting existing leaders and their advancement. Diversity among leadership throughout EI/ECSE is essential to ensuring educational equity for all children and families (Moore, 1997).

DEC strongly encourages and supports the development and dissemination of products that address family cultures, values and languages. To meet the needs of an increasingly diverse number of children, families and professionals in the early childhood field, it is important that materials and products reflect and address different family cultures, values and languages (Santos, et al. 2000). The dynamic nature of our field warrants the development of materials and products that reflect current and state-of-the-art evidence- and value-based practices. The impact of differing values, beliefs and practices must be addressed and infused across all relevant topics in DEC products. A separate section on "diversity" is often insufficient in addressing the full impact on practices. For example, a booklet for families on transition should address how individual family values, beliefs and practices may influence their participation in the transition process, choices of programs, expectations of children's readiness and overall development, and families' relationships with professionals. Finally, it is critical that material developers consider and address cultural and linguistic factors that impact accessibility, appropriateness, and adaptability, not only in terms of the format of materials but also in the information and practices promoted in the products.

Organizations and programs must also give equal importance to creating and implementing an effective dissemination plan. Multiple venues to disseminate information and products must be considered to ensure that needed information reaches all possible audiences.

Accessibility is key to the success of any dissemination activity. Thus, developers of materials must consider the accessibility of their products not only in terms of disability access (e.g., Braille) but also in terms of languages (e.g., Spanish, American Sign Language and other languages), formats (e.g., video, audio, Web-based), readability and comprehensibility.

Likewise, at the organizational level, dissemination in multiple formats is also desirable to reach diverse audiences. For example, information gathering for strategic planning might include specific target groups (e.g., family members, direct service providers, higher education faculty, etc.), and formats for input and discussion might vary (e.g., focus groups, online surveys, conference meetings, Web-based discussion groups, etc.).

As consumers, we need to encourage product developers to bring together a wide range of diverse voices to conceptualize, develop, implement, evaluate and disseminate products. This is an important first step to ensure that materials address different family cultures, values and languages (Corso, Santos, & Roof, 2002). A flexible yet systematic plan must be in place to ensure that multiple perspectives are considered and addressed in all phases of product development, implementation and dissemination. This plan should include concrete steps to recruit and retain individuals from a variety of backgrounds who will participate in all aspects of the development and dissemination of products. For example, a work panel composed of diverse stakeholders could provide continuous feedback to developers on the content and format of the product. Members of the panel could be recruited through agencies that serve diverse children and families who would benefit from the product being developed. The plan also should include a clearly conceptualized formative and summative evaluation plan that promotes and supports meaningful consumer participation. Developers should consider evaluation questions that examine the extent to which their products address the needs of families and children from a variety of backgrounds.

DEC strongly believes in training and dissemination activities (e.g., meetings, events, conferences and publications) that incorporate the impact of family cultures, values and languages. Professional organizations such as DEC play a key role in promoting the transformation of the educational pipeline (from high school through postdoctoral and continuing education) so that the student population reflects the changing demographics of the population at large. Also, higher education and continuing education programs must embed multicultural competence in training, research and practice issues. Within higher education, scholars acknowledge that professionals will not become culturally competent and inclusive until programs are reflective of those values (American Psychological Association, 1997; Morey & Kitano, 1997; Phillips, 1993; Ponterotto, 1996). DEC professional development and personnel preparation activities seek to incorporate family cultures, values and languages. For example, explicit review criteria for conference proposals and publications are steps to ensure that multiple voices contribute to these activities, and the translation of materials is a positive step towards addressing the needs of a linguistically diverse population.

In the broader context, organizations and service programs should engage in interactions with other systems such as human services organizations and higher education institutions. Stakeholders take key values with them as they move within and across systems and organizations. The process of inclusion permeates the organization or service program's product development (e.g., journals, publications, Web site, brochures, etc.), conference planning, meetings, and communication styles at local, state and national levels. For example, human services systems (Focal Point, 1994; Hernandez & Isaacs, 1998), child welfare systems (Child Welfare League of America, 1993), schools (Kalyanpur & Harry, 1999; Lipman, 1998; Nieto, 1999) and communities (Pang, Gay, & Stanley, 1995) recognize a growing need on the part of agencies and institutions to examine their systems with respect to serving increasingly diverse populations. Thus, it is critical that organizations and service programs commit themselves to continuous improvement with regard to family cultures, values and languages. Furthermore, organizations and service programs must engage in a process of ongoing monitoring and recalibration to assure adjustments that reflect our ever-growing appreciation of how to be responsive. Therefore, organizations and service programs should continuously examine and take steps to make necessary changes to ensure that what is projected to the larger community, such as policies, position statements and products, reflect the value placed on the multiple viewpoints that its diverse membership brings.

DEFINITIONS OF SELECTED TERMS

Many fields have long-established definitions and an understanding of concepts around culture and language. Because EI and ECSE as a field are young, there is as yet no general consensus of understanding. In fact many concepts related to culture and language may be unfamiliar to readers. This section provides definitions of selected terms, which we have borrowed from various disciplines such as anthropology, sociology, psychology and counseling. It is important to note that there are local, regional and state differences on which terms are used and how they are used. Each term carries various nuances depending on the user and listener. While this list is not exhaustive, it is our intention to establish some common understanding among EI and ECSE researchers and practitioners around these concepts.

Culture refers to "shared and learned ideas and products of a society. It is the shared way of life of a people, including their beliefs, their technology, their values and norms, all of which are transmitted down through the generations by learning and observation" (Small, 1998, p. 72). It also refers to the "ideations, symbols, behaviors—values, and beliefs that are shared by a human group" (Banks & Banks, 2001, p. 428). "Culture is not a static phenomenon. It is sustained, challenged, or modified over time. Culture is also not a neutral construct. It draws much of its influence from the conviction that its values and practices are inherently right and preferable to those of others" (Shonkoff and Phillips, 2000, p. 69). "Central to greater understanding [of culture] is the need to identify the diverse and frequently overlapping elements of ethnicity, which include national origin, race, minority status, language, and religion.

Ethnicity can be an amalgam of any or all of these . . ." (Shonkoff & Phillips, 2000, p. 63).

Cultural linguistic diversity refers to "behavioral, value, linguistic, and other differences ascribed to people's cultural backgrounds. Cultural diversity almost invariably includes some level of diversity in how language is understood and used . . . [the terms] cultural diversity and cultural linguistic diversity [are often used] synonymously" (Barrera, Corso, & Macpherson, 2003).

Inclusiveness "is the act of encouraging belonging. Leaders of an inclusive organization do more than value diversity—they understand and aggressively eliminate barriers to performance that fall unevenly on different groups. In addition to creating a pluralistic culture, they establish standards of behavior that affirm inclusiveness. These leaders expect all . . . to meet the standards. Inclusive organizations motivate employees and generate intensive commitment, while at the same time leading world-class performance standards. They use diverse teams to solve complex problems that involve highly diverse customer populations" (Norris & Lofton, 1995, pp. 5–6).

Multiculturalism "refers to a condition in which the organization represents, values, understands, and respects several distinct cultures. The classic multicultural situation exists in many international settings, where distinctive ethnic or cultural groups must understand and respect one another if they are to do business together and succeed" (Norris & Lofton, 1995, p. 5).

Values refer to aspects of one's culture (e.g., behaviors, beliefs, language) that are given high positive weight, esteem and/or significance. For example, common values in cultures with Northern European roots include competition, autonomy and individualism. Cultures with roots in South American and non-European countries value intimacy, dignity and deference to elders (Robinson & Howard-Hamilton, 2000).

REFERENCES

23rd Annual Report to Congress on the Implementation of the Individuals with Disabilities Act. 2001. http://www.ed.gov/offices/OSERS/OSEP/Products/OSEP2001AnlRpt/

American Psychological Association. 1996a. *Valuing diversity in faculty: A guide.* Washington, DC: American Psychological Association.

American Psychological Association. 1996b. *How to recruit and hire ethnic minority faculty.* Washington, DC: American Psychological Association.

American Psychological Association. 1997. *Visions and transformations: The final report of the commission on ethnic minority recruitment, retention, and training in psychology.* Washington, DC: American Psychological Association.

Banks, J.A., and C.A. Banks, eds. 2001. *Multicultural education: Issues and perspectives, 4th edition.* John Wiley and Sons, Inc.

Barrera, I. 2000. Honoring differences. *Young Exceptional Children* 3(4), 17–26.

Barrera, I., R. Corso, and D. Macpherson. 2003. *Skilled dialogue: Strategies for responding to cultural diversity in early childhood.* Baltimore: Paul H. Brookes Publishing.

Bayles, P., and J. Parks-Doyle. 1995. *The web of inclusion: Faculty helping faculty.* New York: Jones and Bartlett Publishers.

Block, P. 2002. *The answer to how is yes.* San Francisco: Barrett-Kohler.

Bredekamp, S., and B. Willer. 1992. Of ladders and lattices, cores and cones: Conceptualizing an early childhood professional development system. *Young Children* 47(3), 47–50.

Brown, G., C.V. Ummersen, and B. Hill. 2002. *Advancing women's leadership III: Breaking the barriers: A guidebook of strategies.* Washington, DC: American Council on Education, Office of Women in Higher Education.

Bryant, A.L. 1991. Creating a multicultural association. *Leadership.* Washington, DC: American Society of Association Executives.

Child Welfare League of America. 1993. *Cultural competence self-assessment instrument.* Washington, DC: Child Welfare League of America.

Corso, R.M., R.M. Santos, and V. Roof. 2002. Adapting and evaluating early childhood education and early childhood special education materials at the community level. *TEACHING Exceptional Children* 34(3), 30–36.

Division for Early Childhood. 2004. *DEC strategic plan for 2004–2009.* Missoula, MT: Division for Early Childhood.

Division for Early Childhood. 2002. *DEC position statement on responsiveness to family cultures, values and languages.* Missoula, MT: Division for Early Childhood.

Elliott, K., C. Alvarado, J. Copland, W. Surr, M. Farris, A. Genser, et al. 1999a. *Taking the lead: The power of mentoring.* Boston: Wheelock College, Center for Career Development in Early Care and Education.

Elliott, K., C. Alvarado, J. Copland, W. Surr, M. Farris, A. Genser, et al. 1999b. *Taking the lead: The many faces of leadership.* Boston: Wheelock College, Center for Career Development in Early Care and Education.

Fenichel, E., ed. 1992. *Learning through supervision and mentorship to support the development of infants, toddlers, and their families: A source book.* Washington, DC: Zero to Three/National Center for Clinical Infant Programs.

Focal Point. 1994. *Developing culturally competent organizations* 8 (2). Portland, OR: Bulletin of the Research and Training Center on Family Support and Children's Mental Health, Portland State University.

Gay, G. 2002. Preparing for culturally responsive teaching. *Journal of Teacher Education* 53(2), 106–116.

Hanson, M.J. 1998. Ethnic, cultural, and language diversity in intervention settings. In *Developing cross-cultural competence: A guide for working with children and their families*, eds. E.W. Lynch and M.J. Hanson, pp. 3–22. Baltimore: Paul H. Brookes Publishing.

Harbin, G., and C. Salisbury. 2000. Recommended practices in policies, procedures and systems change. In *DEC recommended practices in early intervention/early childhood special education*, eds. S. Sandall, M.E. McLean, and B.J. Smith, pp. 65–75. Longmont, CO: Sopris West.

Harry, B., M. Kalyanpur, and M. Day. 1999. *Building cultural reciprocity with families: Case studies in special education.* Baltimore: Paul H. Brookes Publishing.

Helgesen, S. 1990. *The female advantage: Women's ways of leadership.* New York: Doubleday.

Helgesen, S. 1995. *The web of inclusion.* New York: Doubleday.

Hernandez, M., and M.R. Isaacs. 1998. *Promoting cultural competence in children's mental health services.* Baltimore: Paul H. Brookes Publishing.

Hood, S.L., and J. Boyce. 1997. Refining and expanding the role of professional associations to increase the pool of faculty researchers of color. In *Diversity in higher education: Mentoring and diversity in higher education*, ed. H.T. Frierson, pp. 141–159. Greenwich, CT: JAI Press.

Isenberg, J. 2000. The state of the art in early childhood professional preparation. In *New teachers for a new century: The future of early childhood professional preparation.* ECI 2000–9038r, pp. 15–58. Washington, DC: U.S. Department of Education, National Institute on Early Childhood Development and Education. Also available at http://www.ed.gov.

Jalongo, M., and J. Isenberg. 2000. *Exploring your role: A practitioner's introduction to early childhood education.* Columbus, OH: Merrill/Prentice Hall.

Kagan, S.L., and B.T. Bowman, eds. 1997. *Leadership in early care and education.* Washington, DC: National Association for the Education of Young Children.

Kalyanpur, M., and B. Harry. 1999. *Culture in special education: Building reciprocal family-professional relationships.* Baltimore: Paul H. Brookes Publishing.

Kegan, R., and L.L. Lahey. 2001. *How the way we talk can change the way we work: Seven languages for transformation.* San Francisco: Jossey-Bass.

Kushner, M.I., and A.A. Ortiz. 2000. The preparation of early childhood education teachers to serve English Language Learners. In *New teachers for a new century: The future of early childhood professional preparation.* ECI 2000–9038r, pp. 125–154. Washington, DC: U.S. Department of Education, National Institute on Early Childhood Development and Education. Also available at http://www.ed.gov.

Lipman, P. 1998. *Race, class and power in school restructuring.* Albany, NY: SUNY Press.

Lynch, E.W., and M.J. Hanson. 1998. *Developing cross-cultural competence: A guide for working with young children and their families.* 2nd ed. Baltimore: Paul H. Brookes Publishing.

Moore, E.K. 1997. Race, class, and education. In *Leadership in early care and education,* eds. S.L. Kagan and B.T. Bowman, pp. 69–74. Washington, DC: National Association for the Education of Young Children.

Morey, A.I., and M.K. Kitano. 1997. *Multicultural course transformation in higher education: A broader truth.* Boston: Allyn and Bacon.

NC TEACH Newsletter (Fall 2001). http://ncteach.ga.unc.edu/docs/NCTeachnewsfall2001.pdf (accessed 10/30/02).

National Association for the Education of Young Children. 1994. A conceptual framework for early childhood professional development (position statement). In *The early childhood career lattice: Perspectives on professional development,* eds. J. Johnson and J.B. McCraken. Washington, DC: National Association for the Education of Young Children.

National Institute on Early Childhood Development and Education. 2000. *New teachers for a new century: The future of early childhood professional preparation.* ECI 2000–9038r. Washington, DC: U.S. Department of Education, National Institute on Early Childhood Development and Education. Also available at http://www.ed.gov.

National Research Council. 2002. *Minority students in special and gifted education,* eds. M.S. Donovan and C.T. Cross. Division of Behavioral and Social Sciences and Education/Committee on Minority Representation in Special Education. Washington, DC: National Academy Press.

Nieto, S. 1999. *The light in their eyes: Creating multicultural learning communities.* New York: Teachers College Press.

Norris, D.M., and M.C.J. Fignolé Lofton. 1995. *Winning with diversity: A practical handbook for creating inclusive meetings, events, and organizations.* Washington, DC: American Society of Association Executives Foundation.

Pang, V.O., G. Gay, and W.B. Stanley. 1995. Expanding conceptions of community and civic competence for a multicultural society. *Theory and Research in Social Education* 23 (4): 302–331.

Phillips, C.B. 1993. *Early childhood reform: Innovative approaches to cultural and racial diversity among families.* Alexandria, VA: National Association of State Boards of Education.

Ponterotto, J.G. 1996. Multicultural counseling in the twenty-first century. *The Counseling Psychologist* 24 (2): 259–268.

Robinson, T.L., and M.F. Howard-Hamilton. 2000. *The convergence of race, ethnicity, and gender.* Columbus, OH: Merrill.

Sandall, S., M.E. McLean, and B.J. Smith, eds. 2000. *DEC recommended practices in early intervention/early childhood special education.* Longmont, CO: Sopris West.

Santos, R.M., S.A. Fowler, R. Corso, and D. Bruns. 2000. Acceptance, acknowledgement, and adaptability: Selecting culturally and linguistically appropriate early childhood materials. *TEACHING Exceptional Children* 32 (3): 14–22.

Shonkoff, J.P., and D.A. Phillips, eds. 2000. *From neurons to neighborhoods: The science of early childhood development.* Washington, DC: National Academy Press.

Small, M.F. 1998. Our babies, ourselves: *How biology and culture shape the way we parent.* New York: Anchor Books.

Turnbull, H.R., and M.J. Stowe. 2001. Five models for thinking about disability: Implications for policy responses. *Journal of Disability Policy* 12 (3): 198–205.

Villegas, A.M., and T. Lucas. 2002. *Educating culturally responsive teachers: A coherent approach.* Albany, NY: SUNY Press.

Wheatley, M.J. 2000. *Turning to one another: Simple conversations to restore hope to the future.* San Francisco, CA: Berrett-Kohler.

Wheatley, M.J., and M. Kellner-Rogers. 1996. *A simpler way.* San Francisco, CA: Berrett-Kohler.

---

*Division for Early Childhood of the Council for Exceptional Children promotes policies and practices that support families and enhance the development of young children who have or are at risk for developmental delays and disabilities.

Division for Early Childhood of the Council for Exceptional Children. "Responsiveness to Family, Culture, Values and Education." 2004. http://www.dec-sped.org/uploads/docs/about_dec/position_concept_papers/ConceptPaper_Resp_FamCul.pdf.

The Effects of Culture on Special Education Services: Evil Eyes, Prayer Meetings, and IEPs

By Suzanne Lamorey*

How does culture affect how educators provide special education services? This is a question that challenges practitioners in the United States and other countries as they provide appropriate assessment and intervention to a multicultural population of children with disabilities and their families.

We need to examine the ways culture affects the development of the following educational processes:

+ Valid assessment measures.
+ The articulation of intervention goals for children that reflect socially and culturally relevant skills and academic skills.
+ Sensitive delineation of roles of family members, as well as the roles of professionals.
+ An investigation of changes in and challenges to the Westernized middle-class notions of child development.
+ The preparation of personnel to assist in the identification of children with disabilities and the provision of services.

Because more countries are sending their promising teachers and researchers to be trained in U.S. colleges of education, the resultant large-scale exportation of the Euro-American cultural values regarding disabilities and educational practices abroad may not be in the universal interests of all children and families.

This article provides a case study of monocultural personnel preparation, discusses various cultural beliefs about disability, and examines the effect of the dualities and dichotomies of parent/professional beliefs about childhood disabilities. In addition, it discusses intervention concerns in developing countries such as Turkey, Ecuador, and India and discusses cross-cultural implications for practitioners seeking partnerships with multicultural families and their children.

PREDOMINANCE OF A MONOCULTURAL PERSPECTIVE IN THE UNITED STATES

According to Kisanji (1995), culture is a broad abstraction that includes the forms of knowledge, belief systems, languages, religion, and values of a society. Each culture has its own explanations for why some babies are born with disabilities, how these children are to be treated, and what responsibilities and roles are expected of family members, helpers, and other members of the society (Groce, 1999).

Understanding and building on a family's cultural interpretations of disability is essential in creating partnerships with parents of children receiving special education services. Parent beliefs about the nature of disability are related to parent beliefs about and participation in treatment and intervention. In the United States (and elsewhere), parents who do not share special education's predominately biomedical belief system have been perceived by professionals as contributors to their children's disability, rather than as partners in the intervention process (Hopfenberg et al., 1993). These parents subsequently become marginalized, alienated, and excluded from participating in the educational decision-making process (Harry, Allen, & McLaughlin, 1995). Optimal outcomes for children with disabilities can only occur when professionals create a bridge from the culture of schooling to parents' multifaceted perceptions of the disability, its cause, its acceptable treatments, and the available sources of formal and informal support.

Take Off the Westernized Blinders

What are some examples of the cultural beliefs that people may have regarding the causes of childhood disability? In a large urban university located in a multicultural metropolis, a group of 31 Euro-American women between the ages of 19 and 25 who were enrolled in an undergraduate teacher training program answered this question with responses that uniformly reflected a Westernized biomedical orientation. Even when specifically urged to relate a family story or folk tale about causes of disabilities, these teachers-to-be did not (could not?) contribute any nonmedical responses other than "disability may be God's will." On the other hand, a group of 17 international graduate students in education, representing a variety of cultural backgrounds, answered this question with a rich collection of beliefs about disability. Their responses included beliefs that reflect the role of supernatural or cosmic causes, fate, magic, and religious beliefs, as well as biomedical reasoning (see box, "Cultural Beliefs").

In light of the implications of the monocultural orientation of the U.S. students, the lack of awareness of other perceptions and the shortcomings in multicultural training experiences, as demonstrated by the responses of these undergraduates, is discouraging. As Garcia, Mendez-Perez, and Ortiz (2000) wrote, "Differences in perceptions are not problematic. . . . The problem is created when the possibility of such differences is not even considered, or when unquestioned assumptions create misunderstandings" (p. 97). Although there exist professional standards for the development of culturally responsive special education programs, there are still far too many U.S. educators—and people from other countries trained in the United States—who wear Westernized blinders, unaware of the rich relationships among beliefs, values, buffers, supports, roles of family members, and child outcomes in non-Western contexts.

Cultural Beliefs about the Causes of Childhood Disability

- If mom cuts her hair during her pregnancy, it will cause a miscarriage or shorten the life of her baby.
- If mom views a person with deformities during pregnancy, she will give birth to a similarly deformed baby.
- Having sex during pregnancy produces a child with disabilities.
- Eating a grape or fish during pregnancy will produce a birthmark in the shape of grapes or fish.
- If mom eats fish during her pregnancy, her child's skin will be scaly.
- If mom eats spleen during pregnancy, it causes a dark birthmark on her baby.
- If mom eats spleen and touches a part of her body then her baby will have a dark birthmark on that area.
- If mom smells certain foods during her pregnancy, she must lick her right hand to prevent the food from causing childhood disability.
- If mom kills a lizard during her pregnancy, the baby will have visual disorders.
- God causes disabilities in order to examine a couple's patience.
- To ward off the evil eye, a parent must spread black coal on the newborn's forehead.
- A new mother should keep a copy of the Koran and a broom close to the newborn to avoid red genies that would disturb the mother and baby.
- No meat should be brought into the home of a newborn for 40 days to avoid newborn disability.
- No women who are menstruating can visit a newborn baby or the baby will become ill.
- The newborn should wear a red ribbon to protect it from harm.
- During pregnancy, mom must avoid greasy foods as the grease collects in the unborn child's brain.
- Messages about the baby and the baby's health come to mom in dreams during pregnancy.
- If mom lies face down to sleep, baby will be deformed.
- Do not take the newborn outside for 40 days or the baby will become ill.
- If mom looks at a dead body during her pregnancy, her baby will have a light-skinned face or she may miscarry.

Multicultural Investigations of Parent Perceptions of Disability

Several studies have examined the perceptions and beliefs that parents use to understand the causes and meanings of their children's disabilities.

+ Cho, Singer, and Brenner (2000) compared the experiences and perceptions of Koreans and Korean Americans who were parenting children with developmental disabilities. Eighty percent of the Korean parents attributed causes of disabilities to their own mistakes relative to prenatal enrichment practices and parenting attitudes (poor "Tae Gyo" which translates to "education during pregnancy") while 63% of Korean American parents attributed the causes to a divine plan (God's will for the family and child) as well as poor "Tae Gyo."

+ From Australia, Gray (1995) reported that 25% of the parents of children with autism mentioned religious, magical, or psychological reasons for the cause of their child's disability.

+ Among Chinese-American parents of young children with disabilities in a study by Ryan and Smith (1989), at least one-third of the parents considered supernatural and metaphysical elements in describing the cause of their child's outcome.

+ According to Mardinros (1989), Mexican-American parents of young children with disabilities perceived the causes of childhood disability to be either a biomedical etiology (health problems, genetic diseases, birth trauma) or a sociocultural view (marital difficulties, divine intervention, past sins, and negative attitudes).

+ In Yoruba society, congenital disability is understood as an indication of family sin that requires punishment by ancestors or gods, and the subsequent need for parental atonement (Olubanji, 1981).

+ According to Serpell, Mariga, and Harvey (1997), in the central region of Africa, some tribal societies attribute disability to magical or religious explanations; however, as in many rural areas characterized by a subsistence economy, these authors point out that individual differences are widely tolerated so that the degree of disability would need to be severe before it would become conspicuous.

+ Caprara et al. (2000) studied the cultural meanings of tuberculosis in Sumatra, and found that TB was actually understood as a "semantic network of illnesses." The disease could be caused by a contagious germ (biomedical category), hard work (poor economic conditions), conflict (social transgressions), and poisoning (supernatural powers).

As this compilation of etiologies of disease and disability shows, there is a wide diversity of attributions that reflect cultural beliefs. Add to these traditional beliefs the impact of industrialization, urbanization, socioeconomic factors, political change, migration, and educational opportunities on traditional family systems, and the outcomes can be complex for both parents and practitioners. Embracing this complexity is key to understanding and supporting the health-and-habilitation seeking behavior of parents of children with disabilities.

THE MULTICULTURAL EXPERIENCES OF PARENTS

In light of this complexity of beliefs, what constitutes effective, holistic intervention among groups who hold different perceptions of disability? Unfortunately, we don't know the answer to this question. Collaborative cross-cultural research is urgently needed to investigate the efficacy of programs that combine culturally informed interventions (e.g., home remedies, religious activities, the services of community healers, and other cures) with Westernized special education services. The fact that researchers have not included these culturally sanctioned interventions in the special education research agenda is telling in itself and illustrates our monocultural understanding of disability.

We know that parents of children with disabilities derive a sense of personal meaningfulness from their cultural beliefs. For example, descriptions of the positive effects of parent beliefs about their children's disability are emerging in the area of parents' religious beliefs. Cho et al. (2000) reported in their study of Korean-American families with young children with disabilities that the majority of these families were members of Korean ethnic churches. The religious influences of the churches appeared to mitigate the self-blame of poor "Tae Gyo" because most families indicated that they experienced a new sense of hope and support through their involvement in their church. Similarly, Gray (1995) found that some of the Australian families with children who had autism had strong religious beliefs that explained their children's disability. These religious parents had higher expectations for their children, and Gray suggests that religious beliefs give disability a special meaning and provide a sense of resilience to parents' day-to-day experiences.

Other researchers have made similar suggestions about the significant role of religion in the lives of families whose children are disabled (Rogers-Dulan, 1998; Weisner, Beizer, & Stolze 1991). This idea of finding hope, support, and resilience through parents' personal beliefs about disability is also reinforced by Kleinman (1988), who noted that in the case of chronic illness, the experience of the illness not only has meaning relative to symptoms, but also serves to make sense of one's life experiences and personal struggles.

Studies have also indicated that parents rely on a duality of beliefs as they seek treatment and educational services for their children with disabilities. According to Ryan and Smith (1989), many of the Chinese-American families they interviewed chose to take advantage of Western medical treatment (as far as language and accessibility to services permitted), as well as used culturally specific cures. These families reported a release of some of their anxieties, fears, and guilt feelings by combining cultural cures with Western treatment. The authors urged professionals to incorporate nonconventional perspectives in their interactions with Chinese-American families, particularly in terms of support systems within the community.

This need for professionals to accept duality is also supported by Stahl (1991), who found that when Jewish-Oriental parents were able to communicate openly and freely to Jewish Israeli teachers about the cultural cures they pursued for their child, a climate of confidence in the schools was nurtured. Trust was established between parents and professionals when pilgrimage experiences were shared by parents. When the professionals replaced the dichotomy of cultural versus "scientific" beliefs with an acceptance of the duality of beliefs, parents no longer felt excluded by the educational system—to the benefit of their child. It is important to learn more about the interaction of dual belief systems for practitioners to perceive and effectively support these systems in intervention contexts.

Finally, there is support for the role of cultural beliefs as protective factors or pathways to resilience. Reiter, Mar'i, and Rosenberg (1986) studied parental attitudes toward disability among Arab communities and found that the more educated and more modernized people had less favorable attitudes, and that the Druse villagers who believe in reincarnation and life-after-death had the most positive attitudes about disability. Perhaps the more traditional parents experienced their cultural beliefs as a source of support in the face of adaptation to a child born with a disability. Studies such as these have a lot to teach us about the role of culture as an important buffer in the lives of families who have a child with a disability.

LESSONS FROM OTHER COUNTRIES

Another way to understand the relationship between culture and disability services is to investigate the ways that practitioners in other countries integrate Westernized intervention beliefs and practices with families' cultural beliefs and practices. One study, in particular, has a lot to offer, particularly in terms of its accomplishments amidst the economical, political, and social struggles of a transitional developing nation.

The Turkish Early Enrichment Project (TEEP; Kagitcibasi, 1996) was established as a mother-training program that sought to culturally contextualize an early intervention program aimed at promoting child competence. It was determined that to facilitate children's success, Turkish mothers needed to become more verbally communicative and responsive with their young children (to enhance cognitive competence) and to promote child autonomy while nurturing a close mother-child relationship (to enhance social competence). These goals were successfully attained by TEEP through building on Turkish family culture and communal support systems, including the development of a culturally relevant curriculum, group meetings of mothers, and paraprofessional home visits. The outcomes for this early intervention project have been impressive over a 10-year follow-up study.

Srinivasan and Karlan (1997), as well as Stuecher and Suarez (2000), described the challenges affecting special education in transitional developing countries, such as India and Ecuador, respectively. These researchers made the point that it is difficult to provide for the health, welfare, and educational needs of all children, including those with disabilities, in countries experiencing severe economic constraints, a high incidence of child poverty, and social inequalities. These authors offer some questions for culturally responsive researchers and practitioners to consider:

+ In planning an intervention program, what are the society's goals and expectations of child-rearing?
+ How does having a child with a disability influence parents' child-rearing goals?
+ How can society justify special education services when children without disabilities are not having their basic needs for food, health, shelter, and education met?

- Can developing countries benefit from some of the special education research and practices advocated by industrialized nations without also buying into the commercialization of disability testing and programming, professional specialization and turf issues, costly technology, and systemwide strategies, such as mandated mainstreaming, which have no place in the countries' culture?
- Can affordable, sustainable, and culturally relevant programs be created in the context of community (e.g., children with disabilities raise food and learn domestic skills, such as sewing and cooking; parents are employed as paraprofessionals; and elders, as well as extended family members, are involved as teachers)?

IMPLICATIONS FOR PRACTITIONERS

Parents and their extended families may have different belief systems relative to the meaning of disability than the typical teachers from middle-class Euro-American backgrounds who provide educational and support services. There may be some aspects of Western acculturation that families from different cultural backgrounds choose to embrace. Attempting to understand a child's disability, however, may occur more securely within the context of a family's familiar traditional cultural ways and supports. When practitioners can accept parents' beliefs, parents may no longer feel the need to hide traditional beliefs from the practitioners and possible combinations of intervention approaches can occur in the context of a duality of belief systems.

As we've seen in the literature, cultural beliefs can be a protective buffer for families. This is an important point for practitioners to remember. By attempting to dissemble a family's "old fashioned," "dangerous," or "foreign" belief system to replace it with best practices in brain research, medical therapies, and behavior guidance programming, practitioners may be tampering with a belief system that has provided generations of meaning to those family members' lives. These beliefs define their goals for their children, their relationships and responsibilities toward each other and toward other members of their cultural community, as well as their relationships with a higher power, ancestors, and an afterlife. Practitioners may want to see their roles not as service brokers or agents of change, but as interpreters or translators of Westernized approaches and resources available within the special education community, and as guides who respectfully offer services that families may or may not choose to embrace.

In terms of training, practitioners might become more effective with multicultural families if they themselves experienced opportunities to travel to other countries. More U.S. colleges of education might consider a summer-abroad option at a sister university. The establishment of relationships with teacher preparation programs in other countries could provide a powerful learning experience for the monocultural young women who fill the majority of undergraduate teaching training programs in the United States. Some universities have coordinated student teacher placements with the Department of Defense schools around the world, further providing an enriching opportunity for teacher trainees to broaden their cultural horizons.

Finally, child development, care, and education occur in cultural as well as socioeconomic and political contexts, as the intervention efforts in Turkey, India, and Ecuador illustrate. Parent child-rearing goals, contextual interpretations of child competence, community support, intergenerational cooperation, practical habilitative programs, and affordable interventions need to occupy central roles in a culturally responsive special education system.

REFERENCES

Caparara, A., Abdulkadir, N., Idawani, C., Asmara, H., Lever, P., & De Virlilio, G. (2000). Cultural meanings of tuberculosis in Aceh Province, Sumatra. *Medical Anthropology, 19*, 65–89.

Cho, S., Singer, G., & Brenner, M. (2000). Adaptation and accommodation to young children with disabilities: A comparison of Korean and Korean American parents. *Topics in Early Childhood Special Education, 20,* 236–250.

Garcia, S., Mendez-Perez, A., & Ortiz, A. (2000). Mexican-American mothers' beliefs about disabilities: Implications for early childhood intervention. *Remedial and Special Education, 21*(2), 90–100, 120.

Gray, D. (1995). Lay conceptions of autism: Parents' explanatory models. *Medical Anthropology, 16,* 99–118.

Groce, N. (1999). Disability in cross-cultural perspective: Rethinking disability. *Lancet, 354,* 756–758.

Harry, B., Allen, N., & McLaughlin, M. (1995). Communication versus compliance: African-American parents' involvement in special education. *Exceptional Children, 61,* 354–377.

Hopfenberg, W., Levin, H., Chase, C., Christensen, S., Moore, M., Soler, P., Brunner, I., Keller, B., & Rodriguez, G. (1993). *The Accelerated Schools resource guide.* San Francisco: Jossey-Bass.

Kagitcibasi, C. (1996). *Family and human development across cultures: A view from the other side.* Mahwah, NJ: Lawrence Erlbaum Associates.

Kisanji, J. (1995). Interface between culture and disability in the Tanzanian context: Part II. *International Journal of Disability, Development, and Education, 42*(2), 109–124.

Kleinman, A. (1988). *The illness narratives: Suffering, healing, and the human condition.* New York: Basic Books.

Mardinros, M. (1989). Conception of childhood disability among Mexican-American parents. *Medical Anthropology, 12,* 55–68.

Olubanji, D. (1981, February 19–21). Traditional attitudes to the handicapped. *Annual general meeting and conference of the Nigerian Society for Handicapped Children.* Alvan Ikoku College of Education, Owerri, Nigeria.

Reiter, S., Mar'i, S., & Rosenberg, Y. (1986). Parental attitudes toward the developmentally disabled among Arab communities in Israel: A cross-cultural study. *International Journal of Rehabilitation Research, 9,* 355–362.

Rogers-Dulan, J. (1998). Religious connectedness among urban African American families who have a child with disabilities. *Mental Retardation, 33,* 226–238.

Ryan, A., & Smith, M. (1989). Parental reactions to developmental disabilities in Chinese-American families. *Child and Adolescent Social Work, 6,* 283–299.

Serpell, R., Mariga, L., & Harvey, K. (1993). Mental retardation in African countries: Conceptualization, services, and research. *International Review of Research on Mental Retardation, 19,* 1–10

Srinivasan, B., & Karlan, G. (1997). Culturally responsive early intervention programs: Issues in India. *International Journal of Disability, Development and Education, 44,* 367–385.

Stahl, A. (1991). Beliefs of Jewish-Oriental mothers regarding children who are mentally retarded. *Education and Training in Mental Retardation, 26,* 361–369.

Stuecher, U., & Suarez, J. (2000). Research in special education from the perspective of a country in development: Ecuador. *Exceptionality, 8,* 289–298.

Weisner, T., Beizer, L., & Stolze, L. (1991). Religion and families of children with developmental delays. *American Journal on Mental Retardation, 95,* 647–662.

---

*Suzanne Lamorey is associate professor and Child and Family Program coordinator at the University of North Carolina.

Lamorey, Suzanne. "The Effects of Culture on Special Education Services: Evil Eyes, Prayer Meetings, and IEPs." *Teaching Exceptional Children* vol. 34, no. 5 (May/June 2002): 67–71.

Used by permission.

Discussion Questions

1. What are cultural barriers in relation to individuals with disabilities?

2. Do you think people with disabilities are viewed differently in different cultures? In what ways?

3. Is it possible for someone with an intellectual disability to be valued in one society and not in another? How about an individual with a physical disability?

4. How does culture play a part in education and the inclusion of families in the decision-making process?

CHAPTER 5:

Reducing Poverty and Social Exclusion

Chapter 5 argues that the exclusion of people with disabilities from international development initiatives reflects and reinforces the disproportionately high number of people with disabilities among the poorest of the poor. The articles explore the links between disability and poverty and discuss ways in which disability is excluded from development policy. They also present ways in which institutions can challenge poverty and exclusion among people with disabilities.

Article 28 of the UN Convention on the Rights of Persons with Disabilities affirms an adequate standard of living and social protection. It requires states to recognize the rights of people with disabilities to an adequate standard of living for themselves and for their families, including adequate food, clothing, and housing. It also requires states to recognize the rights of people with disabilities and their families to continuous improvement of living conditions, including respite care, public housing programs, and retirement benefits.

The first article, "Including Persons with Disabilities in Development: Opportunities and Accessibility," by Iqbal Kaur, shares the commitment of the World Bank to inclusive approaches to development in order to achieve the Bank's primary objective: a world free of poverty. The article concludes by recommending that the World Bank adopt a dual approach to promoting the inclusion of people with disabilities by learning by doing—piloting initiatives that show the benefits of inclusion—and building a knowledge base—undertaking research and analysis of key issues to inform policy dialogues and interventions.

The second article, "Mainstreaming the Rights of Persons with Disabilities in National Development Frameworks," by Teresa Njoroge Mwendwa, Ambrose Murangira, and Raymond Lang, describes the continuing efforts of development practitioners and governments to best ensure the participation in society of people with disabilities and their organizations—especially in the development of strategies for reducing poverty and national development programs. The article describes how recent practices in Uganda effectively include individuals with disabilities in development efforts.

Including Persons with Disabilities in Development: Opportunities and Accessibility

*By Iqbal Kaur**

INTRODUCTION

The [World] Bank has focused increasingly on the importance of inclusive approaches to development. However, activities that specifically focus on the needs and capacities of people with disabilities have been limited in number and often narrow in scope. A number of countries in the MENA Region have made progress in the prevention of disabilities and in the inclusion of people with disabilities in socio-economic activities. Yet, overall, most countries in the region do not adequately promote an inclusive environment for persons with disabilities. On a corporate level, the Bank has expressed its commitment to promoting inclusive development as such an approach is important in achieving the Bank's primary objective—that is, a world free of poverty.

While the Bank as an international development institution primarily focuses on economic growth and development, the Bank's increased focus on inclusive development is drawing guidance from several internationally acceptable frameworks including the Convention on the Rights of Persons with Disabilities (CRPD), which has been ratified by 65 countries worldwide and 8 countries in the MENA Region.[1] The CRPD provides a unique and widely endorsed framework for promoting the inclusion of people with disabilities. The Bank can play an important role in ensuring the integration of people with disabilities through effective labor market policies and by enhancing accessibility. These are two areas where the Bank has made a sizeable investment and has technical expertise. Together, significant progress in these two areas can ensure that people with disabilities gain socioeconomic independence. In addition to reducing unemployment rates, efforts in these two areas can lead to increased productivity, while reducing government transfers and costs borne by families caring for individuals with disabilities.

Regional Context

An estimated 10 to 12% of the population, or approximately 30 million people, are disabled in the MENA Region.[2] Disabilities in the Region are often the result of communicable and non-communicable diseases, limited access to health services, poor nutrition, accidents and violence, amongst other causes. Furthermore, MENA has the highest rate of traffic accidents and job-related injuries, and diseases are currently on the rise. Moreover, a number of countries in the region continue to experience conflict, which means high rates of conflict-related injuries as well as mental disorders (e.g. depression and post-traumatic stress disorders). People with disabilities in MENA, as elsewhere, experience severe socio-economic exclusion as a result of societal stigmatization and face extremely limited opportunities for participation in daily activities. In recent years, and in order to better meet these challenges, the Bank has sought to strengthen its knowledge and cross-sectoral collaboration on promoting inclusive development.

Advancing Bank Engagement on Disability Issues

Consistent with the regional priority of reducing unemployment, the Bank aims to promote inclusive development through two major areas of focus: (i) *promoting employment* of people with disabilities and (ii) *ensuring accessibility* so that people are able to avail themselves of existing opportunities. This focus was further highlighted in the first MENA Disability Learning Event on June 17, 2009.

The MENA Disability Learning Event

The objective of the learning event was to bring together Bank staff and external partners to discuss (i) issues faced in promoting inclusive development; (ii) barriers to promoting inclusive development; and (iii) strategies, policies and concrete steps that might be taken in response to these challenges. The learning event was characterized by broad representation across sectors within the Bank and other organizations including: USAID, Handicap International, US International Council on Disabilities, ACCSES,[3] Half the Planet Foundation,[4] the Advisory Committee on Persons with Disabilities, U.S. Department of State, and Mercy Corps.[5]

Key Messages

A number of key messages emerged from the event with particular focus on issues of accessibility and employment. These provide guidance to Bank teams in their efforts to promote inclusive development in MENA:

Lack of Data: There is a lack of data differentiated by type of disability. Two critical factors have contributed to this situation: (i) at the macro-level, disability is not seen as priority given that the economic rewards of inclusion of persons with disabilities in the development agenda is still little understood; (ii) at the micro-level, stigma relating to disability is still highly prevalent in the developing world, which means that the issue is unlikely to become one around which public opinion forces action.

Recommendations: Specific instruments need to be developed by the Bank and its partners to gather data. Also, mechanisms should be established at the country level to update data at agreed intervals. In this context, international cooperation and the role of people with disabilities as key stakeholders in the design and implementation stages of data collection are critical. Caution also needs to be exercised with regard to using single instruments to gather information on disability as one instrument may not provide the needed information. For example, poverty assessment and census surveys may not capture the precise data needed on persons with disability.

ENFORCEMENT OF DISABILITY DEFINITION

Though a UN definition for disability is available, many people continue to be categorized as disabled based on the understanding applicable to the location and the perceptions of those involved in providing the definition. This can lead to less than sup-optimal interventions.

Recommendation: A universal definition of disability needs to be agreed upon through the collaboration of international actors with buy-in from national stakeholders. This will help in developing a global framework on how various levels of disability are to be approached. This would further be complemented by awareness campaigns designed for specific groups within countries.

Limited Knowledge Base on Disability: Currently, there are not enough evidence-based data or case studies on people with disabilities. There is a need for case studies on good practices and lessons learned documented with the help of disabled people's organizations (DPOs) and other actors in the field.

Recommendations: The Bank should use its convening power among international and national actors to support the gathering of good-practice case studies from around the globe. Here again, people with disabilities will need to be included as key stakeholders both in the identification and design of these case studies.

Operationalization of the CRPD: While many countries have ratified the CRPD, actual implementation lags behind. Even in the U.S., legislation still does not fully reflect the full extent of the challenges addressed in the CPRD—despite the fact that the US' Disabilities Act and the Rehabilitation Act were passed decades ago.

In short, these measures do take time to be realized and do not happen easily or quickly, even in environments with high capacity and resources.

Recommendation: The Bank should work with ratifying countries to share expertise and provide technical support to ensure that the Convention's goals are progressively realized. This is beginning to happen, though slowly. For example, the Government of Bahrain, which has ratified the Convention, has requested Bank support as it moves forward toward implementation.

Building Evidence on Disability and Economic Growth: There is very limited data and analysis on the cost of exclusion of disabled people. This has led to a major gap in establishing the links between poverty and disability as well as broader issues of economic growth. It is estimated that nearly one trillion dollars is lost world wide due to the exclusion of people with disabilities in the economic development agenda. The inability to make this case also means that lending operations and other types of Bank efforts to address these challenges are not brought to the table by client countries, relevant NGOs, or other development partners.

Recommendation: The Bank and its global partners need to focus on generating the analytical data to establish the critical links between disability, poverty and the broader issues of economic growth.

Lack of Integrated approach to Disability: To date, many countries focus on *ad hoc* and stand alone interventions, or those that focus on a partial solution to the challenges facing disabled people.

Recommendation: The Bank needs to more effectively leverage its convening power and bring its global partners together to establish an integrated approach to address these challenges. Such an approach would also have to fit the needs and priorities of specific countries, thus giving the highlighting the importance of local knowledge.

CPRD and the CAS/CSP Process: The ratification of the CPRD by each country should be reflected in the Country CAS or CSP for follow-up action.

Recommendation: All follow-up actions in the ratifying countries should be carried out in close collaboration with internal and external partners, including the Bank, to ensure that the efforts are part of an overall structured plan.

Employment Issues: Many countries have quotas for the employment of persons with disabilities. These quotas are often designed as a social protection tool with little form of career advancement or opportunities for high level entrants. The concept of micro loans for persons with disability is still a new tool yet to be fully exploited in the developing world. These are some exceptions in countries such as India and the Philippines, where again, the scope of lending is often limited to crafts and needle work with limited returns. The promising area of Information and Communication Technologies (ICT) is not harnessed enough to enable the effective inclusion of persons with disability.

Recommendation: The Bank and its global partners should provide equal opportunities to persons with disability by collaborating with local DPOs/microlending NGOs to support persons with disability.[6]

THE WAY FORWARD

It is recognized that disability issues are generally not well covered in Bank lending operations. However, there are exceptions. The Bank's education and transport lending programs have done better in this regard than others. Transport has covered the issue of disability through components in projects on improving access and safety. Education has covered disability issues largely in the context of an inclusive approach to education. In general, however, there has been a tendency to sideline the issue of disability given the general lack of appreciation of the economic and social benefits of economic inclusion, and the inability to correctly prioritize the needs of the disabled in the context of a development agenda that has many urgent needs.

Recommendation: The Bank needs to adopt a dual approach in promoting the inclusion of persons with disabilities: (i) Learning by Doing—Identifying opportunities at hand to pilot operational initiatives to provide concrete examples of the benefits of inclusion; (ii) Building A Knowledge Base—Undertaking research and analysis of specific issues to promote evidence based policy dialogue and inform the design of future interventions.

NOTES

1. Latest list of MENA countries having ratified the CRPD as of August 23, 2009 found at UN ENABLE: http://www.un.org/disabilities/default.asp?id=257

2. This figure is derived from WHO estimates that approximately 10% of the world's population is disabled.

3. On July 1, 2007, the American Congress of Community Support and Employment Services (ACCSES) merged with Disability Support Providers of America (DSPA) to successfully form ACCSES. For more see www.accses.org

4. For more see www.halftheplanet.com

5. www.mercycorps.org

6. For more on employment and the disabled see Fast Brief #31 "Unlocking the Economic Potential of People with Disabilities in MNA" by Gustavo Demarco.

---

*Iqbal Kaur is social protection specialist and regional disability coordinator for the Middle East and North Africa human development branch of the World Bank.

Kaur, Iqbal. "Including Persons with Disabilities in Development: Opportunities and Accessibility." *MNA Knowledge and Learning. . .*, fast brief 32 (August 2009). http://www.wds.worldbank.org/external/default/WDSContentServer/WDSP/IB/2009/10/01/000334955_20091001035519/Rendered/PDF/508630BRI0Fast10Box342008B01PUBLIC1.pdf. Copyright © The International Bank for Reconstruction and Development, the World Bank.

Mainstreaming the Rights of Persons with Disabilities in National Development Frameworks

By Teresa Njoroge Mwendwa, Ambrose Murangira, and Raymond Lang*

1 INTRODUCTION

Debates within contemporary development studies discourse are increasingly critical about the extent to which current aid modalities are really enhancing the livelihoods of the poorest and most marginalised groups within developing countries (Eybern, 2005; Adejumobi, 2006). These include evaluations of the efficacy of the poverty reduction strategy (PRS) process; the extent to which social protection programmes and cash transfer initiatives benefit the chronically poor; as well as the effectiveness of direct budget support. Furthermore, there has been critical reflection on the utility of a rights-based approach to development, and the degree to which poor, marginalised groups effectively participate in the development of poverty reduction initiatives and national development plans (Hickey and Mohan, 2004).

In May 2008, the UN Convention on the Rights of Persons with Disabilities came into force, which ostensibly has the potential to create a paradigm shift in the manner in which disability policy is formulated and implemented. However, this paper will argue that it is far from certain whether such a paradigm shift will occur. It is not the intention here to give a full description of the principles and substantive issues addressed by the Convention, which can be found elsewhere (Hendriks, 2007; Megret, 2008; Lang, in press). The Convention has changed the perception and conditions for persons with disabilities by positioning disability as a specific human rights issue, calling for a new approach to policies—including development policies—and the need to enact them through the removal of barriers. The Convention states it is a 'benchmark for future standards and action'. The consensus is, as stipulated in the Convention, that society has to ensure that persons with disabilities can fully exercise their economic, social, political, civil and cultural rights on an equal basis with non-disabled people. Two of the articles in the Convention—Article 4 on General Obligations and Article 32 on International Cooperation—underline the principles relevant to inclusive development towards achieving poverty reduction. In particular Article 32 (a) reads:

> Ensuring that international cooperation, including international development programmes, is inclusive of and accessible to people with disabilities (UN DESA, 2006).

The Convention offers both a human rights and a development framework to move towards inclusive development. It provides a comprehensive framework that can help national governments to consider the principles and aspects of inclusive development. The concepts must therefore be factored in the processing of any international development framework. The civil and political rights of people with disabilities make little sense without fulfilment of social, economic, and cultural rights. Hence a cross-sectoral approach should be encouraged in the processing of any poverty reduction strategies, or other development agendas. The key is effective implementation, which requires coordinated action by disability organisations; cooperation among States and the mainstreaming of disability issues into development assistance programmes.

Drawing upon original qualitative research, this paper will examine the extent to which disabled people's organisations (DPOs) have been included in the development of such frameworks, with specific examples from Uganda. The paper will also highlight the factors that both enhance and militate against the inclusion of poor and marginalised groups in such initiatives, using the example of DPOs as a case study.

Such an analysis must be contextualised within the broader political and policy context found in many developing countries. Notwithstanding the fact that the UN Convention is premised on the fundamental precepts of human rights, it nevertheless remains the case that many developing countries do not adhere to, or promote such values. Current debates would suggest that effective poverty reduction, good governance frameworks and human rights are inexorably linked (Adejumobi, 2006). However, the lack of good governance, the scant appreciation of the principles of human rights, as well as the lack of robust statistical data is commonplace in many developing countries. This is further compounded by the fact that many civil society institutions are themselves deeply entrenched within a culture of charity approaches to social and economic policy. An example of this comes from Nigeria, where one of the key findings from a recent DFID-funded Disability Scoping Study was found that DPOs function on the basis of charity/welfare, rather than human rights (Lang and Upah, 2008: 21).

2 PARTICIPATION AND GOOD GOVERNANCE IN POVERTY REDUCTION AND NATIONAL DEVELOPMENT PLANNING

Poverty Reduction Strategy Papers (PRSPs) arose from a critique of the structural adjustment policies promulgated by the World Bank and IMF during the 1980s and 1990s. The switch to the PRSP process was meant to ensure that poverty reduction strategies were 'owned' by their respective governments, and that such strategies were developed with the full participation of civil society institutions. In essence then, the PRSP process was instituted to create a nexus between poverty, accountability and governance. Such an approach to policy making is underpinned by the notion that a strong relationship exists between the state and society, whereby each interacts with the other to negotiate national objectives, as well as negotiating modalities for how these will be achieved:

> 'Poverty is a policy issue that exists in the political domain. Poverty, inequality and governance are now seen to be inseparably related because without good governance, bad policy choices will be made, the people would have neither voice nor power, and the economy is likely to deteriorate. Similarly, when poverty and inequality persists in a society it weakens the political process and promotes deficient governance'. (Aduejumobi, 2006: 3)

The ideological shift that underpinned the move from the structural adjustment policies of the 1980s and 1990s to the PRSP process instituted after 1999 could not be more pronounced. The raison d'être underpinning the PRSP process has been to promote ownership, accountability and participation. It can therefore be argued that this will be the most long-standing legacy of this approach. David Booth has convincingly argued that the institution of the process has created a 'new poverty contract', by which political leaders owe new responsibilities to the poor (Booth, 2003: 147). So has the institution of the PRSP process had a positive impact upon the poorest and most marginalised groups within African society? To date, the evidence is mixed; taken at face value, it suggests that for those countries that have fully implemented PRSPs, average per capita income has risen by 2.5%, and that governments are beginning to allocate an increasing proportion of GDP for poverty alleviation. There is also evidence to suggest that significant progress is being made in implementing social welfare policies. For example, primary school enrolment has increased from 6.5 million in 1999 to a projected estimate of 10,000,000 by 2010 (Adejumobi, 2006:19). Notwithstanding these ostensibly positive outcomes, there is nevertheless much discussion regarding the extent to which the PRSP process has fundamentally changed the dynamics in the power relations that exist between the Bretton Woods institutions on the one hand, and government and civil society on the other. Critics of the PRSP process maintain that civil society institutions are 'consulted' rather than 'participate' in the development of poverty reduction strategies. Furthermore, there is strong anecdotal evidence to suggest that governments consult with compliant civil society institutions, who are in broad agreement with government policy and ideology (Booth, 2003). Finally, the PRSP process was developed during the time when the very nature of poverty was being redefined, moving away from a purely economic understanding to one that reformulated poverty as a multidimensional phenomenon, embracing economic, political and social factors, and which perceived poverty reduction in terms of freedom (Sen, 1999). Hence, it is now understood people are poor because they are in essence powerless.

There is little agreement among development practitioners whether the PRSP process has indeed resulted in the democratisation of poverty reduction policy (Eyben, 2008). Given that this is the case for poor and marginalised groups generally, it will not be surprising that this is the case for the vast majority of people with disabilities, whom it is often claimed constitute the 'poorest of the poor'.

The PRSP process is only one instrument which aims to address and alleviate chronic poverty in developing countries. There is insufficient space to discuss these options here, but other important mechanisms include social protection and cash transfer programmes. Bilateral and multilateral donors are now giving increasing consideration to how these can be most efficiently and effectively used to alleviate poverty (Marriott and Gooding, 2007).

3 THE INCLUSION OF PEOPLE WITH DISABILITIES WITHIN POVERTY REDUCTION AND NATIONAL DEVELOPMENT PLANNING

Notwithstanding the challenges and difficulties of including all marginalised and socially excluded groups within poverty reduction and national planning frameworks, it nevertheless remains the case that people with disabilities comprise a significant proportion of the world's population, with some estimates suggesting that they constitute 10% of the global total (Thomas, 2005). Furthermore, there is strong anecdotal [evidence] to suggest that disability is both a cause and a consequence of poverty (Yeo, 2001). Hence, if a person is disabled, it is less likely that they will have benefited from formal education, and more likely to be unemployed: if they are in employment, they will earn significantly less than their non-disabled counterparts (Lang and Upah, 2008). Similarly, poorer people have a greater statistical likelihood of becoming disabled, as those who are poor invariably live and work in unsafe and unsanitary conditions with little access to clean water, rendering them more susceptible to injuries and preventable diseases such as malaria and polio. An ILO study estimated that between US$1.37 trillion and US$1.94 trillion of GDP is lost annually from underemployment of people with disabilities (ILO, 2002). Excluding people with disabilities from development and poverty reduction strategies leads to a loss of productive potential and income for people with disabilities and other family members. Therefore the inclusion of people with disabilities in poverty reduction initiatives is underpinned by compelling economic arguments, as well as those human rights.

The mutual self-reinforcing factors that drive the disability/poverty nexus remain ill defined and under researched. However, what is known is that people with disabilities find it increasingly difficult to access credit from mainstream micro-finance institutions (Mersland, 2008), and that, there are few social protection programmes specifically targeted at persons with disabilities (Mitra, 2008). In summary, persons with disabilities in developing countries are subjected to systemic social exclusion and discrimination, manifested by a multiplicity of environmental, attitudinal and institutional barriers that militate against their participation within contemporary society, and they invariably do not enjoy the same economic, social and political rights as their non-disabled peers.

4 Disability, Inclusive Development and Policy Development

During the past two decades, governments, bilateral and multilateral donor agencies and civil society institutions have increasingly recognised that if persons with disabilities are to be afforded the same fundamental rights as everyone else, then they must be able to access mainstream services. In 2000, the UK Department for International Development (DFID) published its issue paper *Disability, Poverty and Development*, which advocated a 'twin track' to policy making and service provision (DFID, 2000). According to this model, donors would fund specifically targeted services for persons with disabilities, as well as promoting the inclusion of people with disabilities within mainstream programmes. During the past 10 years, increasing emphasis has been put upon mainstreaming. This approach underpins the fundamental rationale of the UN Convention on the Rights of Persons with Disabilities. Yet there is scant agreement as to what are the most effective strategies and modalities for effective mainstreaming. This is particularly the case in developing countries, where with some notable exceptions, disability policy and service provision are premised on the principles of charity/welfare, in stark contrast to the principles of human rights.

The situation is compounded by the fact that most governments still believe that disability is a specialist issue, which is best provided for through segregated institutional provision. Indeed, some disability activists still advocate for specialised service provision, for example, schools catering for blind and/or deaf children, as they argue mainstream education fails these pupils. This can lead to confusion on behalf of policymakers. The Ugandan government supports inclusive development and ratified the UNCRPD on 25th September 2008. It also has a range of policies to promote inclusion and mainstreaming, including in the education sector. Nevertheless, a group of disability activists recently met with the President and lobbied for the creation of more special schools for blind and/or deaf children. The President directed the Ministry of Education to construct more special schools, thereby causing confusion within the ministry who had been building plans and budgets for inclusive education.

Of course, caution should be taken to ensure that disability mainstreaming does not become just another buzzword in the lexicon of development workers, devoid of any concrete meaning, or an excuse for not targeting aid where it is specifically necessary. Notwithstanding the increasing trend towards mainstreaming, it is nevertheless argued that there is still credence in the 'twin track' approach, for it will be many years before mainstreaming, in and of itself, will be sufficient in meeting the needs of persons with disabilities in a plethora of developing countries.

There has been some progress in the last decade, including the continuation of the work done by The African Decade of Persons with Disabilities as well as the UN Convention on the Rights of Persons with Disabilities. However, it must be recognised that the UN Convention, even when it has been ratified, will not be a panacea for ending systemic exclusion and discrimination.

5 THE DISABILITY DIMENSION IN DEVELOPMENT AND POVERTY REDUCTION STRATEGIES AND NATIONAL DEVELOPMENT FRAMEWORKS: THE EXPERIENCE OF UGANDA

Until recently, few Poverty Reduction Strategies had any disability dimension. The number is now increasing, but the extent to which disability issues have been effectively included remains mixed. When the Poverty Reduction Strategy Paper (PRSP) process was first introduced, disability was commonly addressed in national PRSPs under the category of 'vulnerable groups', 'marginalised groups' or even 'disadvantaged groups' (ILO, 2002). However, in January 2006, Handicap International and CBM published a handbook, financed by the World Bank, entitled *Making PRSPs Inclusive*, which has gone some way towards raising the profile of disability issues in the production of poverty reduction strategies in developing countries. (HI, 2006).

This section of this paper analyses the extent to which disabled people's organisations had been involved in the development of poverty reduction strategy in Uganda. It draws upon work already undertaken by one of the authors in his position as Chair of UNAD, as well as interviews conducted in Kampala in March 2009 with Executive Directors of 10 National DPOs, though only five had some experience of the PRSP/PEAP processes members of the Ugandan disability movement. As will be seen, it is a far from straightforward process to ensure that poor and marginalised groups, such as persons with disabilities, are involved the development of poverty reduction initiatives.

In Uganda, there has been some attempt to include persons with disabilities and their representative organisations in developing the PRSP and involvement in the national planning framework, particularly in relation to poverty reduction (Dube, 2006). However, a recent DFID-funded Disability Scoping Study in Uganda found that the disability movement was somewhat disengaged from working with the parliamentarian and civil servants in developing disability policy and have had little impact in ensuring that disability issues were included in mainstream social and economic policy. This was compounded by the fact that there is no reliable and robust statistical data with regard to the livelihoods of persons with disabilities within the country. Consequently, it can be argued that there is a 'democratic deficit' with regard to disability policy formulation and implementation. In the absence of robust statistical data, it is hard to see how civil society institutions, not least DPOs, are able to hold their governments to account for human rights commitments. This scenario is not unique to Uganda though, and is commonplace throughout much of the African continent.

5.1 The Ugandan Experience

In Uganda, PRSP is commonly known as Poverty Eradication Action Plan (PEAP). PEAP is an overall planning framework for guiding public action on development/poverty reduction. It has been implemented on a 3-year basis through its translation into expenditure actions in the 3-Year Medium Term Expenditure Framework (MTEF). The PEAP, which started in 1997 in Uganda, has been revised every 3 years with an aim of incorporating emerging lessons and issues. The latest version of the PEAP was formulated in 2004 and thus expired in 2008. Currently a 5-Year National Development Plan (NDP) is being developed to become the successor plan to the PEAP.

The first submission by the Ugandan disability movement was made during a third review of the PEAP, which took place in 2004. It was made by the National Union of Disabled People of Uganda (NUDIPU) under the auspices of the Uganda NGO forum, with no other DPOs being involved in the process. It is apparent that NUDIPU have never been involved in implementation, monitoring and evaluation of PEAP, meaning that involvement of DPOs ends at consultation/planning level. All DPOs agree that, to date, DPO involvement in the PEAP planning process has been tokenistic. This can be attributed to lack of a strong PEAP advocacy component, and the fact that NUDIPU has been the only DPO involved.

NUDIPU is aware of this. In the 1990s, NUDIPU actively advocated and lobbied for amendments of the constitution and Local Government Act 1997 to ensure that persons with disabilities are represented at lower levels of the governance structure to bridge the gap brought about by decentralisation, which started in 1997. Consequently, since the 2001 elections there have been over 50 000 councillors and 5 MPs representing the interests of persons with disabilities in Uganda. Their role is to ensure that any policy and governance decisions made are inclusive of persons with disabilities.

However, this is often not the case, as one of the research respondents stated:

> 'Despite the fact that Uganda is one of the countries with best laws for persons with disabilities in the world, its unfortunate to note that lives of poor persons with disabilities have remained the same. If I was asked to tell you who has benefited [from this], would say the 'elected' and the 'DPO staff' because they earn salaries and allowances as our representatives and that's all what we get'.

In 2008, a National Report titled 'Disability and Poverty in Uganda: Progress and challenges in PEAP implementation 1997–2007' by the Ugandan Ministry of Finance, Planning and Economic Development indicated that although Uganda has been able to reduce poverty from 56% down to 31% in the last 10 years of PEAP implementation, the overall well being of persons with disabilities has not significantly changed (MFPED, 2008). The main problem identified by the report is that service providers are not aware about the actual needs of persons with disabilities. DPOs have also failed to convince service providers and government employees of the benefits of investing in persons with disabilities. In addition to a rights-based approach, there is a need for DPOs to ensure that the justification for inclusion of disability in PRSP/NDP demonstrates benefits to the community, the state and government as well as the traditional focus on the benefits to persons with disabilities. Many DPOs in Uganda lack a detailed understanding of how government structures work and how issues of disability can be brought on board. It was also surprising to note that some heads of DPOs interviewed were not aware of the ongoing PEAP review process, which started in 2007.

The survey also found out that DPOs and persons with disabilities themselves are more interested and focused on short-term projects whose outcomes can be easily measured: for example, income generating activities such as poultry rearing and making wheelchairs, rather than longer-term projects with fewer immediate results, such as the PEAP/NDP. This is certainly un-derstandable—the chronic poverty facing thousands of persons with disabilities makes them and their representatives prioritise projects that can bring in cash, goods or services in the shortest time possible. One DPO member was honest enough to say that *the process is quite technical and requires a lot of skills, which quite often are not available among NGOs* [in this case, DPOs]*.* They further added: *the process is very long, tedious, engaging and normally demands constant attendance of meetings by the same officer from the same organization. . .'* DPOs interviewed agreed that in order for the rights of persons with disabilities to be effectively included in the NDP, there is a need to form a task force made up of representatives from other national DPOs, not just the umbrella national union. They also suggested that for a task force to have an impact, alliances with civil society organisations or pressure groups and politicians beyond traditional disability circles must be built, and the 'disability agenda' must be clear to everyone.

DPOs are recognised as key stakeholders only by the Ministry of Gender, Labour, and Social Development during the PEAP/ NDP consultation. As a result, DPOs are not actively involved within the National Planning Authority (NPA) or the Ministry of Finance, Planning and Economic Development (MoFPED), despite this being the key Ministry spearheading the PEAP process.

It is evident that [the] disability movement in Uganda lacks the technical capacity to effectively lobby the government to include persons with disabilities in the NDP. Despite many years of DPO advocacy in Uganda, there are no traceable guidelines from any DPOs on how to work with either central or local governments on including persons with disabilities in the national or district development plans/strategies. For example, the researchers were able to access some of the copies of official letters from several DPOs to the Ministry of Gender, Labour and Social Development, and a critical review of these 'advocacy letters' reveals that in most instances, the DPOs just state what they want but not how it can be done. For example, one letter written by an organisation of people with visual impairments demanded 'Brailled drugs'—which led to the official from Uganda National Drug Authority responding: 'How do you expect us to Braille a tablet?'

From the above analysis, it is clear that the vast majority of persons with disabilities and their representative organisations do not have an in-depth understanding of poverty reduction processes. Many DPOs have never participated in the processes of NDP/PRS. They are unaware of when and where such activities take place, and if they are invited to participate at all, they are often invited only when the process has already started, making it difficult to make timely and useful contributions.

6 Conclusion: The Challenges for Effective Inclusion

By way of conclusion, this section will attempt to analyse the generic challenges that are encountered with respect to developing genuinely inclusive poverty reduction strategies and national development plans. At the outset, it is duly acknowledged that this is by no means an easy task. However, if the Millennium Development Goal (MDG) targets stand any chance of being met, then it is imperative that persons with disabilities and their representative organisations are included in such initiatives.

It is apparent that the inclusion of persons with disabilities within such processes has to date been limited and largely ineffective. This can be attributed to a number of factors, including:

+ Policy-makers and senior civil servants not understanding disability issues from a rights-based perspective;
+ The disability movement not having fully comprehended the complexity and dynamics of the policy-making process (including budgeting and macroeconomics);

- The lack of capacity of DPOs to lobby governments effectively; and
- Negative social attitudes *vis-à-vis* persons with disabilities held by the general community limit a willingness to listen to and include DPOs charged with fostering this inclusion.

A number of strategic interventions could be made by national governments and donor agencies to make the development poverty reduction strategies more inclusive, and which would specifically address the difficulties identified above, particularly the lack of dialogue between governments and DPOs. Funding should be provided so that DPOs acquire relevant skills in policy making and should gather substantive data informed by research that will compel policy-makers to act. Furthermore, the capacity of DPOs should be enhanced so that they can effectively advocate and articulate social policy issues in order for them to make the most significant impact on development policy making. Physical and environmental barriers to participation and inclusion must also be removed, such as ensuring meeting places are accessible and that any review materials or documents are available in a variety of formats.

To ensure that disability issues are included in the NDP/PRS, DPOs need to form strong national and regional coalitions to harness their voices. They should prepare well to identify issues that need be included in the plans prior to attending these meetings. DPOs should also seek alliances with other non-disabled colleagues to gain solidarity in pushing anti-poverty agendas within these frameworks.

The various ministries that form Governments are often disjointed and hardly demonstrate any collaboration in addressing disability and development issues. There is a need to strengthen the existing structures within national and local councils and ensure policy and practice is coordinated and coherent. The focal point in each Ministry should be clearly identifiable. To ensure that disability remains a priority in the National Development Plans/PRS, there should be regular engagement between the Government and stakeholders. This should be followed up with regular monitoring and evaluation.

International donors should mainstream disability in all their programmes/projects as advocated in the UN Convention. Furthermore, they should ensure that they include disability as a condition. Indicators should be included to ensure measurable monitoring. There is now a growing body of guidelines around these issues.[1]

DPOs can effectively use the UN Convention to positively influence mainstreaming and inclusion in international donor development plans by holding accountable donor countries and individual governments who are signatories to the Convention to ensure that disability is equally included in all their programs/projects. A shadow audit report should also be made to ensure this is being monitored and reported at country levels.

Despite these challenges, the inclusion of persons with disabilities in the PRSP process and other poverty reduction initiatives provides an opportunity to bring poverty to the centre stage in international politics, and this commitment could eventually have effect at the local and international level. The main focus of the PRSP process is increasingly gaining acceptance and approval and there is a quantitative rise in cooperation between the civil society and government; for example, the Mozambican government recently launched an inclusive PRSP project with the support of the World Bank and other organisations working in the field of disability. This wave of acceptance should be exploited to ensure that DPOs and their allies and partners push the disability agenda into development plans.

One of the main challenges that still needs to be addressed is the lack of capacity of DPOs to engage in the policy-making process. Notwithstanding the growing recognition of DPOs as significant civil society actors in many developing countries, this is indeed one of the most intransigent barriers to inclusion. However, increasingly, there are some good examples where DPO engagement has been effective. In Tanzania, DPO leaders are now regularly invited to District Council meetings to present their plans, and a network has been formed to coordinate all disability organisations and further ensure that they are involved in the National Strategy for Economic Growth and Reduction of Poverty (NSGRP) 2005–2010. However, in many countries, the capacity of DPOs and persons with disabilities representatives' needs to be enhanced in order to engage with government, international donors, the business community and other key stakeholders effectively.

DPOs cannot undertake these challenges alone and must undergo changes themselves in their perceptions and mindsets in terms of why and with whom they build alliances. They often perceive non-disabled people as threatening, or dominating, especially professionals who are capable and willing to provide skills and resources which are needed. What needs to be realised is that there is 'strength in numbers' and that experience has shown that alliances and genuinely inclusive partnerships can provide the necessary critical mass required to generate change. Excellent examples can be found in the cases of Honduras, Tanzania, Cambodia, Vietnam, Bangladesh, Sierra Leone and Uganda. In all these countries, local DPOs such as National Union of Disabled People of Uganda (NUDIPU), Tanzania Federation of Disabled Peoples Organizations (SHIVYAWATA) and the Cambodian Disabled People's Organization (CDPO) have worked with, all of whom have all worked with other organisations towards a common goal. These organisations include Leonard Cheshire Disability, UNICEF, WHO, UN FAO, Handicap International, CBM, Catholic Relief Service (CRS), World Concern and Health Volunteers Overseas (HVO). Now is the time for all who are sincerely committed to promoting genuinely inclusive development policies and modalities to work together towards the materialisation of the UN Convention and hence achieve social development and equality of human rights.

It is fallacious to think that the inclusion of people with disabilities in the development of poverty reduction strategies will be an easy task. However, the undertaking will be much harder if the discriminatory attitudes that previously placed persons with disabilities in a trap of exclusion and spiralling poverty are not challenged and eradicated. Change will require strong political will and the capacity to defend re-allocation of scarce resources against competing demands. The international community, respective governments, civil society, DPOs and the general public need to be fully cognisant of, and committed to, the principles of the UN Convention and to improving the lives of people with disabilities through its mechanisms, rules, regulations, policies and strategies.

Awareness is building globally but not rapidly enough. The voicelessness and powerlessness of persons with disabilities must end. There is no historic example of any excluded or oppressed minority group obtaining recognition of its rights without having had to fight for it. Therefore, DPOs, individual, allies and partners must keep the struggle and the movement strong and alive, and strive for a 'Society for All';—where policy will state clearly the goal of an inclusive society for all that tolerates and celebrates diversity and promotes equity and social justice; a society within which persons with disabilities have a key role to play equal to all other human beings. The UN Convention presents an opportunity to correct the current unjust situation that has prevailed for far too long. Perhaps this is best summarised in the words of the new President of USA who stated:

> 'We must build a world free of unnecessary barriers, stereotypes, and discrimination. . . . policies must be developed, attitudes must be shaped, and buildings and organizations must be designed to ensure that everyone has a chance to get the education they need and live independently as full citizens in their communities'.

> —Barack Obama, 11th April 2008

NOTE

1. See for example the Leonard Cheshire Disability Edamat Tool: www.lcint. org\?lid=3142

REFERENCES

Adejumobi S. 2006. *Governance and Poverty Reduction in Africa: A Critique of Poverty Reduction Strategy Papers.* Economic Community of West African Studies: Abuja.

Booth D. 2003. *Fighting Poverty in Africa: Are PRSPs Making a Difference?* Overseas Development Institute: London.

DFID. 2000. *Disability, Poverty and Development.* DFID: London.

Dube AK. 2006. Participation of disabled people in the PRSP and PEAP process. In *In and Out of the Mainstream? Lessons from research on disability and development cooperation,* Albert B (ed.). The Disability Press: Leeds.

Eyben R. 2005. Who owns a poverty reduction strategy? Power, instruments and relationships in Bolivia. In *Inclusive Aid, Changing Power and Relationships in International Development,* Groves L, Hinton R (eds). Earthscan: London.

Eyben R. 2008. *Power, Mutual Accountability and Responsibility in the Practice of Aid: A Relational Approach.* IDS Working Paper 305. Institute of Development Studies: Brighton.

Handicap International, CBM. 2006. *Making PRSPs Inclusive.* Handicap International and CBM: Munich.

Hendriks A. 2007. Selected legislation and jurisprudence: UN convention of the rights of persons with disabilities. *European Journal of Health Law* 14(3): 281–298.

Hickey S, Moham G. 2004. *Participation: From Tyranny to Transformation.* Zed Books: London.

ILO. 2002. *Disability and Poverty Reduction Strategies: Discussion Paper.* ILO: Geneva; Available at http://www.ilo.org/public/english/employment/skills/disability/download/discpaper.pdf

Lang R. in press. The United Nations convention on the rights and dignities of persons with disabilities. *European Journal of Disability Research.*

Lang R, Upah L. 2008. *Disability Scoping Study in Nigeria.* Department for International Development: London; Available at http://www.ucl.ac.uk/lc-ccr/downloads/dfid_nigeriareport

Marriott A, Gooding K. 2007. *Social Assistance and Disability in Developing Countries.* DFID and Sightsavers International: UK; Available at http://www.ipc-undp.org/publications/cct/Social_Assistance_Disability_Gooding_Marriott.pdf

Mersland R, Bwire F, Musaka G. 2008. *Access to Mainstream Micro-Finance Institutions: Lessons from Uganda*, Paper presented at the Joint UNECA/Leonard Cheshire Disability Conference 'UN Convention on the Rights of Persons with Disabilities: A Call for Action on Poverty, Lack of Access and Discrimination', Addis Ababa, May 2008.

Megret F. 2008. The disabilities convention: towards a holistic concept of rights. *International Journal of Human Rights* **12**(2): 261–277.

MFPED. 2008. *Disability and Poverty in Uganda: Progress and Challenges in PEAP Implementation 1997–2007*. MFPED: Kampala.

Mitra S. 2008. *Social Protection and the Role of Social Safety Nets in Low Income Countries*. Paper presented at the Joint UNECA/Leonard Cheshire Disability Conference 'UN Convention on the Rights of Persons with Disabilities: A Call for Action on Poverty, Lack of Access and Discrimination', Addis Ababa, May 2008.

Sen A. 1999. *Development As Freedom*. Oxford University Press: Oxford.

Thomas P. 2005. *Disability, Poverty and the Millennium Development Goals: Relevance, Challenges and Opportunities for DFID*. DFID: UK.

UN DESA. 2006. *Convention of the Rights of Persons with Disabilities*. UN DESA: New York; Available at http://www.un.org/disabilities/documents/convention/convoptprot-e.pdf

Yeo R. 2001. *Chronic Poverty and Disability*. Action on Disability and Development, Frome: UK; Available at http://www.chronicpoverty.org/pdfs/04Yeo.pdf

---

*Teresa Njoroge Mwendwa is with Friends of the Disabled Foundation, Kenya.

Ambrose Murangira is chairman of the Uganda National Association of the Deaf, Kenya.

Raymond Lang is with the Cheshire Disability and Inclusive Development Centre, University College, London.

Mwendwa, Teresa Njoroge, Ambrose Murangira, and Raymond Lang. "Mainstreaming the Rights of Persons with Disabilities in National Development Frameworks." *Journal of International Development*. vol. 21 (2009): 662–672. Published online at www.interscience.wiley.com.

Used by permission.

Discussion Questions

1. Discuss the correlation between disability and poverty.

2. What are some effective models for developing inclusive policies in developing countries?

3. How does the Convention on the Rights of Persons with Disabilities tie in with the Millennium Development Goals?

4. How does being poor and having a disability increase social exclusion?

CHAPTER 6:

Guaranteeing Deinstitutionalization

Chapter 6 addresses the conditions at several institutions for individuals with disabilities, calls for action on deinstitutionalization, and makes recommendations for community living options. The first article, a report by Mental Disability Rights International, "Torment Not Treatment: Serbia's Segregation and Abuse of Children and Adults with Disabilities," chronicles extensive human rights offenses against people with disabilities warehoused in substandard institutions.

The second article, by Save the Children, "Keeping Children Out of Harmful Institutions: Why We Should Be Investing in Family-Based Care," provides an overview of the harmful practices in institutions. Issues of poverty, social exclusion and discrimination, and cultural taboos are illuminated. Recommendations are made that will require a new era of political leadership to ensure that high-quality, family-centered care alternatives and protection practices are put in and remain in place.

The third article, from the Center for An Accessible Society, is a summary of 1999 U.S. Supreme Court case, *Olmstead v. L.C. and*

E.W., that affirmed the right of individuals with disabilities to live in their communities. The Supreme Court ruled that the unnecessary segregation of individuals with disabilities in institutions may constitute discrimination based on disability. The Court held that the Americans with Disabilities Act may require states to provide community-based services rather than institutional placements for individuals with disabilities. This historic pronouncement makes attainable the goal, long sought by people with disabilities and advocates, of living in their communities.

The final article in the chapter, "Recommendation CM/Rec (2010)2 of the Committee of Ministers to Member States on De-institutionalisation and Community Living of Children with Disabilities," spells out the aim of the Council of Europe to achieve a greater unity among its member states by promoting the adoption of common rules on deinstitutionalization. The report recommends that the governments of member states develop and implement a comprehensive standards-based system that provides community living options and supportive services to children currently institutionalized, consistent with the articles contained in the Convention on the Rights of Persons with Disabilities.

Torment not Treatment: Serbia's Segregation and Abuse of Children and Adults with Disabilities

*By Mental Disability Rights International**

Torment not Treatment: Serbia's Segregation and Abuse of Children and Adults with Disabilities is the product of an investigation spanning four years, by Mental Disability Rights International (MDRI), into the human rights abuses perpetrated against institutionalized children and adults in Serbia. From July 2003 to August 2007, MDRI has documented a broad array of human rights violations against people with disabilities, segregated from society and forced to live out their lives in institutions (all observations in this report are from December 2006 through August 2007 except as noted). Filthy conditions, contagious diseases, lack of medical care and rehabilitation, and a failure to provide oversight renders placement in a Serbian institution life-threatening. MDRI investigators found children and adults with disabilities tied to beds or never allowed to leave a crib—some for *years* at a time. Inhumane and degrading treatment in Serbian institutions—in violation of article 3 of the European Convention on Human Rights (ECHR)—is widespread. Children and adults with disabilities tied down and restrained over a lifetime are being subjected to extremely dangerous and painful "treatment" that is tantamount to torture.

Serbia lacks adequate laws to protect people with disabilities from arbitrary detention in psychiatric hospitals or social care facilities. Despite an improved new guardianship law, people with mental disabilities can still have all their rights stripped away without adequate due process of law or right to counsel. As a practical matter, many people in institutions are detained for life with no legal process or judicial oversight. For more than 11,000 people detained in Serbia's institutions under the Ministry of Labor and Social Policy (MLSP), and for more than 6,200 in psychiatric institutions under the Ministry of Health, these practices violate the right to "liberty and security of person" under article 5 of the ECHR.

Children with disabilities placed in institutions are likely to spend their entire lives incarcerated. Adults with psychiatric disabilities, placed in institutions by family members, are also at risk of spending years, and in some cases their whole adult lives in institutions. There are virtually no supports or services in the community for people with disabilities nor are there supports for families wanting to keep their children born with disabilities with them. Despite a stated policy of ending new detentions, children continue to be separated from parents and placed in institutions because of a lack of support in the community. Authorities have reported to MDRI that physicians still encourage parents to institutionalize children with disabilities at birth.

Since 2000, the government of Serbia, with the support of international donors, rebuilt many of its old institutions. As international support for reform recedes, Serbia is left with a segregated service system and few resources for reform.

The government of Serbia deserves credit for enormous candor in admitting to poor treatment practices in institutions and for recognizing that most people detained in institutions should be properly cared for in the community. As part of a stated commitment to protect human rights and seek integration into Europe, Serbia established a new social welfare policy in December 2006, committing the government to serving people with disabilities in the least restrictive environment suitable to their conditions. The Ministry of Health has adopted a similar policy for the reform of the mental health system. In April 2006, Serbia adopted a progressive new "Law on the Prevention of Discrimination Against Persons with Disabilities."[1] Serbia's new constitution also bans discrimination based on mental or physical disability.

Despite these important government commitments, actual treatment of people with disabilities violates Serbia's own law and policy on a large scale. The service system discriminates against people with disabilities by taking away peoples' rights without due process and segregating them from society. Serbian law calls for people with disabilities to have an opportunity to live in the community, but the creation of community support systems is left to local governments without the funding necessary to implement these programs. At the same time, funds continue to be used to build and expand institutions at Veliki Papovac and Kovin. When the new buildings are complete at the Kovin psychiatric institution, for example, the capacity of the facility will increase from about 600 to 850 patients. While the MLSP has promised to create new 130 community placements for some 500 individuals, these programs will not meet the needs of thousands of children and adults who remain abandoned in overcrowded institutions. Even if current reform plans are fully implemented, the vast majority of people with disabilities now detained in institutions have no hope for returning to the community. **The government of Serbia has no plan or program to end the improper detention of thousands of people with disabilities—or to end the abusive treatment within its institutions.**

> *There is no solution to the situation at Kulina except to close the institution.*—government official, MLSP

The MLSP recognizes that the most abusive institutions, such as Kulina, should be closed. In July 2007, MLSP officials reported to MDRI that they have a plan to reduce the population of Kulina by 20% by moving children to "better institutions." Even if fully implemented, this plan will leave the great majority of children and adults at Kulina languishing at the facility.

While the children transferred may experience some improvement in physical condition, they will still remain in inappropriate congregate care settings. In August 2007, staff at Kulina were unaware of *any* plan to reduce the population at the institution. "An institutional reform plan has existed for years," reports the chief nurse, "but such promises had been made for years without being fulfilled."

> *The state does nothing. Parents get no support. And there is no interest in adopting children even with the mildest of disabilities or Roma children. Most parents would like to keep their children at home.*—doctor, Subotica children's institution

As the European Union (EU) readies to continue talks on a Stabilization and Association Agreement (SAA)—the gateway to EU candidacy for accession consideration—MDRI urges the EU to insist that Serbia must first protect the basic human rights of its most vulnerable citizens.

Summary of Findings
MDRI observed the following conditions in institutions:
+ **Babies, children and adults with disabilities are confined to institutions for a lifetime, in conditions that are dangerous and life-threatening, and that inflict both mental and physical suffering.**—Babies with disabilities spend most waking hours lying in cribs, with little or no human contact. Children and adults who are labeled "immobile" are also doomed to an existence of confinement in metal cribs and beds where they may be left to eat and defecate.

> *There were rows of metal cribs filled with teenagers and young adults. Labeled immobile or bedridden, many of them were kept naked from the waist down on plastic mattresses, covered only with a sheet to facilitate staff clean-up of bladder and bowel incontinence. Staff reported they also eat in the*

cribs and spend all of their time in the cribs. They never get out.—MDRI investigator, Stamnica Institution

Teenagers and young adults confined to cribs in Stamnica Institution were labeled with "blindness, deafness, Cerebral Palsy, Hydrocephaly and mental retardation." The lights were off and it was dark in the room in the middle of the day. The smell of urine and feces was overpowering and there was one staff person in the room for about 25 people. There was no stimulus of any kind—no music, conversation, television or radio—only darkness and silence.

> *I looked into the crib and saw a child who looked to be 7 or 8 years old. The nurse told me he was 21 and had been at the institution for eleven years. I asked her how often he was taken out of the crib and she said "never, he has never been out of the crib in 11 years."*—MDRI investigator, Stamnica Institution

In the Subotica Institution for babies and small children under the age of 7, babies with disabilities lie in cribs where an insufficient number of caregivers can do little but feed and change the children, with no time for playing, rocking or holding. We observed bottles propped rather than hand fed and babies get virtually no human contact.

> *We have long recognized that placing any child in a setting with little human interaction is inherently dangerous. The children we observed in Serbia who are emaciated and immobile may have adequate nutrients offered to them. But in my clinical experience, emotionally abandoned children may stop eating or simply lose the will to live. The research literature backs this up.*—Karen Green McGowan, RN, expert on children with complex disabilities

+ **The use of restraints and seclusion on both children and adults**—There are no enforceable laws or regulations regulating the use of physical restraints in Serbia, and there is no oversight to prevent the abuse of this potentially torturous practice. As a result, individuals may be left in restraints for days, weeks—or *years*. In severely understaffed institutions, restraint is used for the convenience of staff who cannot provide adequate individual attention or treatment to people detained in institutions. On two different visits to the Kulina Children's Institution in July and August 2007, MDRI found dozens of children tied to beds, chairs and cribs, some in 4-point restraints (i.e., legs and arms tied to the four corners of the cribs and beds). We also found extensive use of restraints in the adult facility of Kragujevac, where many residents were tied to beds. In another institution for adults in Curug, MDRI found tiny rooms where people are kept in seclusion with just a cot and a bucket on the floor for a toilet.

> *In the geriatric ward at Kovin, I observed a room filled with about 30 elders, many of them tied to chairs. It was July and one of the hottest days of the year and all were wearing heavy striped pajamas. There was no air conditioning. Old men and women struggled to pull off their clothes, but they could not do so because of the restraints. One woman pulled so hard, her chair tipped over and she hit her head on the ground. Her robe came off to reveal open sores on her buttocks (perhaps from sitting tied to the chair). A nearby man tried to help her stand up, but he too was restrained and could not reach her. The woman lay motionless on the floor for close to ten minutes before staff noticed her and placed her back in the chair. She screamed as they forced her to sit in the chair despite her open sores.*—MDRI investigator, Kovin psychiatric hospital.

+ **Restraints are used instead of treatment or care for self abuse**—Children who grow up in congregate care without love and attention often become self-abusive. In its mildest form, self stimulation may include rhythmic motions or rocking behavior. Over time, children or adults may be driven to more extreme behavior, including head banging or repeated acts of hitting or biting themselves. Left without attention, the practice can become self-mutilating, including children who gouge out their own eyes. MDRI observers witnessed the full range of such practices in Kulina and Stamnica. None of the institutions we visited had any specialized staff or behavior programs designed to assist children with problems of self-abuse. The commonly accepted "treatment" for self-abuse is the use of physical restraints. This practice actually exacerbates the underlying psychological damage to the person, resulting in continued self-abuse and even more physical restraint. Additionally, prolonged use of restraint can lead to muscle atrophy, life-threatening deformities, and even organ failure.

> *At Kulina, staff reported that a 6 year old boy with Spina Bifida was very aggressive towards himself and tried to rip off his own ear. We observed this boy tied to a chair. At Stamnica, a teenage girl, permanently confined to a crib, was observed attempting to gouge her eyes out while staff stood by and did nothing. We observed many children at the institution biting and chewing their own fingers.*—MDRI investigator

• **Lack of rehabilitation and medical care**—There is a broad lack of rehabilitation, physical therapy and medical care for children and adults with disabilities detained in Serbian institutions. Left to languish for years in a state of total inactivity, children or adults who do not become self-abusive become more disabled in other ways. Without activity, movement or physical therapy, children and adults labeled "immobile" can suffer from contorted and atrophied limbs and spines, dislocated bones and breathing problems. Children who receive little or no human contact and are emotionally abandoned can develop "failure to thrive" and are at increased risk of death.

> *MDRI investigators found a 3 year old boy who had recently been permanently placed in Subotica institution by his parents after he contracted Hepatitis B & C. The doctor at the facility stated he was not adjusting well and "he does not want to eat—he is having a difficult time." Staff pointed out another 3 year old child with Down's Syndrome who also refused to eat.*

50% of the children and adults have hepatitis—nurse, Kulina children's institution

Investigators found residents in different institutions in dire need of medical attention. At Curug, a psychiatric social care facility, a man was kept in an isolation room—which lacked heat and had only a tin bucket as a toilet—because of his Tuberculosis, yet he was not receiving any treatment. Many people had no teeth due to lack of dental care. Infants and babies diagnosed with Hydrocephalus lay motionless in cribs, with heads swelled so large they were unable to move. Staff at Subotica institution wondered out loud "why doctors had not drained it"—often a life-saving procedure for children with such conditions.

When MDRI investigators asked staff at Kulina why a 7 year old girl, with an enormous head from Hydrocephalus, was not getting medical treatment that could save her life, a doctor stated:

> **When this girl was born, the doctor advised the parents not to bother with the surgery she needed since she would die anyway. But she is still alive.**—doctor, Kulina

+ **Inhuman, degrading and life threatening physical conditions of facilities people with disabilities are forced to endure**—During the winter, MDRI investigators found institutions with little or no heat, with patients huddling around radiators trying to keep warm. Many wore hats and coats indoors. The director of Curug Institution told MDRI that the facility was infested with rats and mice and the walls of the building were covered with asbestos. Lack of bathrooms and plumbing forced patients to defecate in buckets which they keep under their beds—causing a stifling smell in the room. MDRI found windows that would not open and faulty electrical wiring.

We have three buildings with 204 clients, many of whom are immobile. With the electric wiring I worry about a fire. At night we only have one nurse and one security guard on duty for three buildings.—director of institution, Curug

---

NOTE

1. Ministry of Labour, Employment, and Social Policy, *Three Keys for Equal Opportunities*, 2007, 92–118 (publication in English and Serbian with the full text of the *International Convention on the Rights of Persons with Disabilities, Strategy for Improving the Position of Persons with Disabilities in the Republic of Serbia and Law on Prevention of Discrimination Against Persons with Disabilities*) (herein after *Three Keys for Equal Opportunities*).

---

*Mental Disability Rights International is dedicated to promoting the human rights and full participation in society of people with mental disabilities worldwide.

Mental Disability Rights International. *Torment not Treatment: Serbia's Segregation and Abuse of Children and Adults with Disabilities.* Washington, DC: Mental Disability Rights International, 2007, iii–vii. http://www.mdri.org/PDFs/reports/Serbia-rep-english.pdf.

Used by permission.

Keeping Children Out of Harmful Institutions: Why We Should Be Investing in Family-Based Care

By Save the Children*

SUMMARY

The UN estimates that up to 8 million children around the world are living in care institutions.[1] However, the actual number is likely to be far higher, owing to chronic gaps in information. It is also likely to rise with the increasing impact of conflict, climate change and the HIV and AIDS pandemic on the poorest and most vulnerable families.

In many institutions, the standard of care is poor. Many children are abused and neglected. Children under three, in particular, are at risk of permanent developmental damage by not being cared for in a family setting. For all children, long-term stays in institutions can have a lasting negative impact. The harm that can be caused to children by institutional care has been documented since the early 20th century.

Most children in what are known as orphanages or children's homes are not in fact orphans. At least four out of five children in institutional care have one or both parents alive.

Poverty and social exclusion are two of the main reasons why children are unable to live at home. Families often feel that placing their children into care is the only way to ensure they get an education and enough food and other essentials. Discrimination and cultural taboos also mean that in some countries a disproportionate number of girls, disabled children and children from minority ethnic groups are relinquished or abandoned into care institutions. With support, the parents and extended families of many of these children could care for them.

Greater political and financial commitment is needed to tackle the poverty and social exclusion that drives families to give up their children, and to help build parents' capacity to care for their children. In addition, greater priority must be given to developing good-quality family-based care options—such as foster care and adoption—for children who need alternative families.

Experience shows that where there is political will, children can be well cared for and protected. For example, Indonesia has embarked on a process of widespread reform to improve the quality of care in institutions and to shift policies and resources towards supporting children in their families. Sierra Leone has reunified many children with their families and is addressing its use of care institutions. Croatia has achieved important structural and legal changes to ensure that family and community-based care is given greater priority. South Africa has built social protection and other mechanisms to strengthen families and prevent unnecessary separation. Unfortunately, such examples are few and far between.

The new international *Guidelines for the Appropriate Use and Conditions of Alternative Care for Children*,[2] which were finalised in 2009 after several years of consultation with governments and experts around the world, should be adopted and implemented as a matter of urgency.

The design and delivery of national and local childcare and protection systems must be transformed to enable families to look after their own children and to ensure that children have access to positive care alternatives where necessary.

This will require a new era of political leadership to ensure that positive childcare and protection practices are pursued at every level. To this end, we are calling for:

Every government to make a long-term commitment to building family support services and family-based alternative care, and to

tackling the overuse and misuse of residential care, in line with the *Guidelines*.

This should be reflected in budget allocations, national strategies, and laws and policies that prioritise the prevention of family separation and ensure that children have access to good-quality family-based care alternatives where necessary. Particular priority should be given to ensuring that children under the age of three can stay with their own families or have access to family-based alternative care.

Governments to ensure that all forms of alternative care adhere to the principles and standards set out in the *Guidelines* by:

+ creating and enforcing national minimum quality standards through certification, inspection and monitoring
+ taking legal action against unregistered or unlawful care institutions
+ building an effective cadre of social workers capable of supporting and monitoring the care of children, including re-training institutional care providers where necessary
+ creating coordination mechanisms at every level so that government, care providers and donors can work together effectively to prevent and respond to care and protection concerns.

Donors to ensure that funding is directed at preventative community and family support and at family-based alternative care by:

+ supporting deinstitutionalisation efforts and the development of good-quality family-based care alternatives
+ promoting the training and accreditation of social work professionals
+ initiating or expanding social protection programmes
+ developing community-based services that support families to care for their children.

UN agencies, NGOs and faith-based organisations to raise awareness of the importance of family and community-based care for children. This should include information campaigns to:

+ educate public and private donors
+ make children and families aware of their rights with regard to support services
+ encourage adults to engage in fostering and adoption programmes.

The UN Special Representative on Violence against Children and the UN Special Representative on Children and Armed Conflict to prepare a joint report on the care situation of children without adequate family care in development and conflict situations.

NOTES

1. P S Pinheiro, *World Report on Violence Against Children*, UNICEF: New York, 2006.
2. *Guidelines for the Appropriate Use and Conditions of Alternative Care for Children*, 2009.

Supreme Court Upholds ADA 'Integration Mandate' in Olmstead Decision

By The Center for An Accessible Society*

Washington, DC, June 22, 1999—In rejecting the state of Georgia's appeal to enforce institutionalization of individuals with disabilities, the Supreme Court today affirmed the right of individuals with disabilities to live in their community in its 6–3 ruling against the state of Georgia in the case *Olmstead v. L.C. and E.W.*

Under Title II of the federal Americans with Disabilities Act, said Justice Ruth Bader Ginsburg, delivering the opinion of the court, "states are required to place persons with mental disabilities in community settings rather than in institutions when the State's treatment professionals have determined that community placement is appropriate, the transfer from institutional care to a less restrictive setting is not opposed by the affected individual, and the placement can be reasonably accommodated, taking into account the resources available to the State and the needs of others with mental disabilities."

The 'integration mandate' of the Americans with Disabilities Act requires public agencies to provide services "in the most integrated setting appropriate to the needs of qualified individuals with disabilities." The high court upheld that mandate, ruling that Georgia's department of human resources could not segregate two women with mental disabilities in a state psychiatric hospital long after the agency's own treatment professionals had recommended their transfer to community care.

The lower courts ruled the state violated the ADA's "integration mandate" and Georgia appealed, claiming the ruling could lead to the closing of all state hospitals and disruption of state funding of services to people with mental disabilities.

However, the women were supported by a number of states, disability organizations and others, including the U.S. solicitor general, who said "The unjustified segregation of people in institutions, when community placement is appropriate, constitutes a form of discrimination prohibited by Title II [of the ADA]."

Originally, 26 states had signed onto an Amicus Brief in support of Georgia's position. However, an extensive education campaign by the disability rights movement reduced that number to just seven.

LEGISLATIVE HISTORY...

The Americans with Disabilities Act is a plenary civil rights statute designed to halt all practices that segregate persons with disabilities and those that treat them . . . differently. By enacting the ADA, we are making a conscious decision to reverse a sad legacy of segregation and degradation.

> Statement of Rep. Ron Dellums (D.-Calif.) during the final passage of the ADA in the House of Representatives

I have seen these institutions. The smell of human waste and detergent has stuck in my throat. I have looked into the vegetative eyes of its inmates in their sterile environments, I have heard of the premature death ratio and prevalence of pneumonia and necrotic decubitus, literally allowing them to rot in their beds, these living dead, our imprisoned Americans with disabilities. At a hearing on the bill before the Subcommittee on Select Education of the House Committee on Education and Labor in 1989, Cindy Miller talked about her "realistic," "constant fear" that she might be institutionalized. "Please enact the ADA quickly," she told members of Congress.

"**Getting people . . . out of institutions**" was named specifically by Senator Tom Harkin (D.-Iowa) in his remarks introducing the 1989 version of the ADA in the 101st Congress. Our country had "created monoliths of isolated care in institutions and in segregated educational settings," former Sen. Lowell Weicker testified during 1989 Senate hearings on the bill. Society made disabled people "invisible by shutting them away in segregated facilities" Rep. George Miller (D.-Calif.) said in a Congressional debate on the bill.

Senator Harkin noted that the Act was needed to address the absence of protection against discrimination in "all services provided by State and local governments. . . ." (Statement accompanying his introduction of the ADA bill in the Senate, 135 CONG. REC. 8505, 8508 (1989)

Title II is intended "to cover all programs of state or local governments, regardless of the receipt of federal financial assistance," said a House Judiciary report. (House Judiciary Committee Report at 49, reprinted in 1990 U.S.C.C.A.N. at 472) The Senate Committee report and the report of the House Committee on Education and Labor declared in identical language that the "first purpose" of Title II is "to make applicable the prohibition against discrimination on the basis of disability . . . to all programs, activities, and services provided or made available by state and local governments." (Senate Report at 44; Education & Labor Committee Report at 84, reprinted in 1990 U.S.C.C.A.N. at 366)

One June 22, 1999, the U. S. Supreme Court ruled in the case *Olmstead v. L.C. and E.W.* that the "integration mandate" of the Americans with Disabilities Act requires public agencies to provide services "in the most integrated setting appropriate to the needs of qualified individuals with disabilities." Disabled people segregated in institutions have used it to require states provide services in the community.

Olmstead v. L.C. and E.W. reached the Supreme Court when the Georgia Department of Human Resources appealed a decision by the 11th Circuit that it had violated the ADA's "integration mandate" by segregating two women with mental disabilities in a state psychiatric hospital—long after the agency's treatment professionals had recommended their transfer to community care.

Lois Curtis, 31, and Elaine Wilson, 47, have mental disabilities. Each was hospitalized repeatedly over two decades, with periodic discharges to inappropriate settings—including a homeless shelter—followed by return to the hospital. Only after Atlanta Legal Aid attorney Susan Jamieson brought a lawsuit in 1995 were they moved to a small group home.

ATTORNEYS GENERAL WITHDRAW SUPPORT FOR GEORGIA'S APPEAL

When Georgia asked the Supreme Court to review the decision of the U.S. Court of Appeals for the 11th Circuit, 22 state attorneys general, led by Florida's, filed a supporting brief. They contended that the ruling would lead to lawsuits forcing closure of all state hospitals and disrupting states' funding of services for people with mental disabilities.

However, by the deadline for filing on Georgia's behalf, 12 of the 22 states had withdrawn their support for Georgia's appeal, and more states are continuing to distance themselves from the position taken by Georgia. The 12 were Alabama, California, Delaware, Florida, Maryland, Michigan, Nebraska, New Hampshire, Pennsylvania, South Dakota, Utah and West Virginia, plus the territory of Guam. For the latest updates on which states have removed themselves from the brief, contact the Bazelon Center.

This highly unusual action has prompted news coverage in many states. Among newspapers covering this story, see

The Seattle Times'
"State's legal stance worries the disabled,"
By Dionne Searcey
Feb. 12, 1999

The Boston Globe's
"State's move enrages advocates for disabled,"
By Shelley Murphy
Feb. 26, 1999

FROM THE BRIEFS...

"One of the congressional hearings on the ADA legislation in the
100th Congress devoted considerable attention to institutionalization. Americans with Disabilities Act of 1988: Hearing on H.R.
4498 Before the Subcommittee on Select Education of the House
Committee on Education and Labor, 100th Cong. (1988). Witnesses provided dramatic, and at times graphic, descriptions of the
damaging effects of segregated treatment facilities. Senator Harkin
made the intent to address segregated treatment programs crystal
clear, when, in introducing the 1989 version of the ADA in the
101st Congress, he expressly listed, as one of the intended consequences of the legislation, "getting people . . . out of institutions . . ."

To refute the argument made by the remaining 11 states, Oregon's director of human resources and 57 former commissioners
of mental health and directors of developmental disabilities, representing 36 states and the District of Columbia, have submitted
a brief on behalf of the women. They point out that at least three
quarters of the states are already reorganizing their systems to provide most services for people with mental disabilities in the community, at less than half the cost of institutional care. Therefore,
their brief asserts, Georgia and the states supporting its appeal are
wrong to contend that the lower courts' decision would unreason-
ably burden states or result in "careless deinstitutionalization." . . .

The commissioners' brief and another, filed by 30 national and
seven Georgia organizations, document the cost differential between institutional and community care. For example, the daily
cost of care in the mental retardation unit at Georgia Regional

Hospital-Atlanta, where the women were confined, was $283 in 1996, compared to the daily cost for community services of $118 to $124. National studies cited in the briefs show a similar pattern. For example, one compared community costs, including housing, of $60,000 per year for a discharged psychiatric patient to $130,000 for institutional care.

---

*Center for An Accessible Society is a U.S. organization that works to focus public attention on disability and promotes independent living.

The Center for An Accessible Society. *Supreme Court Upholds ADA 'Integration Mandate' in Olmstead Decision.* News release, June 22, 1999. http://www.accessiblesociety.org/topics/ada/olmsteadoverview.htm.

Used by permission.

Recommendation CM/Rec(2010)2 of the Committee of Ministers to Member States on Deinstitutionalisation and Community Living of Children with Disabilities

*By the Council of Europe**

The Committee of Ministers, under the terms of Article 15. b of the Statute of the Council of Europe,

Considering that the aim of the Council of Europe is to achieve a greater unity between its member states, inter alia, by promoting the adoption of common rules;

Recalling the Third Summit of Heads of State and Government of the Council of Europe (Warsaw, 16–17 May 2005) and the commitment to fully comply with the obligations of the United Nations Convention on the Rights of the Child, to effectively promote the rights of the child and to take specific action to eradicate all forms of violence against children, as well as the consolidation of the Council of Europe's work on disability issues and the support to its work on equity of access to care of appropriate quality and services which meet the needs of the population;

Taking into account the work of the Council of Europe in the field of childhood, family and disability policies and the following legal instruments:

+ the Convention on Human Rights and Fundamental Freedoms (ETS No. 5), which protects the rights of everyone, including children;

- the revised European Social Charter (ETS No. 163), which guarantees, in particular, the right of persons with disabilities to independence, social integration and participation in the life of the community (Article 15); the right of the family to appropriate social, legal and economic protection (Article 16); the right of children and young persons to grow up in an environment that encourages the full development of their personality and of their physical and mental capacities (Article 17);
- the European Convention for the Prevention of Torture and Inhuman or Degrading Treatment or Punishment (ETS No. 126);
- the European Convention on the Exercise of Children's Rights (ETS No. 160);
- the Convention on Contact concerning Children (ETS No. 192);

Bearing in mind Committee of Ministers' Recommendation Rec(2006)5 on the Council of Europe Action Plan to promote the rights and full participation of people with disabilities in society: improving the quality of life of people with disabilities in Europe 2006–2015, which is designed to make decisive progress in ensuring equal rights for people with disabilities and promotes a human rights based, anti-discriminatory approach to improving the lives of all people with disabilities, including children and those with enduring and/or complex needs;

Recalling the Revised Strategy for Social Cohesion (2004), which gives particular attention to the groups at risk of becoming vulnerable and supports an inclusive approach, underlining the active reintegration of citizens and vulnerable groups;

Referring to the "Report of the High Level Task Force on Social Cohesion in the 21st century" (2007), which attaches a fundamental role to human rights as the cornerstone for cohesive societies along with human dignity and recognition, with particular attention to the interests of vulnerable or potentially vulnerable groups;

Recalling the "Building a Europe for and with children" 2009–2011 Strategy, which pursues and enhances the Council of Europe's commitment to children's rights and the eradication of violence against children, with special focus on particularly vulnerable children, without parental care and/or with disabilities;

Taking into account other resolutions and recommendations of the Committee of Ministers, notably:

+ Resolution (77) 33 on placement of children, which stresses that placement should be avoided as far as possible through preventive measures of support to families in accordance with their special problems and needs;
+ Recommendation No. R (79) 17 concerning the protection of children against ill-treatment;
+ Recommendation No. R (84) 4 on parental responsibilities;
+ Recommendation No. R (87) 6 on foster families;
+ Recommendation No. R (94) 14 on coherent and integrated family policies;
+ Recommendation No. R (98) 8 on children's participation in family and social life;
+ Resolution ResAP(2005)1 on safeguarding adults and children with disabilities against abuse;
+ Recommendation Rec(2005)5 on the rights of children living in residential institutions;
+ Recommendation Rec(2006)19 on policy to support positive parenting, which asks public authorities to create the necessary conditions to implement a better reconciliation of family and working life through legal and other provisions, particularly for looking after children with disabilities as well as sick children;

Stressing the importance of the following United Nations conventions:

+ Convention on the Rights of the Child (1989) to which all the member states of the Council of Europe are parties, and the basic principles of this convention should always underlie the upbringing of children;

♦ Convention on the Rights of Persons with Disabilities (2006) stressing the right of children with disabilities to be treated on an equal basis with other children, especially where they face additional disadvantages, including the right to express themselves on matters of concern to them, and the essential need for fully accessible services. States are urged to conduct public awareness campaigns that "nurture receptiveness" to the inclusion of disabled children and to collective responsibility for upholding their right to a life within the community;

Recalling Parliamentary Assembly recommendations, particularly Recommendation 1666 (2004) on "A Europe-wide ban on corporal punishment of children"; Recommendations 1601 (2003) on "Improving the lot of abandoned children in institutions" and 1698 (2005) on "The rights of children in institutions: follow-up to Recommendation 1601 (2003)";

Referring to the Declaration of the European Ministers responsible for Family Affairs at their 28th session (Lisbon, Portugal, 2006), which underlines the necessity to adopt programmes aimed at providing appropriate support for families with children with disabilities;

Bearing in mind that, as provided in the different international legal instruments of the Council of Europe, as well as in Article 3 of the United Nations Convention on the Rights of the Child, the best interests of the child shall be a primary consideration;

Recalling that children are persons with rights, including the right to be protected and to participate, to express their views, to be heard and be heeded;

Being aware of the fact that placing children in institutionalised forms of care raises serious concerns as to its compatibility with the exercise of children's rights;

Recognising the need for major changes in perceptions of people with disabilities and also for major changes to bring about non-discriminatory and inclusive practices;

Noting the need for a cross-sectoral and co-ordinated approach at all levels of government,

Recommends that the governments of member states take all appropriate legislative, administrative and other measures adhering to the principles set out in the appendix to this recommendation in order to replace institutional provision with community-based services within a reasonable timeframe and through a comprehensive approach.

Appendix to Recommendation CM/Rec(2010)2

I. General framework and basic principles

1. To succeed in promoting the deinstitutionalisation of children with disabilities and their life in the community, the following basic principles enshrined in international legal instruments should be taken into account:

   1.1 all children have rights, hence disabled children have the same rights to family life, education, health, social care and vocational training as all children; long-term planning involving all stakeholders will be needed to ensure that children with disabilities are able to exercise the same rights as other children and to access social rights on the same basis as other children;

   1.2 all disabled children should live with their own family, which is the natural environment for the growth and well-being of a child, unless there are exceptional circumstances which prevent this;

   1.3 parents have the primary responsibility for the upbringing and development of the child; they should choose how to meet their child's needs as long as their decisions are informed by, and seen to be in, the child's best interests;

   1.4 in all actions concerning children the best interests of the child take precedence over other considerations and this principle should be upheld in relation to children with disabilities;

1.5 if a family or a service fails to work in a disabled child's best interests, or if a disabled child is being abused or neglected, the state, acting through its public agencies and within general child protection frameworks, should intervene to protect the child and make sure that his or her needs are met; in these exceptional circumstances, if care is to be provided outside the family, such care should be welcoming, well regulated and designed to maintain family ties;

1.6 the state has a responsibility to support families so that they can bring up their disabled child at home and, in particular, to create the necessary conditions to implement a better reconciliation of family and working life: the state should therefore finance and make available a range of high-quality services from which the families of children with disabilities can choose assistance adapted to their needs.

II. Deinstitutionalisation and the transitional process at national level

2. Deinstitutionalisation requires a number of general actions to support the strategic approach at national level involving all stakeholders. Deinstitutionalisation being a long-term process, a well-planned and structured transition process is necessary. The planning should involve government representatives covering all policy areas that affect the lives of children with disabilities. The following are important aspects that should be taken into account:

2.1 a national, multidisciplinary system for identifying and assessing abilities and needs;

2.2 mutual support programmes for parents;

2.3 provision of various services (support for families, psychosocial support, financial support, educational support, pedagogical support, etc.);

2.4 appropriate consideration of the individual needs of children and their families;

2.5 availability of various measures to allow families to take a break and thus to prevent crises;

2.6 continuity of services and planning of periods of transition (childhood to adolescence, pre-school to school, school to adulthood);

2.7 promoting and supporting active involvement in, and ownership of, the situation by families.

3. Building of new institutions should be discouraged by refusing to approve and fund proposals for this type of project.

4. Public authority action, strategic planning and co-ordination at national, regional and local levels in the context of the de-institutionalisation process should include the following four main strategies:
   a. the prevention of institutionalisation;
   b. the prevention of any prolongation of an initially foreseen short-term stay in an institution;
   c. the deinstitutionalisation of those who are currently in institutions;
   d. the creation of community-based services.

5. Deinstitutionalisation should be considered as an ongoing process that is constantly reviewed and there is a need to be vigilant in order to avoid returning to institutionalisation.

6. Transition from institutional to community-based services should be managed, anticipating resistance to change, challenging prejudices and removing barriers. During this period, services may be run in parallel.

7. While the transition is taking place, the commitment to children's rights applies equally to children who currently live in institutions, or in other types of care. Their successful social integration or reintegration should happen as soon as possible and their situation should be subject to periodic review with regard to the child's best interests; the child's parents should be supported as much as possible with a view to harmoniously reintegrating the child into the family and society.

8. Specific legislation mandating the authorities responsible for creating new networks of community-based care provision and setting a deadline at which point the admission of children to institutionalised forms of care will cease should be adopted. Where appropriate, links should be made to policies addressing poverty and the reduction of social exclusion. Measures taken to improve the governance of social services and non-governmental organisations (NGOs) working in the social care field should also be taken into account.

9. All new legislation, policy and guidance should be co-ordinated to ensure that they are applied equitably on behalf of disabled children, and that a commitment to disabled children is implicit in all legislation and government protocols. For this purpose, it would be relevant to appoint, or strengthen, the role of a children's ombudsman or commissioner. Where required, a timescale for legislative change with precise objectives and milestones against which progress can be monitored should be set up.

10. Organisations of parents and NGOs representing them should be included in the development of community-based services and their expertise should be used throughout the process of transition.

11. Funding should be allocated at national level and sought from international bodies, in order to facilitate and maintain the

momentum of this process. Countries that experience difficulties should be able to ask the international community to share their knowledge on the subject or to ask them for other forms of support.

III. Alternatives to institutional forms of care

12. In exceptional cases (for example, where there has been abuse or neglect), when a child cannot live in his or her own family or a foster family, small, homely settings, that are as near to a family environment as possible, should be provided as an alternative to institutionalised forms of care.

IV. Actions as a prerequisite for the main strategies

13. Actions as a prerequisite for the main strategies are decisive for the success of the measures taken in a reform process and should:

13.1 assess each child's specific needs, on a regular basis, in order to design individualised programmes to ensure his or her social inclusion. Community-based services should respond to the needs identified;

13.2 assist those who may be in danger of being placed in an institution and find alternative solutions;

13.3 provide a strong legal base and quality standards for service provision; the quality of service provision should be regularly reviewed or assessed;

13.4 assess the existing services and the needs of all other stakeholders, such as service providers, families, etc.;

14. Adequate human and financial resourcing and continuing staff training as well as raising public awareness of the special needs of children with disabilities are equally important.

15. Funds should be allocated to research, monitoring and evaluation. An authoritative overview of the country's provision for children with disabilities and of those who remain in institutional settings, together with an audit of the community-based provision in place would be the first step in developing a research infrastructure. Aspects of community provision which need to be strengthened can be evaluated by mapping the needs of disabled children and their families and by learning about the pressures which lead families to seek placements away from home.

    a. Prevention of institutionalisation

16. The creation of new institutions and new placements of children with disabilities in institutions should be prevented. For this reason, preventive measures of support for children and families in accordance with their special needs should be provided as early as possible.

17. Measures for the prevention of institutionalisation should include regular assessment and review of children's needs (once or twice a year), the establishment of individualised development plans and the implementation of quality standards for service provision.

    b. Prevention of the prolongation of an initially anticipated short-term stay

18. Measures should be taken to avoid any unnecessary prolongation of an initially foreseen short-term stay in an institution. Short-term stays should remain exceptional, be adequately reviewed and should not lead to institutionalisation. In general, the measures for the prevention of institutionalisation are also applicable to this situation.

    c. Deinstitutionalisation of those currently in institutions

19. Children have a right to regular reviews and reassessment of their placement in institutions so that they can be offered appropriate community services.

d. Creation of community-based services

20. A national action plan and a timetable should be drawn up to phase out institutional placements and replace these forms of care with a comprehensive network of community provision. Community-based services should be developed and integrated with other elements of comprehensive programmes to allow children with disabilities to live in the community.

21. An access mechanism should be put in place, in line with an assessment of needs, in order to direct families towards community-based provision and support.

22. Top priority should be given to funding and developing a range of community-based services for disabled children and their families with the aim of preventing children from being placed in institutions via:

    22.1 timely and sensitive assessment of abilities and needs;

    22.2 well co-ordinated health and social care;

    22.3 early intervention programmes;

    22.4 a range of options for mainstream and specialised education.

23. Some children with disabilities may need more intensive or more specialised service provision in order to meet their complex needs, but this should be seen as a spur to the development of high quality community-based support services and not as a barrier to their inclusion in ordinary settings.

24. A comprehensive family support system (including financial support to compensate for any additional costs incurred as a result of the child's disability, alongside a range of day-to-day support such as day care centres) should enable families to live

a life which offers the same opportunities as families who do not have a disabled child. Services providing some respite and expert advice and counselling should be available for the disabled child's parents, siblings and carers, while at the same time offering developmental opportunities for the child.

V. Mainstreaming

25. Measures to uphold the interests of children with disabilities across all relevant policy domains should be taken. The interests and needs of children with disabilities should be addressed in the work of all ministries and other responsible bodies in line with the concept of mainstreaming or sector responsibility. At national level, there should also be coherent policies supporting the deinstitutionalisation approach across ministries (including in relation to workforce planning and support for training) in order to ensure that specialist expertise is developed, accredited and used appropriately. At regional or local government level, transparent policies for commissioning services on a statutory, voluntary or independent basis should be adopted.

26. Services for children with disabilities should be provided primarily in mainstream settings. Mainstreaming or sector responsibility should be viewed as the norm and not the exception. Agencies working with children should be helped to build their competence and capacity so that they can meet the needs of children with disabilities on an equitable basis.

27. The community should be involved and made aware of its responsibilities and obligations towards children with disabilities.

28. In future, mainstream services, including day care centres, preschool set-ups, places of worship, schools and leisure services should be required to accept children with disabilities and make available the necessary support to aid their inclusion and

participation. Wherever possible, children with disabilities should be educated—in all phases of their schooling—within the schools used by other children and receive the support required to facilitate their effective education or vocational training within the mainstream systems. Where special schools or units are deemed necessary or appropriate, these should be linked to ordinary schools, be helped to build bridges and be open to their local communities.

29. Likewise, health care should be provided by mainstream health-care professionals in ordinary clinics, surgeries and hospitals. When specialist interventions are needed, the preferred option should be for these to be made available locally. Assessments and expert consultations can often be carried out in the disabled children's normal environment, thereby cutting out the need for them to travel long distances and maximising the relevance of any advice offered.

30. One advantage of mainstreaming is that it allows children with disabilities to become more integrated into their local communities and to get to know other children, who in turn learn how to relate to them and see them as children first and foremost. Another advantage is that the care, services and support made available to children with disabilities can be evaluated using criteria that are relevant for all children.

31. All services should be designed and offered in ways that support family ties and foster good relationships between players, whether professional or not.

32. Mainstream professionals in education, health and social care services should receive additional training and assistance from local centres of excellence to equip them to work with children with disabilities, and to support their work with specific individual children. These services should incorporate a range of personalised support to assist disabled children so that they

can aim for the same kind of life and aspirations as their peer group, as they are entitled to growing independence, autonomy, age-appropriate possessions, and assistive technology, especially with regard to mobility and communication, in accordance with their needs.

33. The principles of inclusion and universal design in relation to all public facilities designed for children and all publicly-funded housing and neighbourhood projects should be adopted. Transport systems in particular should be accessible to all children and adults. Co-ordination and quality in service provision should be ensured.

34. Mainstreaming or sector responsibility requires health, education and social care agencies to take children with disabilities into account in all their planning and service delivery from their inception.

VI. Co-ordination and quality in service provision

35. Some children with disabilities need intensive support in a number of domains: health or social care, educational development, technical assistance, psychological support, and help in decision making and in managing everyday life. They require assistance in building or sustaining social networks and in overcoming isolation or social exclusion. Expert co-ordination between professions and agencies should be foreseen, particularly for disabled children who need considerable support and constant assistance.

36. To achieve the right balance of general and expert assistance, centres of excellence, encouraging partnerships between service providers, NGOs, research and teaching institutes should be established and properly resourced in order to:

36.1 pool existing expertise on severe, complex or rare disorders and disabilities, including challenging needs;

36.2 support regular providers of education, health care and social care so that they can set up and implement specialised support programmes;

36.3 enhance work with multidisciplinary partners;

36.4 disseminate research and develop the evidence base for practice, through the work of national and international centres of excellence and university affiliated programmes;

36.5 provide, or facilitate, access to advice, information, counselling and multidisciplinary specialist health-care services for children with disabilities, and their families.

37. At regional level, agencies and professions should work closely together. A special register should be kept to identify those children and families in need of support and this information should be standardised to allow information to be aggregated at regional and national level. This data should be stored in a format that allows it to be accessed in the context of international comparisons and research, subject to appropriate data protection protocols.

VII. Children with disabilities and their families as stakeholders in the process of service development

38. It is essential to change the way in which services to children with disabilities and their families are developed and provided by involving them in the process. Children with disabilities should have a say in the way that they are treated and, as they grow up, they should be allowed to shape their own future.

39. Young people with disabilities should increasingly be encouraged to make decisions for themselves and take control of their day-to-day lives. Close relatives should be involved in their own right, and they should be allowed to influence the development of the services they will be using.

*Council of Europe includes 47 member countries and seeks to protect human rights, pluralist democracy, and the rule of law.

Council of Europe. *Recommendation CM/Rec(2010)2 of the Committee of Ministers to Member States on Deinstitutionalisation and Community Living of Children with Disabilities.* London: Child Rights Information Network, 2010. http://www.crin.org/Law/instrument.asp?InstID=1444.

Used by permission.

Discussion Questions

1. Adults with disabilities who have lived in institutions and are now living in independent living arrangements. Are they really free? Are they really happy?

2. Should government funds be used on an interim basis to improve the living conditions in institutions? How do you balance the horrible conditions in institutions and the need to use funds for building a system of independent living?

3. Many children who are placed in orphanages are not in fact orphans. Should families have the right to choose institutionalization for their child?

4. What policy should be put in place for the restraint and seclusion of individuals in institutions?

CHAPTER 7:

Advancing Education

Chapter 7 focuses on the importance of providing an inclusive education to children with disabilities. Article 24 of the Convention on the Rights of Persons with Disabilities (CRPD) requires states to recognize the right of persons with disability to inclusive education and lifelong learning opportunities that will enable them to realize their potential. The CRPD requires states to institute effective measures to ensure that people with disability are able to realize such right—including through the provision of reasonable accommodations; individualized support; and facilitation of the learning of Braille, sign language, and other means and formats for communication.

Many children across the globe are denied access to education and opportunities to learn. In some countries, however, children with disabilities are attending neighborhood schools that may not have previously been open to them. Fewer students with disabilities are in separate buildings or separate classrooms on school campuses; they are, instead, learning in classes with their peers. We need to reach beyond physical access to the education system and move toward achieving full access to high-quality curricula and instruction to improve education outcomes for children with disabilities.

The first article, "A Context Ripe for Change: The 1980s," by James McLeskey, examines the provision of special education in the United States from a historical perspective. In the late 1960s and early 1970s, Lloyd Dunn and Evelyn Deno advocated for collaboration between those involved in special education and general education. As part of such collaboration, they recommended that children with disabilities be included in the general education classroom and have access to the general education curriculum. McLeskey explores the relationship between general and special education and discusses the reform efforts that grew out of their work during the 1980s. He also traces the rapid evolution of terms and related practices; the change in terminology from "mainstreaming" to "integration" to "inclusion" reflects changes in the focus of education.

The second and third articles, "Teacher Attitudes Toward Inclusion" and "Reflecting on Teacher Attitudes," by Nancy L. Waldron, address teacher attitudes toward mainstreaming and inclusion. Waldron provides a historical perspective related to possible variables of teacher attitudes, including, to name a few, education levels, geographic area, severity of disability, intensity of inclusion, teacher experience, and school context. The articles revealed that most teachers supported inclusion if evidence-based programs were in place, high-quality professional development was offered, and support from administrators was present to ensure effective outcomes for students and the programs.

The fourth article, "Inclusive Education: Moving from Words to Deeds," a statement by the European Disability Forum, offers reflections and recommendations on several key issues in the implementation of Article 24 of the CRPD. The key issues include: moving toward inclusive education; accessing education in practice; learning life and social development skills; training of teachers; and beyond basic education.

Employment and independence are important pieces of anyone's dream. In today's world, achieving goals depends on having the foundation of a high-quality education in inclusive schools and communities.

A Context Ripe for Change: The 1980s

*By James McLeskey**

> When a student with a disability is mainstreamed it is often assumed that the student will do the same work, behave the same way, and so forth, as other students in the class. The student is expected to adapt to the general education classroom, at times with the assistance of the special education teacher, who will record books, read tests to the student, and so forth. . .the bottom line throughout the mainstreaming movement has been that *the student will adapt* and be ready to participate in the general education classroom, and *that the general education classroom will not change.*
>
> —McLeskey and Waldron, 2000 (pp. 13–14)

The changes that Deno (1970) and Dunn (1968) envisioned in the relationship between general and special education that would serve as a foundation for improving education for all students did not readily occur in subsequent years. General and special education remained, for the most part, separate systems, accountable for separate groups of students and that worked together only when the necessity arose.

In the 1980s, a confluence of factors served to create a context where reform was on the mind of many educators. Change of some sort was bound to occur. The context for change in special education was made possible by a reform movement in general education that was driven in large part by concerns about the economic competitiveness of the U.S. in the world market.

In the early 1980s, it was widely recognized that the economies in the most prosperous countries were changing from an industry base to a knowledge base, and that these changes would require increasing levels of technical knowledge and skill of workers were to remain competitive. A *Nation at Risk* (National Commission on Excellence in Education, 1983)—considered by many to be the most influential catalyst in the general education reform movement—captured these emergent changes. This report characterized a rising tide of mediocrity in America's public schools and emphasized the perspective that student achievement in the U.S. was lagging behind student achievement in other highly prosperous nations. The report went on to emphasize the need to raise student achievement levels by reforming schools, thus ensuring that the U.S. would remain competitive in world markets and in the knowledge-based economy (Hocutt, Martin, & McKinney, 1991).

Much concern in *A Nation at Risk*, as well as in other critiques of the educational system (Carnegie Forum on Education and the Economy, 1986; Goodlad, 1984), related to the failure of schools to effectively meet the needs of students with learning problems and those who were at risk for failure in school. Many of these students were members of minority groups and from low-income homes; others were labeled with mild disabilities.

Soon after *A Nation at Risk* was published, concerns were expressed regarding special education. Primary among these concerns was the failure of general educators and special educators to effectively collaborate to meet the needs of all students, including students with learning problems who were not labeled with disabilities. This issue harkened back to concerns and recommendations made by Deno (1970) and Dunn (1968) some 15 years earlier, which had gone largely unaddressed. This lack of progress led to a second wave of special education reform in the 1980s—a wave of reform that laid the foundation for the move we currently call *inclusion*.

Recommendations for Major Change in Educating Students with Mild Disabilities

Changes in the relationship between general and special education that were recommended by Deno (1970) and Dunn (1968) had not occurred by the early 1980s. Moreover, general education and special education remained substantially separate systems with separate accountability systems, separate administrative organizations, and separate teacher education and professional development programs, and both systems were changed little by the mainstream movement.

Will, who at the time was the Assistant Secretary for the Office of Special Education and Rehabilitative Services in the U.S. Department of Education, called for changes in general education and special education that would more effectively address the needs of students with learning problems (e.g., students with mild disabilities, students in compensatory programs, students who were not making adequate academic progress, etc.). Although Will recognized that special education had made tremendous progress since the passage of P.L. 94-142 in 1975, she noted that more progress was needed. Will pointed out that the central problem with special education was the widespread belief that these programs had to be delivered in pull-out or separate special education classrooms—typically resources classes—and could not be delivered successfully in general education classrooms. She also noted that the way the special education system was organized to identify students and deliver services often created barriers to the successful education of these students. These barriers, she said, were related to the following issues:

- Eligibility requirements for special education excluded many students with learning difficulties who needed assistance.
- Poor performance in school was equated with disability. Thus, a student who had a learning difficulty could only receive assistance from special education if he or she were labeled as having a disability.

- Special education services were only available to students after they had failed in school; they were not used to prevent failure.

To address these issues, Will called for a shared responsibility between general education and special education to improve educational outcomes for all students with learning difficulties. More specifically, Will called for experimental trials to develop effective programs that might be used in schools to better meet the needs of students with learning difficulties.

To implement these programs, as well as to ensure the use of educational programs and techniques with demonstrated effectiveness, Will called for empowering building-level administrators to reform schools so that they were better able to address the needs of all student based on individual needs rather than special education eligibility requirements and related labels. Will also stated that these reformed programs should emphasize prevention on early learning difficulties rather than the wait-to-fail model that was widely used in special education.

Reynolds, Wang, and Walberg worked closely with Will in support of these changes, and their 1987 article further developed her proposals. As with the Will article, these authors addressed only students with mild or what they call "judgmental disabilities" (i.e., the disability is not readily identifiable, but rather a professional has made a judgment that the student has a disability). Reynolds and his colleagues suggested that many students fell through the cracks of the special education eligibility system and, thus, did not receive services for learning problems. These authors contended that the reason this occurred was because many separate categories had been developed over time to address specific student needs (e.g., learning disabilities, Chapter I programs, etc.), and little attention had been paid to the overall relationship among these programs. They argued that this disjointed incrementalism led schools to identify increasing numbers of students with judgmental disabilities to ensure that they received needed services, even though the students might not have met eligibility criteria.

From Mainstreaming to Inclusion
The Rapid Evolution of Terms and Related Practices

As the decade of the 1980s progressed, terminology evolved to describe the education of students with disabilities in the least restrictive environment, and these changes, to some degree, reflected changes in focus. Following is a summary of key changes:

- **Mainstreaming:** At the beginning of the 1980s, mainstreaming was a widely accepted term. This term was used only in reference to students with mild disabilities, and suggested that students with a disability had to fit into the general education classroom with little accommodation for the student's needs (McLeskey & Waldron, 2000).
- **Integration:** Advocates who pushed for students with severe disabilities to be part of the reform discussion expressed a preference for the term "integration." Integration was associated with closing separate schools for students with severe disabilities, and relocating classes for these students on regular school campuses and neighborhood schools.
- **Regular Education Initiative:** As more students with mild disabilities were educated in general education classrooms, advocates sought to differentiate these changes through the use of the term Regular Education Initiative (REI) (Teacher Education Division of CEC, 1987). REI was chosen because it reflected the need for general and special educators to work collaboratively, sharing responsibility for students with mild disabilities.
- **Inclusion:** As advocates for students with severe disabilities changed their focus from closing special schools and opening similar programs on neighborhood school campuses to including students with severe disabilities as full members of the school community and providing their education in general education classrooms, the term "inclusion" emerged. These advocates preferred "inclusion" because it more accurately communicated their claim that *all* children need to be included in the educational and social life of their neighborhood schools and classrooms, not merely placed in the mainstream (Stainback, Stainback, & Jackson, 1992). As these changes in terminology were evolving in the area of severe disabilities, similar concerns arose for advocates of students with mild disabilities (Lieberman, 1985; Fuchs & Fuchs, 1994). Overall, the major concerns focused on the fact that the REI did not originate in general education and that typically, general educators were not interested in addressing issues related to special education as part of their general education reform (Lieberman, 1985; Lilly, 1987; Pugach & Sapon-Shevin, 1987). Gradually, advocates for students with mild disabilities adopted the term inclusion from the area of severe disabilities.

The use of the term inclusion to address the work of professionals in both mild and severe disabilities has led to much confusion. Some attempts to clarify this confusion have led to the use of alternative terms (e.g., full inclusion), but there remains much misunderstanding regarding just what inclusion means in practice.

Reynolds, Wang, and Walberg identified the special education categorical system as a related problem. These authors contended that there was little empirical support for separating students into different categories (e.g., learning disabilities, mild mental retardation, students eligible for compensatory education programs such as Title I, etc.). They pointed to evidence showing that the same effective instructional methods worked for all students, thus dismissing the view that different instructional methods were required based on a student's label.

Reynolds, Wang, and Walberg made the following recommendations that expanded on those made by Will (and by Deno in 1970):

+ Creation of a new wave of innovation in which special educators would join others to advance a broad program of adaptive education for all students. This would require the joining of demonstrably effective practices from special, compensatory, and general education to establish a general education system that would be more inclusive and better serve all students, particularly those who required greater-than-usual educational support.

+ A call for federal support for experimental trials addressing the development of effective programs in general education classrooms to meet the needs of students who were being served in segregated settings.

In practice, the recommendations of these authors resulted in what came to be called the Regular Education Initiative (REI) (Teacher Education Division of CEC, 1987). REI constituted the next generation of the mainstreaming movement. It called for dramatically reducing the number of pull-out or resource class programs for students with mild disabilities and the development of programs that could be successfully delivered in general education classrooms through a shared responsibility between general and special education.

Recommendations for Major Change in Educating Students with Severe Disabilities

Changes recommended by Will and Reynolds, Wang, and Walberg only addressed students with mild disabilities. This is particularly noteworthy because, at the same time that REI was emerging, a parallel movement was occurring within the literature base for dealing with severe disabilities. This movement cited many of the same problems cited by advocates for REI and included many similar recommendations for change.

Stainback and Stainback provided a catalyst for extending the mainstreaming movement to the *integration* (a term used prior to the term *inclusion*) of students with severe disabilities into general education classrooms. In their 1984 article, Stainback and Stainback described major problems related to students with severe disabilities, including:

+ There are not two distinct types of students, those with disabilities and those without. Rather, all students differ along a continuum with regard to cognitive ability, academic skill, and social competence.
+ The special education classification system is unreliable, expensive, and lacks educational utility.
+ Good instructional methods work for all students. There are not unique methods that work only for students with disabilities.
+ Curricular options are limited for students with disabilities, who typically do not have access to the general education curriculum.
+ When students have difficulty progressing in school, they are identified with a disability and sent to another educational system (special education) for services. Thus the general education classroom is not expected to change under these circumstances.

The conclusion reached by Stainback and Stainback regarding how these problems might be addressed was, in general sense, similar to the conclusion that was reached by the others addressing this issue—namely, that the relationship between general education and special education needed to be changed.

However, their specific recommendations for change differed from REI advocates in substantive ways. Stainback and Stainback called for:

+ **Changing the relationship between special education and general education.** They recommended merging the separate special education administrative system with that of general education. In rationalizing this merger, the authors stated that a dual system of general education and special education duplicated services, was unnecessarily expensive, and did not provide the appropriate context for successfully addressing the problems described above.

+ **Expanding the range of students who were included in these changes.** Previously, calls for mainstreaming or extending the movement through the REI had been limited to students with mild-to-moderate disabilities. It was widely assumed that the needs of students with more severe disabilities could be met better in segregated settings and homogenous groups (i.e., groups including only students with severe disabilities). However, citing the work of Brown, et al. (1979)—who recommended that separate schools for students with severe disabilities be closed, and that students with severe disabilities be educated in segregated classes on neighborhood school campuses—Stainback and Stainback explicitly recommended the inclusion of students with severe disabilities in the merged systems.

The merged system they recommended would result in the following major changes in general and special education:

+ Personnel no longer would be prepared and certified as special education or general education teachers. Rather, all teachers would be prepared using a unified system. Teachers with specializations in certain areas (e.g., self-care, community living, etc.) still would be needed to meet certain student needs.

- Categorical classification systems no longer would be needed. Rather, students of similar ages would be heterogeneously grouped for much of the school day in general education classrooms. This grouping would include students with disabilities ranging from mild to severe.

Stainback and Stainback's recommendations laid the foundation for the inclusion movement that evolved in the latter part of the 1980s and early 1990s.

DISCUSSION

All three of the articles focused, to a large degree, on the following major themes:
- The need to redefine and improve the relationship between general education and special education.
- The need to improve or dramatically change how the special education categorical system is used to identify students with disabilities.

To a large extent, these articles echoed and extended upon concerns about the special education categorical system and the relationship between general education and special education first described by Dunn (1968) and Deno (1970). Stainback and Stainback introduced new commentary when they called for students with severe disabilities to be educated in less restrictive settings with typical peers.

REFERENCES

Brown, L., Branston, M., Hamre-Nietupski, S., Pumpian, I., Certo, N., & Gruenewald, L. (1979). A strategy for developing chronological age appropriate and functional curricular content for severely handicapped adolescents and young adults. *Journal of Special Education*, 13(1), 81–90.

Carnegie Forum on Education and the Economy. (1986). *A nation prepared: Teachers for the 21st century*. Washington DC: Author.

Deno, E. (1970). Special education as developmental capital. *Exceptional Children, 37*(3), 229–237.

Dunn, L. (1968). Special education for the mildly retarded—Is much of it justifiable? *Exceptional Children, 35*(1), 5–22

Fuchs, D. & Fuchs, L. (1994). The inclusive schools movement and the radicalization of special education reform. *Exceptional Children, 60*(4), 294–309.

Goodlad, J. (1984). *A place called school*. New York: McGraw-Hill.

Hocutt, A., Martin, E., & McKinney, J. (1991). Historical and legal context of mainstreaming. In J. Lloyd, N. Singh, & A. Repp (Eds.). *The Regular Education Initiative: Alternative perspectives on concepts, issues, and models* (pp. 17–28). Sycamore, IL: Sycamore Publishing Co.

Lieberman, L. (1985). Special education and regular education: A merger made in heaven? *Exceptional Children, 51*(6), 13–16.

Lilly, S. (1987). Lack of focus on special education in literature on educational reform. *Exceptional Children, 53*(4), 325–326.

McLeskey, J., & Waldron, N. (2000). *Inclusive schools in action: Making differences ordinary*. Alexandria, VA: Association for Supervision and Curriculum Development.

National Commission on Excellence in Education. (1983). *A Nation at Risk*. Washington DC: Author.

Pugach, M. & Sapon-Shevin, M. (1987). New agendas for special education policy: What the national reports haven't said. *Exceptional Children, 53*(4), 295–299.

Reynolds, M., Wang, M., & Walberg, H. (1987). The necessary restructuring of special education. *Exceptional Children, 53*(5), 391–398.

Stainback, W., & Stainback, S. (1984). A rationale for the merger of special and regular education. *Exceptional Children, 51*(2), 102–111.

Stainback, S., Stainback, W. & Jackson, H.J. (1992). Toward inclusive classrooms. In S. Stainback & W. Stainback (Eds.). *Curriculum considerations in inclusive classrooms: Facilitating learning for all students* (pp. 3–17). Baltimore, MD: Brookes Publishing Co.

Teacher Education Division of CEC (1987). The regular education initiative. *Journal of Learning Disabilities, 20*(5), 289–293.

Will, M. (1986). Educating children with learning problems: A Shared responsibility. *Exceptional Children, 52*(5), 411–415.

*James McLeskey** is a professor in the School of Special Education, School Psychology, and Early Childhood Studies at the University of Florida. His research is focused on school reform and school improvement, with an emphasis on inclusive school programs.

McLesky, James. "A Context Ripe for Change: The 1980's." in *Reflections on Inclusion: Classical Articles That Shaped Our Thinking,* 69–75. Arlington, VA: Council for Exceptional Children, 2007.

Teacher Attitudes Toward Inclusion

By Nancy L. Waldron*

In the history of special education, few topics have been the subject of more extensive study than teacher attitudes toward mainstreaming and inclusion. Shortly after Dunn (1968) and Deno (1970) published their articles, Shotel, Iano, and McGettigan (1972) published one of the most widely cited articles in special education in the 1970s, titled "Teacher Attitudes Associated with the Integration of Handicapped Children" (McLeskey, 2004). The authors used pre- and post-test measures to compare the attitudes of an experimental group of teachers who were implementing a mainstreaming program, with a control group of teachers who were not engaged in such a program. Their results indicated that while the experimental group was generally more positive or optimistic regarding mainstreaming before beginning the program (i.e., on the pre-test), the differences between groups tended to decline on the post-test, demonstrating less support for these programs and raising questions regarding the feasibility of integrating students with mild mental retardation into general education classrooms.

During the next several decades, other researchers found that teachers were very wary (Semmel et al., 1991), if not outright opposed (Coates, 1989) to the development of mainstreaming or inclusive programs. In spite of documented teacher concerns about mainstreaming and/or inclusion programs, inclusion became a major policy initiative for the U.S. Department of Education and many states during the late 1980s and early 1990s. This resulted in the widespread development of inclusive programs and increased numbers of students with disabilities in general education classrooms. For example, whereas in 1988, 32 percent of students with disabilities spent most of the day in a general education classroom, 45 percent did so in 1994 (McLeskey, Henry, and Hodges, 1998).

During this time, students in all categories of disabilities (except those with deaf-blindness) experienced increased placements in general education classrooms, while placements in more restrictive settings declined (McLeskey, Henry, & Hodges, 1999).

As inclusive programs expanded, special educators tended to promote the position that problems associated with the development and implementation of inclusive programs were, in large part, due to the opposition of general education teachers (McLeskey & Waldron, 2000). In the early 1990s, conventional wisdom seemed to hold that general education teachers opposed inclusion, and this opposition had to be overcome if appropriate programs were to be developed. This school of thought prevailed in spite of the fact that special educators actually understood very little about the perspectives these professionals had regarding students with disabilities.

A synthesis of these investigations on teacher attitudes was needed to clarify misunderstandings and misconceptions. This synthesis would need to consider a variety of possible variables related to teacher attitudes (e.g., education levels, geographic area, severity of disability, intensity of inclusion, teacher experience, school context, etc.). The following article achieved those goals:

+ Scruggs, T., & Mastropieri, M. (1996) Teacher perceptions of mainstreaming/inclusion, 1958–1995: A research synthesis. *Exceptional Children*, 63(1), 59–74.

The Scruggs and Mastropieri article provided a synthesis of issues and related research that filled a need for reliable and valid information regarding general education teacher perspectives on mainstreaming and/or inclusion.

REFERENCES

Coates, R. (1989). The regular education initiative and opinions of regular classroom teachers. *Journal of Learning Disabilities*, 22(9), 532–536.

Deno, E. (1970). Special education as developmental capital. *Exceptional Children,* 37(3), 229–237.

Dunn, L. (1968). Special education for the mildly retarded—Is much of it justifiable? *Exceptional Children,* 35(1), 5–22.

Fullan, M. (1993). *Change forces,* Bristol, PA: The Falmer Press.

McLeskey, J. (2004). Classic articles in special education: Articles that shaped the field from 1960 to 1996. *Remedial and Special Education,* 25(2), 79–87.

McLesky, J., Henry, D., & Hodges, D. (1998). Inclusion: Where is it happening? *Teaching Exceptional Children,* 31(1), 4–11.

McLeskey, J., Henry, D., & Hodges, D. (1999). Inclusion: What progress is being made across disability categories? *Teaching Exceptional Children,* 31(3), 60–64.

McLeskey, J., & Waldron, N. (2000). *Inclusive education in action: Making differences ordinary.* Alexandria, VA: Association for Supervision and Curriculum Development.

Scruggs, T., & Mastropieri, M. (1996) Teacher perceptions of mainstreaming/inclusion, 1958-1995: A research synthesis. *Exceptional Children,* 63(1), 59–74.

Semmel, M., Abernathy, T., Butera, G., & Lesary, S. (1991). Teacher perceptions of the regular education initiative. *Exceptional Children,* 58(1), 9–24.

Shotel, J., Iano, R., & McGettigan, J. (1972). Teacher attitudes associated with integration of handicapped children. *Exceptional Children,* 38(9), 677–683.

---

*Nancy L. Waldron** is a professor in the department of educational psychology at the University of Florida. Her research centers around teachers, their attitudes, and how they affect school reform, particularly around providing special education to children with disabilities.

Waldron, Nancy L. "Teacher Attitudes Toward Inclusion," in *Reflections on Inclusion: Classical Articles That Shaped Our Thinking,* ed. James McLeskey, 163–165. Arlington, VA: Council for Exceptional Children, 2007.

Used by permission.

Reflecting on Teacher Attitudes

*By Nancy L. Waldron**

A Brief Review of Scruggs and Mastropieri's Findings

In reviewing research between 1958 and 1995 on teacher attitudes toward mainstreaming or inclusion, Scruggs and Mastropieri found 28 studies that surveyed more than 10,000 teachers and other school personnel. These teachers represented a wide range of U.S. geographic areas and educational experiences. This synthesis provided the best information available to date from the broadest sample of teachers on the issues that faced these professionals when inclusive programs are implemented in their schools. It also clarified several misconceptions regarding this topic.

A key, overarching question regarding teachers' attitudes toward mainstreaming or inclusion related to whether teachers were generally in support of the inclusion of students with disabilities in general education classrooms. As noted previously, conventional wisdom at the time tended to take the perspective that many, if not most, general education teachers opposed inclusion. Scruggs and Mastropieri found that almost two-thirds of all teachers surveyed supported the concept of inclusion, indicating that they generally found inclusion to be a desirable practice. This level of support was extraordinary, considering the controversial nature of inclusion and the difficulty inherent in implementing a complex form of school change that addressed the development of inclusive programs (Fullan, 1993; Sarason, 1990).

Furthermore, given the range of contexts within which the attitudes surveys were conducted, two-thirds was likely an underestimate of level of teacher support. That is, some surveys likely included teachers in programs that were poorly designed, leading them to oppose such programs and presumably oppose inclusion.

It is important that the remainder of the findings from the Scruggs and Mastropieri review be interpreted in light of their finding that teachers were strongly supportive of the concept of inclusion. That is, this finding suggested that opposition to inclusion typically does not result from social prejudice or negative attitudes toward the social or academic inclusion of these students. Rather, concerns of general education teachers regarding inclusion seemed to rest primarily with procedural issues within their classrooms. This led to a key question for teachers, "Can I make inclusion work in my classroom?" It is clear from Scruggs and Mastropieri's synthesis that teachers have many concerns about inclusion, and believed that substantial supports were necessary to enable these efforts to succeed.

Major concerns of teachers regarding inclusive programs that emerged from the Scruggs and Mastropieri synthesis relate to their need for sufficient time and resources (e.g., materials, personnel support, reduced class size, etc.) to effectively manage an inclusive program, and the need for professional development to prepare general education teachers for the diverse needs of students with disabilities. Furthermore, many teachers expressed concern that some students would be included without such support, which would have a negative impact on the general education classroom (i.e., disrupt the learning of other students).

It is noteworthy that all of these concerns are issues that should be raised by all classroom teachers when any innovation is implemented in their classrooms. The Scruggs and Mastropieri article laid the foundation for more recent research that addressed teacher concerns about the implementation of inclusion (e.g., Agran, Alper, & Wehmeyer, 2002; Austin, 2001; Cook, 2001; Cook, Semmel, & Gerber, 1999; McLeskey & Waldron, 2000, 2002a, 2002b; McLeskey et al., 2001; Vaughn et al. 1996; Weller & McLeskey, 2000).

A Brief Review of Recent Research

In the early 1990s, Semmel and colleagues (1991) conducted a survey of teachers' attitudes toward inclusive programs. The results of this survey revealed strong concern on the part of the teachers related to the desirability of inclusive programs, resources to support the programs, and the preparedness of general education teachers to address the needs of students with disabilities. Semmel and his colleagues speculated that these results could be interpreted "to mean that service providers generally tend to resist change when roles and functions are altered, and that it is lack of their positive experiences" (p. 20) with inclusive programs that served as a barrier to the adoption of inclusive program models.

Several years later, McLeskey and Waldron (1996) extended this idea. They noted that asking teachers who were not involved in inclusive programs to respond to hypothetical situations regarding inclusive programs was tantamount to asking teachers "if they would like to become involved in an ill-defined program that would require them to teach the students with the most significant learning and behavior problems in their school. Such a programs would be difficult to design and implement and would result in many frustrating, anxiety-provoking changes in teachers' professional lives" (p. 154).

McLeskey and Waldron (1996) suggested that opposition or resistance to inclusive programs under such circumstances was understandable. Indeed, one might legitimately question the professionalism of a teacher who did not question and exercise caution regarding the development of such a program. As teachers reflected on the survey questions, they identified problems that had to be addressed if successful school change was to occur (Fullan, 1993). To have ignored these questions likely would have resulted in superficial change that ignored core issues of concern to teachers (McLeskey & Waldron, 2002c).

Research since the review by Scruggs and Mastropieri has begun to address these issues. Consider the following examples.

+ Minke and colleagues (1996) surveyed teacher attitudes toward inclusion. Teachers represented two groups—teachers who were engaged in delivering an inclusive program and general education teachers who were teaching in traditional (non-inclusive) classrooms. Results revealed that special education teachers and general education teachers who taught in inclusive programs had more positive perspectives on inclusion than did general education teachers who were not teaching in such programs. Moreover, these teachers had a higher sense of self-efficacy, higher ratings of their own competence, and more positive perspectives on making instructional adaptations to meet the diverse needs of students in their classrooms.

+ McLeskey and colleagues (2001) conducted a study of the attitudes of teachers toward inclusive programs that also addressed this issue. These investigators compared the attitudes of teachers working in an inclusive program with teachers who had not yet worked in such a program. They found that while all teachers agreed that students with disabilities had a basic right to an education in a general education classroom, the non-inclusion teachers had significantly more negative attitudes toward inclusion. Such attitudes especially related to "how well prepared their school is for inclusion; their possible roles and functions in an inclusive program; as well as their less than sanguine feelings regarding the influence of inclusive programs on students" (p. 113).

Although the findings suggested that many concerns regarding inclusion were significantly reduced once a teacher became involved in an inclusive program, it is noteworthy that some concerns remained for all teachers. For example, all of the surveyed teachers were in agreement about the need to maintain special education resources. They also expressed caution or concern regarding the behavior of some students with disabilities, the influence of students with disabilities on other students in the general education classroom, and whether the general education teachers had the expertise to meet the needs of students with disabilities.

The review by Scruggs and Mastropieri and subsequent publications related to teacher attitudes toward inclusion have helped to clarify this topic. As with all professionals, teachers are cautious about change until they are sure that the change is appropriate and manageable, and that it will make them more effective in meeting the needs of students. In general, teachers are supportive of inclusion, and would welcome students with disabilities into their classrooms, given the right circumstances (e.g., teacher involvement in decision making, sufficient support, appropriate professional development, etc.). However, teachers resist having children in their classes when their concerns have not been addressed appropriately (e.g., the students' behavior or severity of the disability is overly disruptive to the education of other students, the student's behavior or severity of the disability makes it difficult if not impossible for the student to benefit from placement in the general education classroom, etc.)

FUTURE RESEARCH: WHAT IS NEEDED?

Although the basic aspects of teacher attitudes toward inclusion seems to have been well investigated, more in-depth information is needed. Some of this information is only indirectly related to teacher attitudes toward inclusion. For example, more research is needed regarding how, when, and under what circumstances students benefit from inclusive programs and how teachers perceive these benefits. Some existing research on this topic suggests that teachers have different perspectives regarding student progress than do administrators or policymakers (McLeskey & Waldron, 2002b), suggesting that this is an important area for further investigation.

More research is needed regarding topics such as:

+ How to ensure that general education and special education teachers have the necessary skills and knowledge to meet the needs of students with disabilities in general education classrooms.
+ How to ensure that general and special education and special education teachers have the necessary time and resources to deliver effective inclusive programs.
+ How inclusive programs can be developed to enhance the academic and social benefits for all students and reduce any possible negative effects.
+ What factors influence a teacher's willingness and ability to include students with more severe disabilities.

A final area of research that merits further study relates to teachers who do not support the concept of inclusion. Scruggs and Mastropieri's review found that approximately one-third of all teachers surveyed did not support the concept of mainstreaming or inclusion. This is likely an overestimate because of the range of experiences teachers had with inclusion. Some teachers were involved in well-developed inclusive programs, some were involved in poorly developed programs, and many of the teachers had not been involved in any inclusion program.

A more reliable measure of teacher opposition to inclusion may come from the study by McLeskey et al. (2001), who surveyed teachers who were teaching in well-designed inclusive programs as well as teachers who were on a waiting list but not yet engaged in such programs. In this study, approximately 10 percent of the teachers involved in inclusive programs were not supportive of the concept of inclusion, while approximately 20 percent of the teachers who had not yet taught in an inclusive program took this perspective.

More research is needed to determine why teachers continue to oppose the concept of inclusion, even when programs are well designed.

CONCLUSION

Teacher attitudes toward inclusive programs have long been an issue of discussion in the field. What the Scruggs and Mastropieri article revealed is that most teachers supported inclusion if programs were well developed and if teachers received appropriate training and support to ensure the success of these programs. It is appropriate that teachers expect adequate supports and exercise caution as inclusive programs are being developed and implemented to ensure appropriate services are provided to all students.

While several areas related to teacher attitudes and inclusion require further investigation, perhaps it is most important to gain a better understanding of why some teachers do not support the concept of inclusion, even when programs are well developed. This lack of support may result from previous experiences with poorly implemented programs. Regardless of the cause, it is important to understand why some teachers do not support inclusion, and how the reasonable concerns that these teachers express may be addressed.

REFERENCES

Agran, M., Alper, S., & Wehmeyer, M. (2002). Access to the general curriculum for students with significant disabilities: What it means to teachers. *Education and Training in Mental Retardation and Developmental Disabilities, 37*(2), 123–133.

Austin, V.L. (2001). Teachers' beliefs about co-teaching. *Remedial and Special Education, 22*(4), 245–255.

Cook, B. (2001). A comparison of teachers' attitudes toward their included students with mild and severe disabilities. *The Journal of Special Education, 34*(4), 203–213.

Cook, B., Semmel, M., & Gerber, M. (1999). Attitudes of principals and special education teachers toward the inclusion of students with mild disabilities: Critical differences of opinion. *Remedial and Special Education, 20*(4), 199–207.

Fullan, M. (1993). *Change forces,* Bristol, PA: The Falmer Press.

McLeskey, J., & Waldron, N. (1996). Responses to questions teacher and administrators frequently ask about inclusion. *Phi Delta Kappan, 78*(2), 150–156.

McLeskey, J., & Waldron, N. (2000). *Inclusive education in action: Making differences ordinary.* Alexandria, VA: Association for Supervision and Curriculum Development.

McLeskey, J., & Waldron, N. (2002a). Professional development and inclusive schools: Reflections on effective practice. *Teacher Educator, 37*(3), 159–172.

McLeskey, J., & Waldron, N. (2002b). Inclusion and school change: Teacher perceptions regarding curricular and instructional adaptations. *Teacher Education and Special Education, 25* (1), 41–54.

McLeskey, J., & Waldron, N. (2002c). School change and inclusive schools: Lessons learned from practice. *Phi Delta Kappan, 84*(1), 65–72.

McLeskey, J., Waldron, N., So, T.H., Swanson, K., & Loveland, T. (2001). Perspectives of teachers toward inclusive school programs. *Teacher Education and Special Education, 24*(2), 108–115.

Minke, K., Bear, G., Deemer, S., & Griffin, S. (1996). Teachers' experiences with inclusive classrooms: Implications for special education reform. *The Journal of Special Education, 30*(2), 152-186.

Sarason, S.B. (1990). *The predictable failure of educational reform.* San Francisco: Jossey-Bass.

Scruggs, T., & Mastropieri, M. (1996) Teacher perceptions of mainstreaming/inclusion, 1958–1995: A research synthesis. *Exceptional Children, 63*(1), 59–74.

Semmel, M., Abernathy, T., Butera, G., and Lesary, S. (1991). Teacher perceptions of the regular education initiative. *Exceptional Children, 58*(1), 9–24.

Vaughn, S., Schumm, J., Jallad, B., Slusher, J., & Saumell, L. (1996). Teachers' views of inclusion. *Learning Disabilities Research & Practice, 11*(2), 96–106.

Weller, D., & McLeskey, J. (2000). Block scheduling and inclusion: Teacher perceptions of the benefits and challenges. *Remedial and Special Education, 21*(4), 209–218.

---

*Nancy L. Waldron** is a professor in the department of educational psychology at the University of Florida. Her research centers around teachers, their attitudes, and how they affect school reform, particularly around providing special education to children with disabilities.

Waldron, Nancy L. "Reflecting on Teacher Attitudes," in *Reflections on Inclusion: Classical Articles That Shaped Our Thinking,* ed. James McLeskey, 183–187. Arlington, VA: Council for Exceptional Children, 2007.

Used by permission.

Inclusive Education: Moving from Words to Deeds

*By the European Disability Forum**

1. INTRODUCTION

The European Disability Forum (EDF) is the umbrella body of the European disability movement representing the interests of 50 million disabled Europeans and their families—a diverse group made-up of persons with disabilities ranging from physical and sensory disabilities to intellectual disabilities, mental health problems and people with complex and multiple disabilities.

EDF has actively participated in the negotiations of the United Nations Convention on the Rights of Persons with Disabilities, including its article 24. EDF believes that this article is at the core of the Convention and illustrates the paradigm shift from persons with disabilities as defined by their impairments and denied access to mainstream life to persons with disabilities as rights holders empowered to fully participate in all aspects of life, where the barriers that prevent their equal participation are addressed.

With this as the fundamental approach, Article 24 challenges current policies on the basis of a clear right, and demands a new understanding and review of current thinking and practices, which will need time and planning to implement.

Education must be recognised as a fundamental right implying that persons with disabilities have the right to receive education of the same quality as any other person, in an environment that takes into account their needs. In order to achieve this, policies and legislation must address access, not only to schools, and universities, but to all other education opportunities in a lifelong learning perspective.

EDF also realises that some children with disabilities still face restrictions in access to any kind of education, and that inclusive education cannot be achieved within a fortnight, but should be part of a planned transition process. Furthermore, good practice and skills regarding special education should be adapted to work in the general education systems, and should inspire new pedagogical tools.

It is also necessary to point out that the discrimination of girls and women with disabilities on multiple grounds with regards to their access to education is a widespread phenomenon in Europe. When we look at the situation of girls and women with disabilities in Europe from a general perspective, we find that they have less access to school, they have higher rates of school drop outs, higher illiteracy rates and therefore decreased access to employment. It is therefore necessary to take special measures towards girls and women with disabilities in order to fulfil the objectives of inclusive education.

In some countries, pupils with disabilities are still excluded from public schools, and they are obliged to go to private ones. This results in the exclusion of children with disabilities from poorer backgrounds from education altogether, as their families cannot afford private tuition.

The funding of the education system should allow for greater flexibility to open up for the varying support needs of learners with disabilities, and the allocation of funds should not just be based on the number of pupils/students involved.

This is also true for special schools that need to have a high number of students either with disabilities or learning difficulties (e.g. immigrants) to receive funding. This is to the detriment of the programmes quality and of the possibility to develop individualised approaches. Furthermore, this hinders the transition to mainstream schools. All such barriers to the development of a fully inclusive education system should be identified and addressed.

To put all pupils with different kinds of disabilities in one class segregated from other pupils is tantamount to both ignoring the specific needs of different children with different disabilities and a continuation of the distinction between children on the one hand and children with disabilities on the other.

In new EU countries, there are additional problems to achieving inclusive education in mainstream schools. There is no support within the mainstream system; on the contrary there is strong support to specialised education which means that pupils/students with disabilities are directed towards this type of education. Such education systems will need to develop transition plans to be backed by adequate training and resources.

Even in mainstream schools, there is confusion between integration and inclusion. Integration is a matter of location—the placing of students with disabilities in mainstream schools where they have to adapt to existing teaching and learning and organisation of the school. Inclusion, on the other hand, requires adapting the system to meet the needs of the pupil/student with disabilities. The environment, teaching and learning and organisation of the school and education system are systematically to be changed in order to remove barriers to pupils/students with disabilities, so that they can maximise their academic and social achievements. An inclusive approach is beneficial to all students, whether they are disabled or not, or whether they have learning difficulties or not. Lack of progress to inclusion is also due to the fact that there is often a lack of technical and human resources in mainstream education. In addition, there is often a failure to understand what reasonable accommodation means, and students needs for adjustments are often only partially met.

We must realise that in order to change the system, and ensure the inclusion of pupils with disabilities in mainstream schools, a revolution must occur in peoples' minds including families and organisations of disabled people, in addition to public authorities, schools directors, staff, and trade unions.

It is important to ensure that the ratification process of the CRPD produces and changes legislation, and policies, in order to respond to the goals set out in the Convention.

These legislative acts and policies must be developed in close cooperation with organisations of persons with disabilities, and by fostering dialogue with governments, teachers' unions and parents associations and institutes of higher education which train teachers.

There are different pathways to achieve inclusive education which should be developed within and according to the general education system, traditions and cultures in each country, without any compromises with the principle of equal opportunities. It is critical that policies and practices are individualised and responsive to specific needs of children whatever their impairments.

In order to understand and implement inclusive education, it is essential to develop exchange programmes, which involve civil servants, teachers, school directors, parents and, organisations of persons with disabilities, as well as people working on special needs education.

In a human rights perspective, inclusive educations should not be seen only as an obligation, but also as an opportunity to educate all children on human rights and respect for all.

This document is meant to contribute to the implementation of Article 24 of the Convention on the Rights of Persons with Disabilities (CRPD) at all levels through concrete guidelines and actions.

Recommendations for actions are presented according to the different provisions of this article.

2. MOVING TOWARDS INCLUSIVE EDUCATION

> *24.1 States Parties recognize the right of persons with disabilities to education. With a view to realizing this right without discrimination and on the basis of equal opportunity, States Parties shall ensure an inclusive education system at all levels and lifelong learning directed to:*
>
> *(a) The full development of human potential and sense of dignity and self-worth, and the strengthening of respect for human rights, fundamental freedoms and human diversity;*
>
> *(b) The development by persons with disabilities of their personality, talents and creativity, as well as their mental and physical abilities, to their fullest potential;*
>
> *(c) Enabling persons with disabilities to participate effectively in a free society*

The UN Convention does not explicitly define what 'inclusive education' is. Inclusive education should not be confused with integration. The Integration concept implies just an adaptation of the person to fit, and not changes of the environment, pedagogy and organisation. Inclusion is broader and implies a progressive change and adaptation of the educational system, so everybody can have their needs met and thrive.

EDF believes that the Salamanca Declaration adopted in 1994 provides a good starting point with its acknowledgement that Inclusive education means that the school must and can provide a good education to all pupils irrespective of their varying abilities. All children must be treated with respect and guaranteed equal opportunities for learning together.

Inclusive education is an on-going process. Teachers must work actively and deliberately to reach its goals. Inclusive education is a process of addressing and responding to diversity of needs of all learners through increasing participation in learning, cultures and communities, and reducing exclusion within and from education. It involves changes and modifications in content, approaches, structures and strategies, with a common vision which covers all girls and boys of appropriate age range based on the conviction that it is the responsibility of the regular system to educate all children.

The Salamanca Declaration should be used as a reference, in consistence with the principle explained above. We believe that Member States should also refer to this document and subsequent UNESCO guidance when developing new action plans or legislation on education. Moreover, EDF believes that the provisions of the Salamanca declaration should be developed further to take account of the needs of all groups of pupils/students with varying disabilities.

EDF also stresses that education is to be considered as a lifelong process, and persons with disabilities should be provided with the same opportunities as non-disabled people to access education or training during all the phases of their life, and according to the situation in which they live. In addition, the principle of non-discrimination should be applied in access to both formal and informal education.

Purposive Inclusive education in rural areas is still rare in the European Union. Education policies should be targeted to all areas within a country.

3. Accessing Education in Practice

> 24.2 *In realizing this right, States Parties shall ensure that:*
>
> *(a) Persons with disabilities are not excluded from the general education system on the basis of disability, and that children with disabilities are not excluded from free and compulsory primary education, or from secondary education, on the basis of disability;*
>
> *(b) Persons with disabilities can access an inclusive, quality and free primary education and secondary education on an equal basis with others in the communities in which they live;*
>
> *(c) Reasonable accommodation of the individual's requirements is provided;*
>
> *(d) Persons with disabilities receive the support required, within the general education system, to facilitate their effective education;*
>
> *(e) Effective individualized support measures are provided in environments that maximize academic and social development, consistent with the goal of full inclusion*

We recommend that the following constitutional and legislative measures should be undertaken to ensure equal opportunities and access to the right to education:

+ Within all countries there must be a constitutional guarantee (or equivalent) of free and compulsory basic education to all children;

+ Any existing legislation which defines any group of children with disabilities as 'uneducable' should be repealed;

+ Anti-discrimination legislation covering access to education on the ground of disability, as well as the multiple grounds of gender, ethnic origin, race, sexual orientation, age and disability, should be adopted. Such legislation should ensure that failure to accept a disabled pupil/student in a mainstream school is a criminal offence based on anti-discrimination laws. Dissuasive

sanctions to perpetrators of discrimination acts should be foreseen and backed by comprehensive training programmes;

+ The Ministry of Education should be responsible for the provision of all education, including for all children with disabilities.
  They are often under the competence of the health or social affairs ministry;

+ Children with disabilities should be able to attend their local
  school and receive the support they need alongside their non-
  disabled peers;

+ Legislation prohibiting discrimination in employment should
  be enforced in order to enable young women and men with disabilities to become teachers and made consistent with legislation or rules governing access to teaching;

+ Legislation on non-discrimination, as well as on accessibility of
  public buildings and ICTs should include requirements on the
  accessibility of school buildings, equipment and materials;

Reasonable accommodation should include the provision of accessible transport for children, and students with disabilities, on
the same conditions as other children.

In addition to legislation, policies and positive actions must be
taken to support the implementation in practice of these principles:

+ States should ensure a transition to an inclusive education system through action plans with concrete targets. Following the
  recommendation of the Council of Europe Social Charter committee *"When the achievement of one of the rights in question is
  exceptionally complex and particularly expensive to resolve, a State
  Party must take measures that allows it to achieve the objectives
  of the Charter within a reasonable time, with measurable progress
  and to an extent consistent with the maximum use of available resources. States Parties must be particularly mindful of the impact
  that their choices will have for groups with heightened vulnerabili-
  ties as well as for other persons affected including, especially, their*

families on whom falls the heaviest burden in the event of institutional shortcomings.";

+ Policies should be developed in order to ensure transition from special schools to mainstream schools and the transfer of pupils/students. Close cooperation between all types of schools is a precondition to inclusion;

+ Girls and boys with disabilities (and their parents) should have the same opportunities as all other children and must be able to choose the type and length of education they wish;

+ Committees for early identification and assessment of children with disabilities should support and guide children, teachers and schools, thereby enabling full access to education with the educational support and services needed from the earliest possible age, but should never decide for children with disabilities. This is unfortunately often the case.

Measures should be put in place to identify persons with disabilities in need of lifelong learning, and economic, as well as academic, support schemes should be set up in order to encourage and facilitate life long learning for these persons.

Accountability mechanisms to monitor school registration and completion by children with disabilities should be developed. States should adopt and revise reporting mechanisms to disaggregate data on school participation, achievement and social acceptance.

+ The funding of the education system should allow for further flexibility and should not just be based on the number of students. The failure to do this is detrimental to the quality of programmes and of the possibility to develop individualised approaches. In addition, sufficient funding should be dedicated to making school buildings fully accessible, for acquiring accessible materials, and for hiring or developing human support and assistance. The funding system of special schools should create incentives for the transition to mainstream inclusive schools. Adequate financial resources for accommodation and support to students with disabilities should be allocated and identifiable within the general education budget. It is important to stress that funds dedicated to inclusive education should be available on a permanent basis, not only in the face of transition;

+ Individualised support and support in the general educational system should be combined in order to facilitate the inclusion of the pupil/student in the mainstream educational system;

+ Schools should be given a certain autonomy to achieve this, but also responsibilities to which they should be held accountable;

+ Peer support and respect should be encouraged in the school curriculum, for both non-disabled children and children with disabilities;

+ Social interaction between disabled and non-disabled peers should be encouraged, and friendships promoted by the intentional building of relations, also with the aim of challenging bullying;

+ Parents and students/pupils should be involved in the definition of individual educational plans. And parents should be given advice on how to deal with the education of their daughters and sons;

+ A definition of Reasonable accommodation within education, including both human and technical aids, should be developed, so that it really serves the needs of pupils with disabilities;

+ As all other students, students with disabilities, including those with learning disabilities, should receive individual accreditation and certificates as a result of their performance and tests that should enable them to access higher grades and levels where possible. Within that process, individual abilities should be considered;

+ There is a need to ensure coordination between ministries (mainly education and health), and to move responsibility for education of children with disabilities from the ministry of health or social welfare to the ministry for education.

The development of Inclusive education is a process which requires that the conditions are established to enable it. Furthermore, there are already positive experiences of implementation of inclusive education around Europe which should be a source of inspiration and learning through in-site study visits and other forms of training such as showcasing by DVD and on the internet.

- Projects to ensure exchange of good practices in education among different EU countries should be developed and further disseminated. The main actors of such processes: teachers, students, parents, disabled peoples' organisations, people working on special needs education, and local authorities should be involved;
- Training of teachers on inclusive education should be one of the priorities of the relevant EU training and education programmes;
- Organisations of persons with disabilities must initiate discussions with teachers' unions to ensure that teaching methodologies include awareness on inclusive education;
- Pupils/students with disabilities need individualised academic and non academic programmes as their non disabled peers. They should not be systematically directed towards alternative spare activities.

The European Union can play a great role in this respect and should:

- Ensure that new member states receive support from the European Union to develop inclusive education policies.
- Develop International cooperation which should include the issue of inclusive education in the international cooperation strategies. EU should apply the same principle.
- EU structural funds should be used to favour the transition from special to mainstream education in countries receiving cohesion funding through the structural funds, and to ensure that

all children regardless of the area they live in (urban or rural) receive the same opportunities to access education.

+ The EU strategy on education and lifelong learning should have as one of its priorities the promotion of inclusive education and education for all, including girls and women with disabilities.

4. Learning Life and Social Development Skills

> *24.3 States Parties shall enable persons with disabilities to learn life and social development skills to facilitate their full and equal participation in education and as members of the community. To this end, States Parties shall take appropriate measures, including:*
>
> *(a) Facilitating the learning of Braille, alternative script, augmentative and alternative modes, means and formats of communication and orientation and mobility skills, and facilitating peer support and mentoring;*
>
> *(b) Facilitating the learning of sign language and the promotion of the linguistic identity of the deaf community;*
>
> *(c) Ensuring that the education of persons, and in particular children, who are blind, deaf or deafblind, is delivered in the most appropriate languages and modes and means of communication for the individual, and in environments which maximize academic and social development.*

Education should be seen as a holistic process which includes both academic attainment, and the development of life and social development skills.

This means that educational programmes must be individualised, as far as possible, in order to allow full inclusion of all students and in particular those with disabilities.

It is through academic and non academic activities that inclusion can be fully developed, as well as through interaction among students. It is only through this approach that exclusion, abuse, bullying and violence can be prevented.

Adequate support and communication modes must be developed which allow for participation of all students with disabilities. Reference to blind, deaf and deaf blind persons in the text of the Convention are to be considered as examples which should also be applied to other groups of disabled children.

In light of the issues pointed out above, EDF believes that:

+ Educational systems should develop flexible curricula in order to ensure the possibility of individual educational paths for all children, including those with disabilities. Such educational path should include non-academic and vocational activities;

+ There should be an explicit definition of inclusion in terms of the necessary training, support, policies, resources and facilities to enable children with disabilities to realise an effective education in an inclusive environment;

+ It is important to start applying new technologies for teaching processes in mainstream schools, as this facilitates the participation of children with disabilities, in particular those with intellectual disabilities, mental health problems and sensory disabilities;

+ There should be opportunities for children with disabilities to learn life and social development skills to facilitate full and equal participation in education including:
    + learning of Braille, alternative script, augmentative and alternative modes, means and formats of communication and orientation and mobility skills
    + peer support and mentoring
    + learning of sign language
    + social awareness and empowerment;

+ Human rights education should be taught within the school curriculum to promote greater respect for the rights of every child, including children with disabilities;

- Awareness of disability and gender should be taught to all pupils/students based on the human rights paradigm contained in the relevant UN conventions and other human rights instruments;
- Methodologies and activities of peer support as the most preferred assistance by pupils with disabilities should be developed.

Measures to identify and address the specific needs of girls and women with disabilities with regards to education should be put in place. This should among other things include:
- Information to parents about the importance of providing girls with disabilities with opportunities for high quality education;
- Information to girls and women with disabilities about available programmes, grants etc. of relevance to especially girls from the migrant community and other groups who could be expected to have limited access to education;
- Programmes with the objective of providing women with disabilities with further skills and knowledge later in life, in particular targeted at rural areas.

5. Training of Teachers

24.4 *In order to help ensure the realization of this right, States Parties shall take appropriate measures to employ teachers, including teachers with disabilities, who are qualified in sign language and/or Braille, and to train professionals and staff who work at all levels of education. Such training shall incorporate disability awareness and the use of appropriate augmentative and alternative modes, means and formats of communication, educational techniques and materials to support persons with disabilities.*

- Training on Braille and sign language, as well as all other alternative and augmentative communication modes, should be promoted, and included in the general teacher's training, and education studies curricula;
- Teachers should receive both pre-service and in-service training, so that they are better equipped to respond to diversity in the classroom;
- Teacher training syllabuses should include inclusive training methodologies;
- The recruitment and training of people with disabilities to become teachers and support staff in education should be actively encouraged;
- Adults with disabilities should be invited to participate in the training, so as to transfer their experience of being independent, despite environmental and attitudinal barriers;
- Adequate funding should be provided to ensure the above;
- Human rights education should be part of the general teachers' training and education curricula.

6. Beyond Basic Education

24.5 States Parties shall ensure that persons with disabilities are able to access general tertiary education, vocational training, adult education and lifelong learning without discrimination and on an equal basis with others. To this end, States Parties shall ensure that reasonable accommodation is provided to persons with disabilities.

In order to develop inclusive education strategies, access needs must be considered from the outset. This should be done through:

- The appointment of inclusive coordinators within the educational system who could support the development of more inclusive strategies;
- Universal access should be applied in any reform of schools or any adaptation of the school environment;
- In order to ensure further inclusion of pupils/students with chronic illnesses, it is necessary to develop coordination and synergies between social and health services on the one hand and educational establishments on the other. When possible separated solutions should be avoided;
- All schools should be required to introduce student bodies, such as school councils, which provide a forum for children to express their views on matters affecting their schooling, and the opportunity to have their views given due weight in accordance with the age and maturity of the children;
- Lifelong learning strategies for disabled people, is an area of utmost importance (mainly for people with intellectual disabilities) to ensure retention of knowledge and the development of professional careers;

All appropriate initiatives to eliminate discrimination against women and girls with disabilities should be taken, in order to ensure to them equal rights with men and boys with disabilities in the field of education and to ensure the same conditions for:
- Career and vocational guidance
- Access to studies and for the achievement of diplomas in educational establishments of all categories, in rural as well as in urban areas

---

*European Disability Forum is an independent non-governmental organization that represents the interests of 65 million disabled people in the European Union.

European Disability Forum. *Inclusive Education: Moving from Words to Deeds Statement*. Brussels: European Forum, 2009.

DISCUSSION QUESTIONS

1. Why is it important for a shared responsibility between general education and special education in the education of children with disabilities?

2. Discuss the key differences between the following three words: mainstreaming, integration, and inclusion. Reflect on the status of special education services according to these key terms in the community where you attended school.

3. In some countries across the globe education for children without disabilities is not a reality. As countries develop systems of education for all, what are the conditions that must be present?

4. If you were a student with a disability, would you prefer receiving your education in a general education classroom or a self-contained special education classroom? What factors affect your attitudes toward education in inclusive schools?

CHAPTER 8:

Supporting Independent Living

Chapter 8 focuses on the issues encountered by people with disabilities living independently and their efforts to be included in the community. The Convention on the Rights of Persons with Disabilities requires states to recognize that persons with disability have a right to live in the community with choices equal to others. It also requires states to ensure that persons with disability have access to specialized and generic services necessary to support living and inclusion in the community and to prevent their isolation or segregation from the community.

The first article, "Deinstitutionalisation and Community Living—Outcomes and Costs: Report of a European Study," gives data from 28 European countries—including the number of people with disabilities living in institutions and a cost comparison between community living and institutional living. Recommendations for change are presented in a 16-step proactive transition plan that seeks to replace institutional living options with community living options.

The second article, a research paper from the European Network on Independent Living (ENIL), "ENIL Research Paper on Community Living and the Support of Independent Living for the Disabled Women, Men and Children of Europe," advocates for the right of every person with a disability to have the freedom to choose and be supported in an independent community living option. The article includes background on existing European policy, discusses research findings from the United States and Europe, shows financial cost differences and the differences in quality of life and skills between institutionalization and community living, reveals the benefits of personal assistance, and makes recommendations for effective implementation.

The chapter concludes with a report from the National Council on Disability, "The State of Housing in America in the 21st Century: A Disability Perspective." The report details the state of housing for people with disability in the United States and offers recommendations for expanded options and improved services. The current housing needs and options for people with disability are revealed through a question-and-answer format. While tremendous progress has been achieved in making available community living options that are affordable, accessible and appropriate, much remains to be learned.

Deinstitutionalisation and Community Living—Outcomes and Costs: Report of a European Study

*By Jim Mansell, Martin Knapp, Julie Beadle-Brown and Jeni Beecham**

1. Introduction

This project aimed to bring together the available information on the number of disabled people living in residential institutions in 28 European countries, and to identify successful strategies for replacing institutions with community-based services, paying particular attention to economic issues in the transition. It is the most wide-ranging study of its kind ever undertaken.

Increasingly the goal of services for people with disabilities is seen not as the provision of a particular type of building or programme, but as the provision of a flexible range of help and resources which can be assembled and adjusted as needed to enable all people with disabilities to live their lives in the way that they want but with the support and protection that they need. This is characterised by several features:

♦ *Separation of buildings and support*

The organisation of support and assistance for people is not determined by the type of building they live in, but rather by the needs of the individual and what they need to live where and how they choose. High levels of support can be provided in ordinary housing in the community, for example.

♦ *Access to the same options as everyone else*

Instead of, for example, determining that all disabled people must live in group homes, policy is framed around people having access to the same range of options as everyone else with regard to where they live and receiving the support they need wherever they may choose.

+ *Choice and control for the disabled person and their representatives* Help is organised on the principle that the disabled person should have as much control as possible over the kind of services they receive, how they are organised and delivered, to fit in with the person's own aspirations and preferences. This means supporting people's decision-making to achieve the best balance between their wishes and society's responsibility for their care.

This approach is sometimes referred to as 'supported living' or 'independent living'. These services support people to live as full citizens rather than expecting people to fit into standardised models and structures.

Supporting disabled people to live in the community as equal citizens is an issue of human rights. The segregation of disabled people in institutions is a human rights violation in itself. Furthermore, research has shown that institutional care is often of an unacceptably poor quality and represents serious breaches of internationally accepted human rights standards. Evidence from research and evaluation of alternatives to institutional care also supports the transition to services in the community. Where institutions have been replaced by community-based services, the results have generally been favourable. However, experience shows that moving to community-based services is not a guarantee of better outcomes: it is possible to inadvertently transplant or recreate institutional care practices in new services. Developing appropriate services in the community is a *necessary*, but not a *sufficient*, condition for better results.

The overall aim of this project was to provide scientific evidence to inform and stimulate policy development in the reallocation of financial resources to best meet the needs of people with disabilities, through a transition from large institutions to a system of community-based services and independent living.

The objectives of the project were to:

1. Collect, analyse and interpret existing statistical and other quantitative data on the number of people with disabilities placed in large residential institutions in 28 European countries.
2. Analyse the economic, financial and organisational arrangements necessary for an optimal transition from a system of large institutions to one based on community services and independent living, using three countries (England, Germany and Italy) as case studies to illustrate the issues involved.
3. Report on the issues identified, addressing the results of the project, the adequacy of the data available in each country, and making recommendations for the cost-effective transition from institutions to community-based services.

2. Method

For the purposes of this study, the European Commission defined a residential institution as an establishment in which more than 30 people lived, of whom at least 80% were mentally or physically disabled. Informants were asked to supply information about all residential care establishments serving disabled people in each country, to permit examination of the current balance between institutional and community care. The study covered all age groups and all kinds of disability, including mental health problems.

The study involved a number of elements:

+ Existing European and international data sources were reviewed to identify material relevant to the study. These included official reports, reports from non-governmental organisations as well as specific studies.
+ Existing national data sources were identified and collated, using published material augmented by telephone and email contact and visits.
+ Definitions, completeness and quality of the data was checked.
+ The data were analysed and prepared for presentation.

- The sequence and process of service development was described in three countries selected as case studies—England, Germany and Italy.

- As part of this review, particular attention was paid to the roles of different actors (national, regional and local tiers of government), the role of disabled people, their families and representatives and the role of staff and their organisations.

- Evidence about the economic implications of shifting from institutions to services in the community was collated from available research in England, Germany and Italy. Attention was paid to ensure 'like for like' comparison, taking account of the level of disability of residents, the range and level of quality of services achieved and the balance between costs met by public agencies and those met by others, especially the families of disabled people.

- The available evidence was examined to understand the extent to which transitional cost (eg 'double-running' expenditure) issues were important.

- The different strategies used in each of the three countries used as case-studies to manage the cost and wider economic issues arising during the transition from institutional to community-based care were examined.

- The interim report, final report and executive summary were prepared by the University of Kent and the London School of Economics. Interpretation of the results and their implications was strengthened by using the reference group as a 'sounding-board' and by discussion of the report with project partners and with the European Commission.

3. CONCLUSIONS AND RECOMMENDATIONS

The main report of the study is presented in Volume 2, with the detailed reports for individual countries in Volume 3. The following

section of the report summarises the conclusions of the study, starting with the conclusions and recommendations drawn from the review of existing information. It will then present the conclusions drawn from the analysis of the process, costs and outcomes of developing effective services in the community to replace institutions and the recommendations for how governments can take forward this agenda for change.

Review of Existing Sources of Information

Article 31 of the UN Convention on the Rights of Persons with Disabilities requires States to collect data 'to enable them to formulate and implement policies to give effect to the present Convention'. Such information 'shall be disaggregated as appropriate' and used to address the barriers faced by disabled people in exercising their rights. States 'shall assume responsibility for the dissemination of these statistics and ensure their accessibility to persons with disabilities and others'.

It is clear that the countries taking part in this study have some way to go to meet this requirement. At present, comprehensive information is not available for all types of residential services provided nor for all the client groups involved, nor is there clarity about the definition of kinds and characteristics of services provided or people served. Where such information exists, it is not always collated at national level. The data presented here form a starting point—both in terms of specifying what is currently available and in terms of estimating the numbers of disabled people in residential care—on which future efforts will have to build to enable countries to fulfil their obligations.

RECOMMENDATIONS

1. *Agree a harmonised data set at European level*

    1.1 The European Commission should promote joint work between Member States and Eurostat to define a minimum data set for residential services (defined broadly) for people with disabilities.

1.2 The data set needs to include information that will permit the review of Member States' progress in the closure of institutions and of the growth of independent living and services in the community.

1.3 The data set needs to be workable both for countries which still have services largely based in institutions, where the distinction between institutional care and care at home is very clear, and for countries which are in the advanced stages of replacing institutions with community-based services and independent living. This is likely to require a combination of information about numbers of places in services (eg how many places are there in residential establishments where more than 30 people live, of whom at least 80% are mentally or physically disabled?) with information about people (eg how many people live in a house or apartment they own or rent, with what amount of staff support each week?).

1.4 The data set needs to include sufficient information about the people served (gender, ethnicity, primary disability) to enable States to ensure that everyone is benefiting from the transition away from institutions to better alternatives in the community.

2. *Publish statistics demonstrating progress in each country*

2.1 The European Commission should work with Eurostat towards the regular publication of statistics demonstrating progress in each country in the transition away from institutions to better alternatives in the community. These statistics should be available on the world-wide web and should be freely available to disabled people, other members of the public, disabled people, non-governmental organisations and governmental organisations, so that they may use them in commenting upon and assisting in the development of better services.

2.2 The publication of statistics should be accompanied by an assessment by Eurostat of their accuracy and completeness for each country.

2.3 The Commission should work with Member States to identify a single source of information at national level in each country, competent to provide the information needed for the minimum data set and should promote the publication in print and on the world-wide web of the information available for each country.

The Change Process in Three Countries

Perhaps the most striking characteristic of the process of service development in the three countries studied in depth is the importance of coordination of different agencies involved in the transition process. The number of agencies involved, their geographical spread and the involvement of different tiers of government all make good coordination essential. It is simply not feasible to leave to the institution, or the local authorities involved, the task of dismantling institutions which serve people from many different municipalities. Regional and national governments have an important role in driving the process forward, both through their own actions in setting the legal and policy context and through the way they construct and manage the framework of incentives.

Creating new roles for actors in the process is also a major part of the transition task. Traditional service providers—organisations and the people who work in them—need to be offered new roles, either in providing modern services in the community or through leaving the provision of care. New actors—organisations of service users and their families, non-governmental organisations wanting to be involved in providing new models of service, public authorities who have not hitherto played a role in helping their disabled citizens—also need to be involved.

The difference in pace between Germany on the one hand and England and Italy on the other seems to have been influenced by the depth of dissatisfaction among decision-makers with institutions. In both Italy and England, the vision of alternatives and the revelation of very poor conditions in institutions was clearly influential in the transition process.

Finally, England and Germany illustrate an important reason to involve disabled people in the process of service development and to listen and respond to their views and wishes. Service-led reform in these countries has essentially involved redesigning existing service structures to humanise them—replacing institutions with group homes, for example. Disabled people, once given the chance, identified and pursued the considerably more ambitious goal of independent or supported living, organised as 'self-directed services' using individual budgets. Service-providing agencies on their own are likely to be constrained by their past and present ways of thinking and working; the new models of service require a partnership between disabled people (and those who help and represent them) and agencies planning and providing services.

Cost-Effectiveness of Community versus Institutional Models of Residential Care and Change over Time

SYSTEM STRUCTURES

There are four main things to remember about care system structures to take forward into planning the transition from institutional models of care to services in the community:

- Most support for disabled people comes from families, friends and neighbours, but the inputs, responsibilities and burdens of family and other unpaid carers often go unrecognised and unsupported. If family care is not available, then paid staff will need to be employed at greater direct cost to the care system.

There are however well known constraints on the availability of family carers (see below).

+ The needs of disabled people often span more than one care or service 'system', and consequently many different agencies or sectors can be involved in community-based care, including health, social care, housing, education, employment, transport, leisure, criminal justice and social security.

+ There are different ways to raise the finances that will fund these services, including through taxes, social insurance (linked to employment), voluntary insurance (at the discretion of the individual or family) and out-of-pocket payments by service users and their families. Most countries have a mix of arrangements, which can lead to difficulties because of the incentives and disincentives they can create.

+ The complex context of most care systems (multiple services, multiple agencies, multiple funding sources and routes) generally means that there are no simple financial 'levers' to pull to bring about wholesale changes in service delivery.

POLICIES AND PLANS

Closing institutions would be more straightforward if one had little concern for what happens to residents. The challenge is to build good services in the community and, as noted in reviewing transition in England, Germany and Italy, this implies the need for coordination and planning.

+ Ideally, the transition from institutions to services in the community will have a national mandate. At the very least, there need to be local agreements between all potential service provider sectors. This plan should not just specify that an institution will close and indicate the target date, but should also include a detailed vision of the future care system. Consultation should be wide, and users and families should be involved throughout.

+ The local plan needs to be based on relevant knowledge and robust evidence. Decision makers should understand not only which care arrangements and treatment interventions are effective and what they cost (and to which budgets), but also which are cost-effective.

+ Carrying out a good cost-effectiveness analysis or other economic evaluation—to inform national policy or local plans—can be expensive and time-consuming. However, much can be gleaned from previously completed analyses if carefully interpreted in the local system context. It is important to understand *for whom* is a particular service or intervention likely to be cost-effective. For example, is cost-effectiveness achieved only for the health service and at the expense of higher costs for another agency? If so, this could put barriers in the way of system-wide improvements.

Costs, Needs and Outcomes

The (complex) links between costs, needs and outcomes sit at the heart of the evidence base on which to build a strong economic case for making the transition from institutions to services in the community.

+ In a good care system, the costs of supporting people with substantial disabilities are usually high, *wherever* those people live. Policy makers must not expect costs to be low in community settings, even if the institutional services they are intended to replace appear to be inexpensive. Low-cost institutional services are almost always delivering low-quality care.

+ There is no evidence that community-based models of care are inherently more costly than institutions, once the comparison is made on the basis of comparable needs of residents and comparable quality of care. Community-based systems of independent and supported living, when properly set up and managed, should deliver better outcomes than institutions.

- Costs in the community range widely—over many service areas and policy domains—in response to the multiple needs of individual disabled people. Families can also carry quite a high cost responsibility. It is therefore important to ensure that all local stakeholders are aware of, and obviously preferably agree with, the policy or plan.

- Costs are incurred to provide services, in response to needs, and in order to achieve outcomes. It therefore makes little sense to compare costs between two service systems without also looking at the needs of the individuals and the outcomes they experience.

- People's needs, preferences and circumstances vary, and so their service requirements will also vary. Consequently, costs are unlikely to be the same across a group of people. This has at least two crucial implications. First, from a methodological point of view, comparing costs between two settings or service arrangements should be undertaken carefully unless it is known that the people supported in those different settings are identical in all relevant (cost-raising) respects, or that statistical adjustments are made to achieve equivalence. Not to do so risks dangerous under-funding of provision.

- Individuals' needs change over time, especially in the initial few months after moving from an institution to a community placement. Service systems need to be able to respond flexibly to these changing needs. A linked requirement is for care systems to be able to respond to changing preferences, as long-term residents of institutions will have little experience at the time they move out on which to form preferences about their lives in the community.

- The second implication of this inherent variation is that it opens up the possibility for purposive targeting of services on needs in order to enhance the overall ability of a care system to improve the well being of disabled people from fixed volumes of resources.

+ Usually it is relevant to consider a range of outcome dimensions: not just symptoms (for people with mental health needs) or personal independence (for people with intellectual disabilities) for example, but also whether a changing care system improves an individual's ability to function (for example to get back to work or to build social networks) and their broader quality of life. It is generally the case that spending more on the support of disabled people will lead to better outcomes, but the relationship is not simple and decision makers may need to think carefully (and together with disabled people) about which outcomes they wish to prioritise within the care system.
+ A new care arrangement (such as community-based care) could be more expensive than the arrangement it is replacing (such as long-stay hospital provision) but still be more cost-effective because it leads to better outcomes for service users and perhaps also for their families, and those improved outcomes are valued sufficiently highly to justify the higher expenditure.

For decision-makers contemplating a policy of changing from institutions to services in the community, some key effects are summarised in Figure 1. If existing institutional care is relatively less expensive, decision-makers can expect that transfer of the less disabled residents to good services in the community will be achieved at the same or lower costs and at the same or higher quality; cost-effectiveness in the community will be the same or better. More disabled residents in less expensive institutions will cost more in good community services but the quality will be higher and so cost-effectiveness in the community will be the same or better (and decision-makers should not assume that they can keep institutional costs low).

	After transition to services in the community		
	Costs	Quality	Cost-effectiveness
Less expensive institution			
Less disabled person →	Same or lower	Same or higher	Same or better
More disabled person →	Higher	Higher	Same or better
More expensive institution			
Less disabled person →	Lower	Same or higher	Better
More disabled person →	Same or lower	Higher	Better

In more expensive institutions, decision-makers can expect that transfer of the less disabled residents to good services in the community will be achieved at lower costs and at the same or higher quality; cost-effectiveness in the community will therefore be better. More disabled residents in more expensive institutions will cost the same in good community services but the quality will be higher and so cost-effectiveness in the community will be better.

SUPPLY CONSTRAINTS

+ Family care may not be readily available to support people with disabilities. This could be because they have lost contact during the period of institutional residence. Or it could be because the burden of unpaid family informal care is too great. Unsupported family carers can experience many adverse consequences, including disrupted employment and lost income, out-of-pocket expenses, poor health and stress.

+ Support can be provided to families in various ways, including through direct or indirect financial support, employment-friendly policies, educational programmes, counselling and respite services. These can help to reduce carer burden and make it more likely that disabled people can be supported by their families, if this is what they wish.

+ A commonly found barrier to the development of community-based care systems is a shortage of suitably skilled staff. Transferring staff from institutions to the community is a possibility, but not everyone wants to make the move and these might not be the right people anyway.

+ Paying higher salaries to attract better community care staff is one way to address shortages but obviously pushes up overall costs.

+ Recruiting and training staff for community services needs to be done *before* disabled people start to move out of the institutions. The planning of future human resource needs should obviously be a key part of any local plan and national policy.

LOCAL ECONOMIC DEVELOPMENT

+ Closing a large institution could have a major impact on local employment patterns if it is the only or main local employer. Building community accommodation for disabled people in the same communities in order to offer replacement work might not be a sensible option. Residents of the institution may come from other parts of the country and may wish to return to their local community. Local economic development considerations will need to be taken into account.

OPPORTUNITY COSTS OF CAPITAL

+ Many of today's institutions have low value in alternative uses because the buildings are old or in disrepair, and because the land on which they are located is not in high demand for redevelopment. Closing an institution might not therefore generate much additional money for ploughing into the necessary capital investment for community services.

+ Even when a building or site has high economic value in alternative uses, the proceeds from their sale will generally not be realised until the institution has completely closed down. Consequently, some 'hump' costs will be needed—funds made available quite early for investment in new community facilities to get them underway. Double running costs will also be needed to resource both the old and the new services in parallel for a few years until the institution has fully closed down.

FUNDING FLOWS

+ Concerns about the loss of budgets/resources into other parts of the care system or elsewhere following closure of an institution might be addressed by partial or temporary ring-fencing. Thus, for example, the budget currently allocated to a psychiatric hospital might be protected for the development of community-based services for people with mental health needs. Protection of this kind can provide protection and stability, and may help to 'kick-start' a new care initiative.

+ Centralised budgets may be better vehicles for implementing national policies or priorities, but devolved budgets make it easier for local needs and preferences to shape local services. In turn this could make it easier to alter the balance of care away from institutionally oriented services and in favour of community care.

+ Funding tied to individuals rather than institutions would help to break down one of the barriers to shifting the balance of care away from inpatient services.

+ The commissioning environment—the way that services get procured—will have a substantial influence over the performance of a care system, including the balance of care. Decision-makers need to choose the style of commissioning carefully so as to create the appropriate incentives for improvement.

+ Major year-on-year changes in budgets should be avoided, because they can be so disruptive. On the other hand, it may be necessary to move away from a gradual, *incremental* approach to change in order to challenge the status quo.

Multiple Funding Sources

+ Because many disabled people have multiple needs, they may require or request support in the community from a range of different services, perhaps delivered by different agencies out of different budgets. This multiplicity must be recognised. The inter-connections (actual or potential) between services and agencies could put up substantial barriers to effective and cost-effective care.

+ Joint planning and joint commissioning are among the approaches that can be used in an attempt to bring two or more budget-holding agencies together to improve service coordination and its impacts.

+ Devolving certain powers and responsibilities to case/care managers, or even to individual service users via self-directed care arrangements, might also help overcome these difficulties.

Dynamics of Change

+ The dynamics of change are complex and can send out misleading signals about changing costs and outcomes. Decision makers must ensure that they take the long view.

Recommendations

These conclusions imply a central role for vision and leadership by national and regional governments, working in close collaboration with representatives of users and their families. They imply the need for a comprehensive, long-term perspective, which considers all the costs and all the benefits of the process of transition. They underline the need for creativity in developing solutions to the wide range of implementation problems which may emerge and learning from the process as experience and knowledge are gained of how to provide good services in the community. They also confirm that the available evidence is that, once comparison is made on the basis of comparable needs of residents and comparable quality of care, there is no basis for believing that services in the community will be inherently more expensive than institutions.

How can governments take forward this agenda? Change requires that governments, with other actors:

1. Strengthen the vision of new possibilities in the community
2. Sustain public dissatisfaction with current arrangements
3. Create some practical demonstrations of how things can be better
4. Reduce resistance to change by managing incentives for the different actors in the process

This list is not a sequence—attention needs to be given to each area throughout the process. Precisely what steps governments take, and the appropriate balance between different actions, will differ between countries depending on their circumstances. But these four issues will need to be addressed over the whole period of transition. Although other actors (for example, organisations of users and their families) will play an important role, the responsibility for planning, coordinating and managing the process will rest with governments.

The recommendations set out under each of these headings below are derived not only from the evidence presented in this report but also from the growing literature on modernising services for disabled people and from the authors' experience as actors in this field.

STRENGTHENING THE VISION OF NEW POSSIBILITIES IN THE
COMMUNITY

3. *Adopt policies in favour of inclusion*

   3.1 Set out the goal that all disabled people should be included in society and that the help they receive should be based on the principles of respect for all individuals, choice and control over how they live their lives, full participation in society and support to maximise independence.

   3.2 Commit to stop building new institutions or new buildings in existing institutions, and to spending the majority of available funds to develop services in the community.

   3.3 Specify the overall timetable and plan for transition from institutions to services in the community.

4. *Develop legislative support for inclusion*

   4.1 Adopt legislation that promotes independent living and social inclusion.

   4.2 Ratify the UN Convention on the Rights of Persons with Disabilities.

   4.3 Prohibit discrimination against disabled people in services and facilities.

   4.4 Prohibit use of public monies to build new institutions.

   4.5 Ensure that government agencies responsible for serving the population in a defined local area are made responsible for serving disabled people as well.

5. *Strengthen the voice of disabled people, families and their advocates in policy*

   5.1 Support groups that commit to inclusion and the replacement of institutions with community services.

5.2 Appoint disabled people, family members and their advocates who are personally committed to inclusion to official bodies.

5.3 Provide training for disabled people and their families in how policy-making works and how they can influence it.

5.4 Require policy-makers and civil servants to regularly meet disabled people, family members and their advocates who are personally committed to inclusion and to identify how to strengthen their voice in policy.

6. *Require professional bodies to make their policies consistent with supporting inclusion*

6.1 Require that bodies representing or training or accrediting the professional practice of personnel working with disabled people adopt a commitment to supporting the inclusion of disabled people in their work. This should include both specialist staff working with disabled people and others who may provide services to disabled people in the course of their work (eg police officers, nurses in general hospitals).

6.2 Ensure that arrangements for training (including continuing professional development as well as initial training) and accreditation include disabled people and are based on the principle of inclusion.

7. *Encourage media interest in and support of inclusion*

7.1 Promote the policy of replacing institutions with services in the community through official information and public education programmes.

7.2 Help people providing good-quality services in the community and the people they serve to publicise their work.

8. *Learn from best practice in other countries*

   8.1 Support visits by disabled people, families, advocates, service providers and decision-makers to learn from good practice in community-based services in other countries, and reciprocal visits from those countries; instead of visits to and from providers of institutional care.

   8.2 Support participation in international networks (such as the European Coalition for Community Living) which will enable people to learn about best practice.

   8.3 Require that professional training for personnel working with disabled people includes the study of best practice in services in the community in other countries.

SUSTAINING PUBLIC DISSATISFACTION WITH CURRENT INSTITUTIONAL ARRANGEMENTS

9. *Open institutions to independent scrutiny*

   9.1 Require institutions to permit members of the public, non-governmental organisations and the media to visit them and to meet residents, families, advocates and staff who wish to do so.

   9.2 Encourage institutions to promote their replacement with services in the community.

10. *Create inspectorates to protect and promote the rights of individuals*

   10.1 Create inspectorates (which include disabled people and other 'experts by experience') to visit services, meet residents, families, advocates and staff and monitor their living conditions and quality of life.

   10.2 Publish the results of inspection visits.

   10.3 Enforce the findings of these inspectorates where individuals require protection or redress.

11. *Emphasise comparisons of quality of life*

11.1 Encourage the description of living conditions and the quality of life of residents in institutions compared with (i) non-disabled members of the population and (ii) people of similar levels of disability receiving services in the community (elsewhere in the same country or in other countries); instead of the comparison with the same institutions in the past or with other institutions elsewhere.

CREATING SOME PRACTICAL DEMONSTRATIONS OF HOW THINGS CAN BE BETTER

12. *Create innovative services*

12.1 Fund the development of independent and supported living in the community, using ordinary housing and providing the level of staff support each individual needs.

12.2 Ensure that demonstration projects reflect best practice both in how they are set up and how they are run.

12.3 Ensure that demonstration projects both bring people back home from institutions and serve local people on 'waiting lists', so that members of the community in which services are developed are more likely to be supportive and helpful.

12.4 Ensure that demonstration projects include options both for accommodation and for occupation (education, employment or other day-time activities) to increase the likelihood of success.

12.5 Support new forms of training and professional qualification to ensure that there are sufficient staff to support people well as new services develop.

12.6 Monitor the quality and costs of new services.

13. *Include everyone from the start*

13.1 Ensure that schemes include people with more severe or complex disabilities early in the development process, so that experience of meeting their needs is gained from the outset.

Reducing Resistance to Change by Managing Incentives for Different Actors in the Process

14. *Create new funding opportunities*

14.1 Set up mechanisms for individual budgets so that people can be supported to plan their new lives in a personally-tailored way.

14.2 Create opportunities for new organisations to get involved in providing services in the community, outside the existing framework of institutional care, to pioneer the new models of support needed.

14.3 Create financial incentives for local government to get involved in the inclusion of disabled people in their own community.

15. *Remove obstacles to development of services in the community*

15.1 Create arrangements for contracting for innovative, local services, so that existing rules designed for institutional care systems are waived or modified to permit the development of services in the community.

15.2 Review rules for other relevant services such as planning, housing, employment, social security and health care to ensure that disabled people supported in the community can get equal access.

15.3 Work with the European Commission to ensure that EU rules on employment, health and safety and other areas of EU competence support rather than hinder the development of good services in the community.

16. *Make funding of new services contingent on quality*

16.1 Ensure that new services are only funded if they are of good quality, that quality is reviewed (using the experience of disabled people supported by the service as the primary measure of quality) and that funding is discontinued if services do not maintain acceptable standards.

16.2 Resist pressure to redevelop institutions or build new institutions as 'temporary' expedients.

16.3 International bodies, such as the World Bank and the European Commission, should not permit use of their funds to redevelop institutions or build new institutions.

---

*Jim Mansell is professor of the applied psychology of learning disability at the University of Kent.

Martin Knapp is professor of social policy at the London School of Economics.

Julie Beadle-Brown is senior lecturer in learning disability at the University of Kent.

Jeni Beecham is professorial research fellow at the Personal Social Services Research Unit, London School of Economics.

Mansell, Jim, Martin Knapp, Julie Beadle-Brown, and Jeni Beecham. Deinstitutionalisation and Community Living—Outcomes and Costs: Report of a European Study, Vol. 1, Executive Summary. Canterbury: Tizard Centre, University of Kent, 2007. © European Communities, 2007.

ENIL Research Paper on Community Living and the Support of Independent Living for the Disabled Women, Men and Children of Europe

By the European Network on Independent Living*

> *Lack of proper service provision is not about lack of funds or bad administration. It is about prioritizing the rights of the individual and ensuring that in a democratic society those rights are enshrined and implemented. (Hurst 1995:533)*

INTRODUCTION

This paper elaborates the human rights argument for the full support of community living and independent living for all disabled people that is: living in the community independently in a place of one's own choice with financial and local support and with access to personal assistance. The paper argues that disabled people do not need to live in institutions excluded from their communities or have their human rights abused.

The European Network on Independent Living (ENIL) welcomed the European Action Plan which states that disabled people must move from the role of 'patient to citizen'. Action 8 in the Action Plan is devoted to promoting and enacting community living. In addition, the more recent UN Convention on the Rights of People with Disabilities promotes independent living through Article 19 of the UN Convention which states that disabled people should live where they wish and with whom they wish.

However, these demands for disabled peoples' human rights and freedoms are not new, nor were they first voiced through the above documents, they have been a demand of National and European disabled peoples' movements since the early 1970s (Barnes, Mercer and Shakespeare 1999).

In 1989 community living and personal assistance was one of the key demands of the newly formed European Network on Independent Living—an organization run and controlled by disabled people. In 2003 a set of demands were presented at Strasburg by ENIL and were re-presented in 2007. Indeed, the European Network on Independent Living and national disability movements around Europe and beyond have been demanding full support for community living and de-institutionalization for decades.

There have been some welcome changes, with the closure of some large institutions in some European countries, but these advances are marred by the building of group homes which house a smaller number of disabled people representing the institution and its systemic problems in microcosm. The records of some newly ascending European member countries, some of whom see institutionalization as the only option for many disabled women, men and children also present challenges to these demands. While community living and the support of disabled people and children is clearly the wish of the European Community, the United Nations and the disabled peoples' movement, the progress is slow and as you read this millions of disabled people and children are likely to be incarcerated in institutions around Europe. This is a situation which many agree must change. The claim of the Council of Europe in the European Action Plan (2006–2015) that disabled people must move from the role of patient to citizen can only be achieved by prioritizing the rights of the individual and ensuring that those rights are enshrined and implemented.

EXISTING INTERNATIONAL AND EUROPEAN POLICY BACKGROUND

The UN Convention on the rights of people with disabilities has been signed and ratified by a number of countries but is still awaiting ratification from others (see www.enil.eu for summary) Article 19 says:

> "Persons with disabilities should have access to a range of in-home, residential and other community support services, including personal assistance necessary to support living and inclusion in the community and to prevent isolation or segregation from the community".

As noted, both the European Action Plan (2006–2015) and the UN Convention have guiding principles which must become realities for these things to happen and for disabled people to achieve basic human rights as equal citizens. The three guiding principles of the UN Convention are:

1. Respect for inherent dignity and individual autonomy, including the freedom to make one's own choices, and independence of persons;
2. Full and effective participation and inclusion in society; and
3. Respect for difference and acceptance of persons with disabilities as part of human diversity and humanity.

Whilst the European Action Plan is guided by three very similar principles:

1. Disabled people achieving the same rights as everybody else
2. Society ensuring access to human rights for all citizens
3. Disabled people becoming equal citizens

In addition, Action line 8 of the European Action Plan states that disabled people should be given full support for community living and independent living in the same way that article 19 of the UN Convention does.

The implementation of article 19 and action 8 will be the duty of national and local jurisdictions in particular countries. Both of these measures support the European Resolution on the Rights of Disabled People (1996) which said that disability rights must be treated as a civil rights issue, which discouraged the building of new institutions and demanded that no person was institutionalized, against their will. In addition, the Charter of the Fundamental Rights of the European Union (2000) said that states should ensure disabled peoples' independence, participation and inclusion at local, national and European level.

In spite of numerous declarations, policies and demands, continuous problems and barriers have been raised by politicians and local authorities on the costs and outcomes of the full deinstitutionalization of disabled people. In addition, other groups who have a vested interest in the continuation of the institutional system are likely to protest against deinstitutionalization, often developing existing local prejudices in the process and thereby gaining further impetus to violating the human rights of disabled people. These groups can include those service providers/charities who would lose contracts, donations, and government subsidies, other groups and individuals with a financial stake in the institution who gain from the system, staff within the institutions and existing trade unions who may wish to protect staff jobs, professional bureaucrats at local, national and European levels as well as those who claim that closures will have a negative affect on the local economy.

Three key discriminating arguments which act against both the European Action Plan and the UN Convention on the rights of people with disabilities persist

a) The costs of de-institutionalization and community living are higher than institutionalizing disabled people.

b) Disabled people, especially those with perceived higher support needs will be unable to support themselves outside the institutional context, be it a large institution or a small group home institution.

c) The process of community living and independent living will take time and require a change in the local systems.

The form of these arguments can vary due to state and local processes, systems of government, levels of decentralisation, economics, and any welfare systems already in place, while these factors are beyond the scope of this paper they are factors that should be considered in any protest or challenge around deinstitutionalisation.

In the next section we will explore current research and findings on de-institutionalisation.

A Summary of Research and Findings from the United States of America and Europe

The United States of America program and policy of deinstitutionalisation effected a change to the numbers of disabled people incarcerated in institutions from 1977 to 1998. For example large state run institutions decreased numbers of residents from 154,638 to 52,488. Institutions with 16 or less people with perceived intellectual or cognitive impairments decreased from 52,718 to 35,247 but institutions with 6 or less people increased from 20,400 to 202,266 over the same period (Prouty and Lakin 1999). Effectively while the larger institutions were closed those holding 6 or less individuals increased, however differences were made to the overall population with many living in the community with support.

In Europe research has been conducted which shows decreases in the numbers of disabled people institutionalised in large institutions of many established European countries. However, figures from different countries vary in availability and validity (Mansell et al 2007). For example there were clear problems in obtaining information and usable data from Greece, Cyprus, Malta and Austria at the time of the Mansell et al study. However, the study found that in most countries data was available on the types of institution and how they were funded. For example in 16 of 25 countries state funds were being used to support institutions of more than 100 places. In 21 of 25 countries state funds supported institutions of more than 30 places, and in 12 of 25 countries partial state funding was supporting institutions of 1–30 places, with the remainder provided by non-governmental organisations. Yet, as in the U.S., countries which decrease populations in large institutions often show an increase in the building of smaller group homes or supported homes.

In addition, newer European Union countries and ascending post-communist countries can continue to build larger institutions (Holland 2003, 2008, Vann and Siska 2006). The publicity around the often harsh conditions endured by women, men and children is welcome to provide advocacy for those individuals and raise publicity of human rights abuses, yet we should not be misled into thinking that this makes the situations of adults and children in institutions elsewhere acceptable. The next section begins to tackle the first argument against deinstitutionalisation by examining the financial cost differences of institutionalisation and community living.

FINANCIAL COST DIFFERENCES: INSTITUTIONALISATION VS. COMMUNITY LIVING

In the U.S. the average cost per person per annum for those housed in state institutions was $104,000 but for those living in the community it was $30,000 in the late nineteen nineties. The cost of living in the community for those with cognitive impairments was therefore on average 66% cheaper than the costs of their counterparts living in institutions (Pouty and Larkin 1999). Similar findings have been replicated elsewhere, for example an Australian study comparing costs per patient per day, showed that cost savings were made of between one half and one third when individuals were moved from long-stay institutions to the community (Lapsley et al 2000).

American studies clearly show the improvements in quality of life and self-determination, the lower cost of community living and that the economic contributions of disabled people are maximised once they begin to live independently in the community with the proper support. In many cases European studies confirm this view (Zarb 2003, JAG 2006, Evans and Hasler 1996), however some living costs can be higher in the community (Mansell et al 2007), this can be linked to the escalation of costs over-time rather than the comparative costs of institutionalisation and community living, but it also highlights the fact that the worst institutions will reduce their running costs to unacceptable levels.

That is, the cheapest institutions achieve the illusion of economic efficiency only through the severest violation of 'residents' human rights by bypassing basic needs such as adequate nutrition, clothing, heating, basic health needs and clean environments. Sitting on a chair all day or being tied to a bed in these conditions does indeed save money. In these situations community living will appear more costly, and in instances where countries and localities do not have a service infrastructure to provide adequate community support, cost differences on the budget sheet will be more pronounced. The human costs of maintaining what can be perceived as the 'cheap' options are limitless while the costs of maintaining institutions per se are incalculable in terms of dignity, human rights and individual choice.

Without fail all institutions, including those smaller institutions called 'group homes' or the inappropriately named 'community living homes' deny individual choice. They deny choice, independence, basic rights, dignity and privacy. For example the time to get up, go to bed, the time to eat (and what to eat) what to do with one's own money, as cash and government benefits can be withdrawn from individuals and siphoned into the institution, the option to go into the community, the likelihood of education, training, employment, developing skills, and the right to social relationships (Evans 2002). In addition, they increase the likelihood of abuse against residents.

QUALITY OF LIFE AND SKILLS: INSTITUTIONALIZATION VS. COMMUNITY LIVING

A large number of studies examining the effects on the skills of individuals moving from institutionalization to community living show improvements in quality of life and self esteem as well as improvements in communication, academic and social skills. Comparative studies have also found that physical health and life span increases when using a comparative grouping of those in institutions and those living in the community, with those living in the community securing health and longevity gains. Those in institutions suffer greater health costs in both physical and psychological health (Shaville et al 2005, Michelle et al 1990, Roberts et al 2005). Forester-Jones et al (2002) studied people who were institutionalised and assessed their views twelve years on when they had engaged in community living. The findings show positive aspects on several counts for individuals, for example: individuals noted immeasurable gains in terms of self determination and choice, independent living, sociability, employment, leisure and training. These represent economic gains for the community as they validate that those living in the community are able to contribute in a number of ways to the local economy.

These findings can be combined with longitudinal studies taken over a number of years (Kim et al 1999) which provide positive outcomes for individuals living in the community in terms of social contributions, economic contributions and health outcomes which represent a long-term cost saving on health system resources (see

Evans 2002 for a breakdown on the costing). Taken together, existing research provides strong evidence not only on the human rights and equality arguments for deinstitutionalisation, but also on the lowered long-term costs and better economic outcomes for individuals and their communities. These gains and the gains which promote independent living can be achieved in a number of ways with the most effective being personal assistance (PA) support.

Personal Assistance and Independent Living

Personal assistance is a system to enable independent living and it should be paid for by the state. It is a system which should take the place of the dated and abusive system of institutionalisation and be funded accordingly.

"Personal assistance" means that:

+ funding of services follows the person and not the service provider,
+ users are free to choose their preferred degree of personal control over service delivery according to their needs, capabilities, current life circumstances, preferences and aspirations.

Their range of options includes the right to custom-design their own services, which requires that the user decides who is to work, with which tasks, at which times, where and how.

Therefore, a policy for "personal assistance", among other solutions, enables the individual to contract the service of his or her choice from a variety of providers or to hire, train, schedule, supervise, and, if necessary, fire his or her assistants. Simply put, "personal assistance" means the user is customer or boss.

(Ratzka 2004: 2-4)

Moreover eligibility should be granted universally as an independent living need and not dependent on income or assets of the potential user or their family. Disabled women, men and children should fill out a self-assessment form in which they assess their needs and the time that particular tasks may take (with support if necessary), as they are the experts on their needs. The funds for their personal assistance must extend to any equipment or technical aids that will make independent living a reality, and they should be given support in handling the employment of their own chosen Personal assistants from those with experience of employing personal assistants.

The Swedish organisation of disabled people JAG conducted a three year study into these issues and found that personal assistance was cheaper than group homes or the smaller institutions. This was true of all types of impairment including those perceived as 'high need'.

Personal assistance goes beyond community living it is a process where an individual chooses and employs a personal assistant to provide support so that they can live independently, thus generating employment for others, contributing to the national income through payment of national taxes and giving the option for the individual themselves to be employed. Those with perceived higher support needs can effectively become contributors to society through the employment of a team of P. A.s, instead of a perceived drain on resources while imprisoned in institutions. One of the key issues in the deinstitutionalisation argument is that Personal Assistance schemes are available to all throughout Europe (ENIL 2007). It is only through personal assistance that financial and humanity gains are maximised for the individual, the community and the economy.

There is therefore an overwhelming amount of evidence that community living and personal assistance represent the best options to achieve independent living, gains in financial costs and in human rights, equality and independence. However this is not about institutionalising disabled people and children in smaller 'group homes' or community homes, and saying they are living in the community—it is about support from the community for personal assistance schemes and full control, independence and dignity.

TABLE 1. IMPACTS OF INSTITUTIONALISATION, COMMUNITY LIVING AND PERSONAL ASSISTANCE

Impacts on disabled people and localities of institutionalisation, community living and Personal Assistance

Institutionalisation		Community Living		Community Living and Personal Assistance	
Cost	–	Cost	+	Cost	++
Independent Living	–	Independent Living	+	Independent Living	++
Human Rights	–	Human Rights	+	Human Rights	++
Autonomy	–	Autonomy	+	Autonomy	++
Equality	–	Equality	+	Equality	++
Inclusion	–	Inclusion	+	Inclusion	++
Contributions	–	Contributions	+	Contributions	++
				Generation of employment	++
				Economic contribution	++

Key: – negative, + positive, ++ extremely positive with enhanced economic contributions to the locality

CONCLUSIONS: INSTITUTIONALISATION, COMMUNITY LIVING AND PERSONAL ASSISTANCE

Through the media we have consistently witnessed how many disabled adults, older people and children in large institutions have been exposed to human rights abuses both in the established states and the newly emerging European states (Vann and Siska 2006,

Holland 2003, ECCL) and how some within the institutions attempt to silence those that have been subject to such abuses (Malacrida 2006). Research on community living shows many gains for the individual and for the community, whilst research on Personal assistance schemes shows additional gains for the individual and the locality.

Clearly, institutionalisation in large or small settings is often more costly in financial and quality of life terms for localities and for disabled people. Institutionalisation contravenes article 19 of the UN Convention on the rights of people with disabilities and the European Action Plan whether that institution holds 600 people or 6.

Community Living and Personal Assistance systems promote independence, better health outcomes and allow disabled people freedom of choice and greater equality, as well as allowing them to contribute to the local and national economies as active and valued citizens.

Where systems have been slow or negligent in developing PA options, laws and full human rights for disabled people this has been caused by the failure of the deinstitutionalisation process, and a failure in setting up adequate alternatives and supports rather than the failure of community living and independent living options per se (Hudson 1991).

The key issues often raised by politicians and others on cost and the inability of those with perceived higher support needs to obtain independent living outside of institutional settings have been severely undermined by academic research and by the actions and existing schemes undertaken by disabled people to make independent living a reality.

Will the process require a change in local systems? Yes it will. It will require monies currently used for institutionalisation to be transferred to support community living and personal assistance schemes, it will require formal laws where they do not already exist on the right to personal assistance for all disabled people in Europe; it will require mobilisation of the independent living community to launch extensive peer support programs and training schemes for disabled people

The idea that it 'will take time' is a cliché. The process will be speeded by listening to disabled experts on inclusion and independent living policies many of whom have organised and developed schemes of Personal assistance and by allowing them to advise and help develop schemes in those areas that lack the knowledge or will to appreciate the human rights of disabled people. Clearly, time must be taken to ensure that such schemes are effective and efficient but not as an excuse to delay the process or avoid beginning the planning process for deinstitutionalisation, personal assistance and independent living not for satisfying article 19 of the UN Convention on the rights of people with disabilities.

RECOMMENDATIONS FOR EFFECTIVE IMPLEMENTATION OF INDEPENDENT LIVING IN ALL MEMBER STATES

Base line data for all EU member states on number of institutions and size of institutions needs to be compiled to monitor change and identify actions on achieving the goals of independent living.

Monies paid by governments to run institutions needs to be effectively monitored to ensure ring fenced budgets are transferred to the aims of independent living and the development of personal assistance schemes, and training of personal assistants programs run and controlled by disabled people.

States that do not have a Personal assistance law need a target date to develop one in consultation with national or European organisations of Independent Living which are run and controlled by disabled people.

Training in the social model and training for personal assistants needs to be developed along with support mechanisms for those that wish to use personal assistance.

Independent Living organisations run and controlled by disabled people and their members should be consulted at local, national and European level, as they are the experts on disability.

It is only with well resourced Personal assistance systems for all types of impairments that the criteria of UN Convention and European Action Plan on independent living can be achieved by member states.

Disabled people have a role to play in monitoring their governments and asking them what they are doing to achieve independent living.

Continuous excuses are unacceptable because the solutions are available, the blueprints are there and the expertise is there to make community living and personal assistance for all disabled people in Europe possible.

REFERENCES

Barnes, C., Mercer, G. and Shakespeare, T. (1999) Exploring Disability: a sociological introduction, Polity Press, Cambridge.

Council of Europe Action Plan to Promote the Rights and Full Participation of People with Disabilities in Society: improving the quality of life of people with disabilities in Europe 2006–2015 (adopted April 2006) http://www.coe.int/t/e/social_cohesion/soc-sp/Rec_2006_5%20Disability%20Action%20Plan.pdf accessed 14th Jan 2009.

Evans, J. (2002) How Disabled People are Excluded from Independent Living, Presentation to European Disabled People Conference, Madrid.

Evans, J. and Halser, F. (1996) Direct Payments Campaign in the UK Presentation to ENIL seminar, Stockholm. Available at http://www.independentliving.org/docs2/enildirectpayment.html accessed Jan 14th 2009.

Forester-Jones, R., Carpenter, J., Cambridge, P., Tate, A., Hallam, A., Knapp, M. and Beecham, J. (2002) The Quality of Life of People Twelve Years after resettlement from Long-stay Hospitals users' views on their living environment, daily activities and future aspirations, Disability and Society Journal 17, 7, 741–758.

Holland, D. (2003) Grass roots promotion of community health and human rights for people with disabilities in post communist Central Europe: a profile of the Slovak republic, Disability and Society Journal 18, 2, 133–143.

Holland, D. (2008) The Current status of Disability Activism and non-governmental organisations in post-communist Europe: Preliminary Findings based on reports in the field, Disability and Society Journal, 23, 6, 543–555.

Hudson, B. (1991) Deinstitutionalisation: What went wrong? Disability and Society Journal 6, 1, 21–28.

Hurst, R. (1995) Choice and Empowerment, Disability and Society Journal, 10, 4, 529–534.

JAG (2006) The Price of freedom of choice, self determination and integrity cost analysis of different forms of support and service to people with extensive functional impairments, available at http://www.jag.se/eng/eng_index.html accessed Dec 30th 2008.

JAG A Life in Freedom (undated) available at http://www.jag.se/eng/eng_index.html accessed Dec 30th 2008.

Kim, S., Larson, S.A. and Lakin, K.C. (1999) Behavioural outcomes of deinstitutionalisation for people with intellectual disabilities: a review of studies conducted between 1980 and 1999, Policy research brief University of Minnesota: Minneapolis, Institute on Community Integration 10, 1.

Lapsley, H.M., Tribe, K., Tennant, C., Rosen, A., Hobbs, C. and Newham, L. (2000) Deinstitutionalisation for Long-Term Illness; cost differences in hospital and Community Care Australian and New Zealand Journal of Psychiatry 34, 3, 491–495.

Malacrida, C. (2006) Contested Memories: efforts of the powerful to silence former inmates' histories of a life in an institution for 'mental defectives', Disability and Society Journal, 21, 5, 397–410.

Mansell, J., Knapp, M., Beadle-Brown, J. and Beecham, J. (2007) Deinstitutionalisation and community living—outcomes and costs: report of a European Study. Volume 2 main report, Canterbury: Tizzard Centre, University of Kent.

Michell, D., Braddock, D. and Hemp, R. (1990) Synthesis of research on costs of institutionalisation and community based care; cost studies in long-term care reviewed, Mental Health Administration 17, 2, 171–83.

Prouty, R. and Larkin, K.C. (1999) Residential services for people with developmental disabilities: status and trends through 1998, Minneapolis, University of Minneapolis, Research and Training Centre on Community Living, Institute on Community Integration.

Ratzka, A. (ed) (2004) Model National Assistance Policy available at http://www.independentliving.org/docs6/ratzka200410a.html accessed 13th Jan 2009.

Roberts, E., Cummings, J. and Nelson K. (2005) A review of economic evaluation of community mental health care, Medical Care research and review 62, 5, 503–43.

Shavelle, R., Strauss, D. and Day, S. (2005) Deinstitutionalisation in California; mortality of persons with developmental disabilities after transfer into community care, 1997–1999. Journal of Data Science 3, 371–380.

Stratton R.J., Thompson R.L., Margetts B.M., Stroud M., Jackson A.A. and Elia M. (2002) Healthcare utilisation according to malnutrition risk in the elderly: an analysis of data from the National Diet and Nutrition Survey of people aged 65 and over. Proceedings of the Nutrition Society: 20A.

Vann, B. H. and Siska, J. (2006) From Cage Beds' to inclusion: the long road for individuals with intellectual disability in the Czech republic, Disability and Society Journal 21, 5, 425–439.

Zarb, G. (2003) The Economics of Independent Living available at http://www.independentliving.org/docs6/zarb2003.html#footnotes accessed 11th Jan 2009.

For further issues on deinstitutionalisation see European Coalition for Community Living http://www.community-living.info/index.php?page=214 Especially http://www.community-living.info/index.php?page=286.

See also European Network on Independent Living http://www.enil.eu/enil/index.php?option=com_content&task=view&id=111.

I would like to acknowledge the helpful comments and contributions of Ines Bulic and Kapka Panayotova on an earlier draft of this paper

---

*European Network on Independent Living** is a forum for individuals and organizations promoting independent living for the disabled and the general population.

European Network on Independent Living. *ENIL Research Paper on Community Living and the Support of Independent Living for the Disabled Women, Men and Children of Europe.* N.p.: European Network on Independent Living, 2009.

The State of Housing in America in the 21st Century: A Disability Perspective

By the National Council on Disability*

Executive Summary

While great strides have been made by the National Council on Disability (NCD) and others to advance the notion of livable communities for all, there are still gaps in the knowledge about what exactly is needed to transform our communities. Affordable, accessible, and appropriate housing is a critical and integral part of making any community more livable for people with disabilities. This report looks at the state of housing for people with disabilities with the intent to provide recommendations that can improve housing opportunities. The research contained in this report provides a comprehensive overview of the state of housing in the 21st century and answers to seven important questions about the current housing needs and options for people with disabilities living in the United States.

1. What are the types and extent of housing needs of people with disabilities and what is currently available to meet those needs?

+ **Total Households:** Currently, about 35.1 million households have one or more people with a disability—nearly one-third of all U.S. households in 2007. In addition, about 1.6 million people live in nursing homes and another half million in group homes.

- **Affordability:** The greatest need is the ability to afford housing. On average, the income level of people with disabilities is lower than that of people without disabilities. As a result, an estimated 14.4 million households with at least one person with a disability cannot afford their housing—this is 41 percent of all households with disabilities.
- **Worst-Case Need:** A recent report, *The Hidden Housing Crisis: Worst Case Housing Needs Among Adults with Disabilities*, estimates that about 2.4 million households with nonelderly people with disabilities, including 1 million families with children, have worst-case housing needs—nearly 40 percent of all worst-case housing needs in the United States. In addition, another 1.3 million "elderly households" (age 62 years or older) have worst-case housing needs, with many likely also to have a disability. Most are very low income and paying more than half their monthly income for rent.
- **Homelessness:** A recent government report estimated that at least 43 percent of the homeless adults that stayed in a shelter—about 421,000 people—had a self-reported disability. This does not include homeless children with disabilities in shelters or the estimated 282,000 people homeless each night who are living on the streets, in abandoned buildings, or elsewhere not intended for human habitation. While estimates vary, a large portion of this total is likely to include veterans.
- **Physical Accessibility:** National housing survey data indicates that hundreds of thousands of people with disabilities need some form of modification to make their homes accessible. The majority need grab bars and ramps, which cost relatively little to greatly improve people's lives.
- **Environmental Sensitivities:** About 11 percent of the U.S. population has some level of chemical sensitivity (CS) that is likely to require housing that is free of disabling environmental triggers. Unless housing is universally designed to accommodate

different sensitivities, it is better for some with CS to live in segregated housing that ensures control over potential exposures.

+ **Mental Health Issues:** More than 300,000 people with psychiatric disabilities currently living in segregated housing could benefit from more integrated and least restrictive housing options.

+ **Public Housing:** While Section 504 of the 1973 Rehabilitation Act requires a portion of public housing units to be accessible—5 percent for mobility impairments and 2 percent for hearing and visual disabilities—but we do not know if this is the case. If all public housing developments were compliant to this minimum, then about 68,000 could be accessible. There are potentially another 46,000 accessible units in rural multifamily developments if all were compliant. However, many of these units are likely to be in age-restricted developments (62 years and older), and therefore not available to all people with disabilities, even if accessible.

+ **Private Sector Housing:** Similar patterns are found in federally subsidized housing operated by private sector nonprofit and for-profit groups. While about 156,000 units of the U.S. Department of Housing and Urban Development (HUD) multifamily housing portfolio (11% of total) are accessible, less than half (73,000 units) are designated for people with disabilities. While there are about 195,000 "year-round beds" in permanent supportive housing, which often targets people with disabilities, these can benefit only people who are homeless first. Furthermore, many of these programs link housing with services, which can restrict choice and independence.

2. What are the profiles of users for housing program supports and what is the quality of life of people relying on housing-related programs and supports?

Most people with disabilities in federally subsidized housing programs are without children and living alone. While there also may be children with disabilities, these families are not considered "disabled," so they are not included in the numbers above.

A key concern is that need far exceeds the supply of accessible units. In 2008, about 211,000 nonelderly and 135,000 elderly (62 years and older) public housing households were identified as having disabilities. We know nothing about the type of disability or if the housing is appropriate for their needs. Similarly, we do not know how many of the households with disabilities using Housing Choice Vouchers—544,561 nonelderly families with disabilities and 374,265 elderly families—live in appropriate accessible units, or if they are integrated into the community.

Relatively little is known about the quality of life of people living in federal housing other than statistics that generally show public housing residents tend to have poorer health (mental and physical) than the general population and experience higher-than-average rates of crime and violence. Still, research shows that not all public or federally subsidized housing is dangerous, though it is likely to be poor quality due to poor construction and deferred maintenance, which has led to the demolition of nearly 150,000 units in the past 10 years.

Finally, while the Section 811 program has produced about 27,000 housing units specifically for people with disabilities, most are segregated. Recent changes in the program, coupled with innovative strategies, such as buying condominiums in market-rate developments for people with disabilities, are encouraging. Still more is needed in terms of legislation, education, and capacity to scale up these ideas.

3. What is the geographic dispersion of housing and related programs and expenditures?

The federal resources needed for affordable accessible housing are not sufficient to meet the needs in most, if not all, communities. Most entitlement funding is based on formulas designed to reflect need on a per capita basis rather than relative need.

The States with the largest estimated number of noninstitutionalized people with disabilities are California (4,279,000 people), Texas (3,050,000), Florida (2,610,000), New York (2,533,000), and Pennsylvania (1,865,000). These same States have the largest number of renters with mobility impairments and housing problems in the United States, and also the largest share of HOME and Community Development Block Grant dollars annually. In comparison, Puerto Rico has the highest disability prevalence rate at 27 percent of its population (963,000 people), followed by West Virginia (24%), Kentucky (21%), Arkansas (21%), and Mississippi (21%).

Funding for subsidized housing units for people with disabilities—both public housing and multifamily housing—is not subject to formula but instead comes from direct grants and loans from the Federal Government. Looking across the States, we find the following:

+ New York—and particularly New York City—has long had the largest share of public housing (205,000 units) in the United States, with four times the number of units than in Pennsylvania (52,000), which is the next largest supplier. Furthermore, New York has the most public housing for people with disabilities, elderly people (ages 62 and older), and families, and the largest supply of federally funded multifamily housing (108,000 units), though only second and third, respectively, for units designated for people with disabilities and designated units for the elderly. The State ranks lower for Housing Choice Vouchers.

- California, while home to nearly twice as many people with disabilities as New York, has relatively little public housing (less than 40,000 units). Instead, the State has the largest number of Housing Choice Vouchers (290,000), with 78,000 being used by people with disabilities, 28,000 by elderly households, and 55,000 by households that are both elderly and with disabilities. California also has the largest number of federally subsidized multifamily housing units designated for elderly (39,000) and for people with disabilities (5,000).
- States that rank consistently in the top 10 across all categories of housing based on the number of units developed include Illinois, Ohio, Pennsylvania, and Texas.
- States ranking consistently in the bottom 10 across all categories of housing, based on the number of units, are Alaska, Idaho, Montana, North Dakota, South Dakota, and Wyoming, along with the District of Columbia.

4. What barriers and gaps prevent people with disabilities from attaining accessible and affordable housing?

Creating and sustaining safe, accessible, affordable, and integrated housing continues to involve challenging and complex barriers that arise from the interaction of poverty, inaccessibility, funding rules related to acquiring supportive services, and a disability policy system rooted in the outmoded model of segregating people with disabilities from the community mainstream.

Affordability is a key challenge. For prospective buyers this includes securing financing, which is even more daunting with tighter rules guiding both conventional lending and affordable homebuyer programs. The single greatest barrier to rental housing in the private market may be the combination of too little subsidized housing and inadequate funding for Housing Choice Vouchers to close the gap between very low incomes and rental costs. Even if affordable, most market-rate housing lacks basic accessibility features. Some private building industry groups oppose additional mandatory accessibility requirements for new home construction, and bureaucratic complexities tied to funding supportive services add additional challenges and layers of difficulty.

A key challenge to putting housing and community services together is the difference between systems and funding mechanisms, their differing groundings and philosophies, and the complexity of housing and community living choice at the legislative and policy levels. States face several challenges when trying to create "real choice" in accessing affordable, accessible, and integrated housing. This includes differences in:

- Definitions related to housing and community living/integration, which make it hard to show need, coordinate services, and compare across States.
- Qualification and eligibility criteria, which are set by funding sources that often use different thresholds to determine initial and continuing eligibility (e.g., HUD uses median income in relation to national poverty and income thresholds, while Medicaid uses income/asset thresholds determined by individual State statute).
- System funding levels and disparities related to funding of housing and community living supports, as well as disparities between different disability and aging constituencies in accessing this funding.
- Information access, quality, and coordination, especially for people with disabilities who may be trying to access information during times of housing or health crises or emergencies, or from within settings where information access is difficult, unavailable, or withheld.
- Coordinated, consumer-directed system delivery, especially across housing and community services, but even within each.
- Monitoring and enforcement across systems.

5. What means are available to people with disabilities to enhance their capacity to choose and sustain accessible and affordable housing?

Potential best practices and models that respond to current barriers almost always involve public policy that supports (or can be interpreted to support) a particular solution, multiple public and private funding sources, local ingenuity and community commitment, and, in some situations, the courts. We do see "promising practices" that have been or are being implemented by and within States in the areas of systems change, information access, legislation, monitoring and enforcement, and research related to housing and community living. These include:

Systems Change and Coordination

One of the most promising trends has been the increasing cross-co-ordination of housing with community living and support systems, funding, and service delivery. Referred to as Single Access Points, One Stop Shop, No Wrong Door, and Comprehensive Entry Point, these systems enable consumers to enter through many different "doors" in order to receive coordinated housing and community living supports and services. Many of these initiatives, which often require new policies to enable coordinated service delivery, are based on a Money Follows the Person (MFP) framework to offer cross-system, consumer-directed choice.

Cross-System Navigation

Several of these systems change initiatives have formally incorporated coordination with regional Aging and Disability Resource Centers, Area Agencies on Aging, and Centers for Independent Living (CILs) to provide information, case management, peer mentoring, legal assistance, and connection to related community living, transportation, social participation, and employment opportunities. Several States are using CILs and peer mentors to support consumers in navigating complex housing and community living systems and programs. Coordination also involves continuous education of staff across systems and delivery programs.

PROMOTING INTEGRATED AND LEAST RESTRICTIVE CHOICE

Several States have targeted initiatives to create and expand integrated housing choices. For example, Washington is using federal demonstration grant funding to collaborate with local housing authorities throughout the State to develop more integrated and less restrictive (four or fewer beds/units) community living choice models. Oregon continues to expand community housing in small neighborhood homes, and is also developing individual apartment housing in which consumers can share support services with other consumers with developmental disabilities. Virginia is working to revise legislation and policies to enable people with developmental disabilities to share an apartment or single-family home with supports.

INCREASING INFORMATION ACCESS WITH HOUSING LOCATOR SYSTEMS

A number of States have developed housing locator systems that allow online searches of affordable housing units. These systems range from minimal databases of State-financed developments to more sophisticated Web sites with multiple search options, detailed accessibility information, updated vacancy and occupancy status, and links to local service agencies and resources. Some States, such as Louisiana, have incorporated housing locators into housing developer contracts to make it easier for individuals to identify available housing options and to improve marketing of affordable and accessible units to consumers.

As a result of disability advocacy, some States have enacted legislation to rebalance Medicaid monies toward community-based options. For example, Texas Rider 37 enables the Texas Department of Human Services to allow money to follow the person from a nursing facility to the community, enabling the transfer of funds from nursing home appropriations. As of 2007, an estimated 13,300 people transitioned from nursing homes to the community via this initiative. Passed in 1996, Vermont Act 160 allows funds appropriated for nursing home care to be used for extensive home- and community-based services, and created a statewide system of Long-Term Care Community Coalitions to action plan methods to improve the infrastructure for Medicaid waiver and the long-term services and supports programs.

6. What practices exist that improve the housing status of people with disabilities?

In addition to the promising practices above, specific examples of effective housing solutions exist; however, they generally are not yet sufficiently scaled to meet the need. At a minimum, long-range solutions must include comprehensive changes in public policy. Such changes include substantially increasing funding for housing vouchers, creation of incentives for inclusion of housing units for very low income people with disabilities in all federal and State programs that support housing development and construction, and adoption of accessibility standards and universal design principles for all home construction by States, counties, and cities, as well as by the building and housing construction industry.

Although serious problems remain, some notable successes suggest that momentum is building for broader reforms. For example, the movement for housing to be constructed according either to universal design or visitability principles appears to be gaining currency. Designers, architects, and homebuyers are growing increasingly interested in these principles. Thirty-seven cities across the nation have adopted either mandatory or voluntary policies that are beginning to generate results: because of such policies, roughly 30,000 homes have been constructed with some level of accessibility. These advances are serving as models for other locales, demonstrating that accessibility and visitability can be achieved without undue cost or administrative burden.

For-profit and nonprofit developers are creating exemplary models of scattered, affordable, accessible mixed-income and mixed-use housing that set the bar for what can be accomplished. Other housing models are evolving that hold promise for people with disabilities, including Naturally Occurring Retirement Communities (NORCs) and Limited-Equity Cooperatives (LECs). Supportive living programs ensure that people with disabilities receive the help they want and need to live as independently as possible in their own homes. The evolution of these programs nationwide has helped significantly reduce the number of people who are forced to live in restrictive institutions. Much remains to be done, but these and other areas of progress reveal that an important shift is taking place that eventually will lead to an increase in and improvement of housing and supportive services options for people with disabilities.

7. What lessons have been learned from national emergencies, such as Hurricane Katrina, regarding the provision of accessible and affordable housing in the wake of national disasters and emergencies?

1. **Hurricane Katrina revealed stark gaps in emergency housing for people with disabilities.** Progress toward closing these gaps has come from community and organizational initiatives and post-Katrina legislation that have led to the creation of guidance and planning materials. To this end, several promising and best practices are emerging that follow three principles:

2. **Forethought and planning for disabilities and special needs should serve as the main strategy.** This begins by taking a

functional approach to special needs, which centers on communication, medical needs, independence, supervision, and transportation (C-MIST model). This approach is now supported through various guidance and planning materials, including the U.S. Department of Justice *Guidance for Emergency Shelters: ADA Best Practices Toolkit for State and Local Governments*, and the Federal Emergency Management Agency (FEMA) *Comprehensive Planning Guide*.

3. **Include and actively involve people with disabilities, disability organizations, and advocates to help planners and those involved in all aspects of emergency housing identify problems and address solutions.** In January 2009, FEMA approved a National Disaster Housing Strategy, which includes sections specifically on building partnerships to assist in the evaluation and identification of special needs. At a formal level, FEMA's National Advisory Council has recommended the creation of Regional Disability Coordinator positions for each of the 10 FEMA regional offices to serve as liaisons between State and federal levels and to increase personnel available to coordinate and support outreach to victims with special needs.

4. **Ensure sufficient resources to support initiatives, including relocation and rebuilding.** Internet-based search tools provide a resource for both individuals and case managers to search for suitable emergency housing. Also, HUD has developed programs to help people relocate relatively easily to other communities while maintaining their housing assistance. For homeowners, the Mortgage and Rental Assistance Act of 2007 can help low- and moderate-income families keep their homes after a disaster. An example for rebuilding, Louisiana plans to create 3,000 new supportive housing units for people with disabilities using multiple sources of funding.

*National Council on Disability is an independent U.S. federal agency that promotes policies and programs, that guarantee equal opportunity for all individuals with disabilities, with the ultimate goal of enabling them to lead independent lives.

National Council on Disability. *The State of Housing in America in the 21st Century: A Disability Perspective*. Washington, DC: National Council on Disability, January 10, 2010, 9–19. http://www.ncd.gov/newsroom/publications/2010/NCD_Housing_Report508.pdf.

Discussion Questions

1. Independent living services support people to live as full citizens rather than expecting people to fit into standardized models and structures. What are the pros and cons of supporting people's decision making to achieve the best balance between their wishes and society's responsibility for their care?

2. Developing appropriate services in the community is a necessary but not a sufficient condition for better results. How does one ensure that institutional care practices are not inadvertently transplanted or recreated in the new services?

3. Build a strong economic case for making the transition from institutions to services in the community, keeping in mind the complex links between costs, needs, and outcomes.

4. Identify the merits of improvements in quality of life and self-esteem in community-living options for individuals with disabilities.

CHAPTER 9:

Accessing Employment

This chapter discusses the effects of employment among people with disabilities, a U.S. Supreme Court case concerning employment and the Americans with Disabilities Act (ADA), and the provision of personal assistance to individuals with disabilities in the workplace. These articles highlight successes and challenges in implementing the provisions of work and employment under the Convention on the Rights of People with Disabilities (CRPD).

The CRPD requires states to recognize the right of persons with disability to work in freely chosen or accepted employment in a labor market and work environment that are open, accessible, and inclusive; and requires states to safeguard and promote realization of this right by measures such as prohibiting discrimination on the ground of disability in all aspects of employment; ensuring access to general technical and vocational education; providing assistance with job searches, career development, and business development; and employing persons with disability in the public sector.

The first article, "The Difference a Job Makes: The Effects of Employment among People with Disabilities" by Lisa Schur, affirms the historic low employment rates for people with disability, which result in social exclusion and discrimination. The ADA has enabled more people with disabilities to be gainfully employed, thus contributing economically, politically and socially to their communities and countries.

The second article, "Overview—Supreme Court Ruling in *Alabama v. Garrett*," from the National Association of Protection and Advocacy Systems, reports that the Court ruled that state workers cannot sue state governments for monetary damages for on-the-job discrimination under Title I of the Americans with Disabilities Act. The Court's decision will affect not only the legal scope of the ADA, but also the balance of power between the federal government and the states.

The third article, "The Applicability of the ADA to Personal Assistance Services in the Workplace" by Robert Silverstein, suggests that personal assistance services provide a reasonable accommodation to enable an employee with a disability to perform the functions of a job. Personal assistance services may include reading handwritten mail to an employee with a visual impairment or ensuring a sign language interpreter is available during staff meetings to accommodate an employee with a hearing impairment. The provision of personal assistance services can help individuals with disabilities and specifically those individuals with significant disability maintain current levels of functioning, more fully participate in society—including employment—and prevent institutionalization.

The Difference a Job Makes: The Effects of Employment among People with Disabilities

By Lisa Schur*

How does employment affect the lives of people with disabilities? While employment can have a variety of benefits for all individuals, it may play an especially positive role for members of minority groups who have been socially marginalized and often denied access to jobs. People with disabilities have especially low employment rates, partly reflecting a history of social exclusion and discrimination (US Commission on Civil Rights 1983; Yuker 1988). In the past two decades there have been significant efforts to improve employment opportunities for people with disabilities, shown most clearly by the growth of the disability rights movement and the passage of the Americans with Disabilities Act (ADA) in 1990. Employment of people with disabilities has been promoted not only for its economic benefits but also because it can improve their skill levels and integrate them more fully into mainstream society.

Using the Survey of Income and Program Participation and two recent national household surveys, this paper provides new evidence on the effects of employment for people with and without disabilities. Comparisons are made not only on economic measures but also on a variety of social, psychological, and political measures in order to gain a more complete picture of the particular value that employment can have for people with disabilities and of the importance of policies to increase their job opportunities.

LITERATURE REVIEW

Disability has been consistently linked to labor market difficulties in many studies. About 8 percent of working-age Americans report having a "work disability" (a health condition that limits the kind or amount of work they can do), of whom only one-third are employed in the course of a year (Burkhauser et al. 2001). Using a broader definition based on activity limitations and functional impairments (more closely reflecting the ADA's definition), 17 percent of working-age people have a disability, of whom about half (49 percent) are employed in a given month compared to over four-fifths (84 percent) of working-age people without disabilities (McNeil 2000). The figure is much lower among those with severe disabilities, of whom only one-fourth (24 percent) are employed in a given month. Among those who are employed, a variety of studies have estimated that people with disabilities earn 10–25 percent less on average than otherwise-comparable people without disabilities (summarized in Baldwin 1997, 43). Negative effects of disability on employment and earnings have been found in both cross-sectional and longitudinal comparisons before and after disability onset (Burkhauser and Daly 1996). The low employment rates contribute to lower levels of household income and higher rates of poverty among people with disabilities (Kruse 1998).

While a portion of the employment and earnings gaps is probably due to lower productivity associated with many disabilities, prejudice and discrimination may also play a role, as suggested by the finding that wage gaps are higher for people who have disabilities that elicit the most negative social attitudes (Baldwin 1997). In addition, the work disincentives provided by government disability income programs also appear to contribute to the low employment rates of people with disabilities (Bound and Waidmann 2000).

Along with the employment gaps, people with disabilities have lower education levels (Kruse 1998) and experience greater social isolation. They are less likely to be married, more likely to live alone, and less likely to socialize with friends outside the home or to be involved in religious, recreational, or other groups or activities (Louis Harris and Associates 2000). They are also less likely to vote and take part in other political activities (Schur et al. 2002). Many people with disabilities experience transportation difficulties, which contribute to their isolation (Louis Harris and Associates 2000). The lower resource levels and greater isolation contribute to lower life satisfaction levels reported by people with disabilities (Louis Harris and Associates 2000).

Employment may not only reduce the income gaps between people with and without disabilities but also reduce the gaps in social and psychological measures. Most jobs involve interactions with co-workers or members of the public, which can help decrease social isolation and build social capital (Putnam 2000). Employment often increases civic skills and exposure to political recruitment and has other resource and psychological effects that can increase the likelihood of political participation (Schlozman et al. 1999). Finally, employment may increase life satisfaction through increased resources, decreased isolation, and a greater sense that one is filling a valuable social role. While the social and psychological benefits of employment are often proclaimed, there has been very little study of the existence and extent of those benefits and of whether employment plays a more important role among members of marginalized groups such as people with disabilities.

Data and Methods
This paper makes use of two datasets. The first is the 1999 disability supplement of the Survey of Income and Program Participation (SIPP), which is used for employment, earnings, income, and poverty comparisons between individuals with and without disabilities. The disability definition is based on a series of questions that identify a variety of impairments and activity limitations (McNeil

2000). The second data source comes from two national household surveys conducted following the November elections in 1998 and 2000. The surveys, conducted by the Rutgers Center for Public Interest Polling, included a variety of questions on employment, political participation, civic skills, political efficacy, group activities, life satisfaction, and disability discrimination. The final samples included 1,242 US citizens of voting age in 1998 and 1,002 in 2000. To ensure a sufficient sample for analysis of disability issues, the samples were stratified to oversample people with disabilities, resulting in an overall final sample of 1,132 citizens with disabilities and 1,112 citizens without disabilities. The disability screening questions were based on the six disability questions used in the 2000 US Census, plus two questions from the Harris disability survey. Where more than one person in a household was identified as having a disability, the interviewer asked to speak to the person with the most recent birthday. (All survey questions are available on request.) The figures in this paper are based on those of working age (18–64), comprising 668 citizens with disabilities and 924 citizens without disabilities.

To explore the effects of employment, this paper first presents comparisons of employment variables between people with and without disabilities (table 1) and then compares economic, social, psychological, and political outcomes between employed and non-employed people separately for the disability and non-disability samples (table 2). A comparison of simple gaps in outcomes may be a biased estimate of the effects of disability or employment due to omitted variables—for example, the lower employment and earnings levels of people with disabilities are partly explained by their lower levels of education. To control for important omitted variables, regressions were run estimating the disability gap in employment variables (in table 1) and the employment gap in economic, social, psychological, and political variables (in table 2). In addition to controlling for education and other demographic variables, the regressions control for types and severity of disability, since (as will be seen) these are highly related to employment. Rather than including full regression results, the tables present just the coefficient showing the estimated disability or employment effects. The resulting figures provide a guide to the likely effects of disability and employment, although it must be recognized that selection effects or other unobserved variables may also help to account for the observed relationships.

RESULTS

Consistent with other studies, both the SIPP data and the 1998/2000 Rutgers surveys show that employment rates are especially low among people with disabilities. As shown in table 1, significantly less than half of the working age people with disabilities are employed in the United States (46.3 percent were employed in the last month according to SIPP and 45.5 percent in the last week according to the Rutgers surveys), compared with more than 80 percent of the working age people without disabilities (82.2 percent in the last month and 81.9 percent in the last week). These gaps are reduced but remain very large and strongly significant when controlling for demographic and disability characteristics (column 3). Among those who are employed, workers with disabilities are more likely to work part time, and both their hourly and annual earnings are significantly lower than those of their non-disabled counterparts. The remaining earnings gaps may reflect a combination of lower productivity associated with many impairments, and employer discrimination against people with disabilities (Baldwin 1997).

The 2000 survey also asked employed respondents whether they had performed several skill-enhancing tasks at work in the past six months. As shown in table 1, employed people with disabilities were significantly less likely than those without disabilities to have given a presentation or speech at work and less likely (although not significantly so) to have participated in decision making, planned or chaired a meeting, or written a letter. These results combined with the lower earnings of people with disabilities indicate that simply having a job does not eliminate some of the economic and skill gaps they face.

Do employment rates vary according to the type or severity of disability? People with more severe disabilities are more likely to have health problems that limit the time and energy they can devote to work and are less likely to drive a car, which can make commuting to work more difficult. The data in table 1 show that employment is most common among those with sensory impairments (which includes visual or hearing impairments) or "other type" of impairments (which includes such conditions as high blood pressure and cancer). It is lowest among those with mobility and mental impairments, particularly among those with the most severe impairments—those who have difficulty going outside alone or performing activities inside the home, and those who need help with daily activities. Given that people with more severe activity limitations are less likely to be employed, it is important to account for differences in type and severity of disability when estimating the potential effects of employment on other outcomes.

How does employment affect economic, social, psychological, and political outcomes? Consistent with the idea that employment may have stronger effects among members of marginalized groups, employment seems to have a stronger effect on several outcomes among people with disabilities. Even though people with disabilities have lower earnings on average, employment is estimated to raise their household income levels by 49 percent compared to only 13 percent among people without disabilities (table 2, columns 3 and 6). This reflects greater access to other sources of income (such as from a spouse) among non-disabled people who are not working outside the home. Perhaps more importantly, employment has a slightly larger effect on the probability of escaping poverty

TABLE 1. EMPLOYMENT AND DISABILITY

	With Disability (1)	Without Disability (2)	Disability gap with controls^ (3)
Data from 1999 SIPP survey			
Employed last month	46.3%	82.2%	-21.3%***
If employed:			
Part-time schedule	23.6%	14.3%	6.5%***
Annual earnings	$25,504	$33,088	-17.9%***
Hourly earnings	$14.68	$16.38	-10.2%***
Data from 1998/2000 Rutgers surveys			
Employed last week	45.5%	81.9%	-36.4%**
If employed, work part-time schedule	26.7%	14.6%	12.2%**
If employed, have done following in job in last 6 mos.:			
Participated in decision-making	60.6%	71.4%	-10.9%
Planned or chaired a meeting	32.6%	40.7%	-9.2%
Given presentation or speech	35.1%	46.7%	-15.4%*
Written letter	46.1%	57.1%	-13.1%
Employment rates among those with:			
Sensory impairment	41.1%		
Mobility impairment	36.3%		
Mental impairment	33.6%		
Other type of impairment	66.0%		
Difficulty going outside alone	18.5%		
Difficulty with activities inside home	23.8%		
Need help with daily activities	24.3%		
Sample sizes			
1999 SIPP survey	7309	36713	
1998/2000 Rutgers surveys	668	924	

*Significant difference at $p < .10$.

**$p < .05$.

***$p < .01$ All data limited to working-age (18–64).

^From disability coefficients in regressions that control for gender, age, age-squared, race, marital status, education, and the impairments and activity limitations listed above (excluding "other type of impairment"). To estimate percentage differentials, the logarithm of income was used as a dependent variable for the income variables.

among people with disabilities, lowering their poverty rate by 20 percentage points, compared to 17 points among people without disabilities. (It is important to note, however, that the poverty rate of employed people with disabilities remains higher than among employed people without disabilities, due to their lower work hours and earnings.)

Employment also appears to play a large role in alleviating social isolation among people with disabilities. While employed people with disabilities have less time to participate in groups, they are still about 10 percentage points more likely to meet regularly with groups than those who are not employed. However, their participation in disability groups is similar, reflecting the importance that disability groups can have in providing support to many non-employed people with disabilities. Interestingly, there is no significant difference in group attendance between employed and non-employed people without disabilities, indicating that the lack of employment is more isolating for people with disabilities.

Measures of psychological well being are particularly low among non-employed people with disabilities. Employment appears to increase overall life satisfaction and the feeling of being useful and needed, while decreasing feeling "down-hearted and blue," to a greater extent among people with disabilities than among non-disabled respondents. However, these questions were only asked in the 2000 survey and the sample size is too small to yield statistically significant differences.

Employment can help people develop a variety of skills that are useful not only in the workplace but in other areas of life, such as community and political participation. These "civic skills" were measured by asking respondents, "Compared to most people are you not as good, about the same, better, or much better at the: a) ability to work with others? b) ability to speak in public? c) ability to lead a group? d) ability to compose an effective letter to an elected official? e) communicating your ideas to others?" An index was created by giving one point for each skill for which the respondent

TABLE 2. ECONOMIC AND SOCIAL OUTCOMES ASSOCIATED WITH EMPLOYMENT

	With disability			Without disability		
	Employed	Not Employed	Difference with controls^	Employed	Not Employed	Difference with controls^
	(1)	(2)	(3)	(4)	(5)	(6)
Financial resources						
Household income (mean)	$51,782	$31,629	49.3%***	$65,033	$57,131	13.1%**
In poverty^^	7.5%	29.7%	-20.0%***	5.0%	23.2%	-17.2%***
Social isolation						
Regularly meet with any groups	48.1%	32.2%	9.7%**	55.2%	57.6%	-2.8%
Regularly meet with disability groups	7.8%	6.0%	0.4%			
Psychological well-being^^^						
"Very satisfied" with life in general	48.5%	35.2%	10.8%	56.3%	66.5%	-3.5%
Down-hearted and blue good part of time	11.4%	21.0%	-1.3%	0.9%	1.8%	-0.6%
Feel useful and needed most of time	70.7%	49.8%	11.5%	75.5%	74.2%	3.7%
Civic skills (0–5 scale)	2.48	1.82	0.34**	2.72	2.31	0.18
Political participation and efficacy						
Internal political efficacy (3–15 scale)	9.64	9.12	-0.14	10.20	9.89	-0.08
External political efficacy (2–10 scale)	5.73	5.13	0.24	6.10	6.38	-0.43
Perceive that people with disabilities:						
Get equal respect from public officials	3.36	2.97	0.26*	3.60	3.58	-0.11
Have equal influence in politics	3.84	3.39	0.42***	3.96	3.87	0.03
Participation index (0–8 scale)	2.14	1.57	0.45***	2.26	1.95	0.25*
Active on disability issue in past year	17.0%	17.3%	2.2%			
Disability discrimination and response^^^						
Perceived disability discrimination in past 5 yrs.	21.2%	30.3%	-4.5%	1.6%	2.6%	-0.7%
Took action against perceived discrimination	5.9%	13.1%	-5.9%	0.7%	2.6%	-1.5%
Sample size	308	359		748	175	

*Significant difference at p <.10.   ** p <.05.   ***p <.01.   All data limited to working-age (18–64).

^From employment coefficients in regressions that control for gender, age, age-squared, race, marital status, education, and the impairments and activity limitations listed in table I. To estimate percentage differentials, the logarithm of income was used as a dependent variable for the income variables.

^^Data calculated from 1999 Survey of Income and Program Participation, Disability Supplement. Other data are from the Rutgers 1998/2000 surveys.

^^^These measures are available only in the 2000 survey, so the sample sizes are smaller.

said that he or she was better than average. As shown in table 2, employment seems to play an especially important role in increasing the civic skills of people with disabilities, although they remain below the level of employed people without disabilities.

In addition to civic skills, perceptions of political efficacy have been shown to influence political involvement. Internal political efficacy is the belief that one is competent to participate in politics, while external political efficacy is the belief that the political system is responsive to one's interests. While there were no significant differences in overall measures of political efficacy between employed and non-employed respondents, employed respondents with disabilities were significantly more likely than their non-employed counterparts to say that people with disabilities get equal respect and have equal influence in politics. These results reveal the political alienation experienced by many non-employed people with disabilities, which can be expected to discourage conventional participation but may sometimes motivate disability activism. Employment appears to contribute to a greater sense of inclusion in mainstream society, which can increase perceptions that people like oneself have influence and are respected by politicians.

As noted earlier, people with disabilities have relatively low levels of voter turnout and other forms of participation. These data indicate that the lower levels of participation are concentrated among non-employed people with disabilities. A political participation index was constructed using eight activities that the respondent may have done in the past year (such as voting, contributing money to a campaign, and attending a political meeting). As can be seen in table 2, employed people with disabilities have done significantly more of these activities than non-employed people with disabilities. The effect of employment on participation is also positive, but smaller, among the non-disabled respondents. A separate analysis of these data shows that the effect of employment operates mainly through increased income and political recruitment at work (Schur 2001). While overall political participation is greater among employed people with disabilities, levels of disability activism are similar between employed an d non-employed people with disabilities, probably reflecting the greater number of disability-related problems faced by non-employed people with disabilities.

What is the relationship between employment and experiences of discrimination? About one-fifth of employed respondents with disabilities reported encountering disability discrimination in the past five years, compared with almost one-third of the non-employed people with disabilities. Interestingly, employed respondents were less likely to take action against perceived discrimination, perhaps reflecting the belief that they had too much to lose by challenging unjust treatment. While it is encouraging that a majority of people with disabilities did not report experiencing disability discrimination, the results of this survey can be extrapolated to estimate that about 4.2 million people with disabilities believe they have experienced discrimination in the past five years.

CONCLUSION

Employment may play a particularly important role among members of historically marginalized groups, such as people with disabilities, who often have low employment levels that contribute to high poverty rates, social isolation, political alienation, and low levels of civic skills and political participation. The results of this analysis support the idea that employment can have special benefits for people with disabilities. Not only does it increase incomes and help lift people out of poverty, it also helps people overcome the social isolation that often accompanies disability. In addition, employment can lead to the development of civic skills that facilitate participation in a variety of community and political activities outside the workplace. It also increases the perception that people with disabilities receive equal respect and have equal influence in the political system, reflecting their greater sense of inclusion in mainstream society. Finally, employment appears to have especially strong effects on the political participation of people with disabilities, counteracting the alienation experienced by many non-employed people with disabilities.

These estimates probably provide an upper bound on the actual effects of employment since, despite the controls for disability type and severity, the results may be explained by selection effects or unobserved variables. While this clearly deserves further research (ideally with panel data), these initial findings nonetheless provide some additional support for public policies designed to increase employment among people with disabilities.

Given the important benefits to be gained from working, the persistent low employment levels among people with disabilities are especially troubling. These findings suggest that increased employment will significantly reduce the economic and social disparities facing people with disabilities, helping them gain economic security and become more fully integrated and engaged in mainstream society.

REFERENCES

Baldwin, Marjorie L. "Can the ADA Achieve Its Employment Goals?" *Annals of the American Academy of Political and Social Science* 549 (January 1997): 37–52.

Bound, John, and Timothy Waidmann. "Accounting for Recent Declines in Employment Rates among the Working-Age Disabled." Research Report 00-460, Population Studies Center, Institute for Social Research, University of Michigan (October 2000).

Burkhauser, Richard V., and Mary C. Daly. "Employment and Economic Well-Being Following the Onset of a Disability." In *Disability, Work, and Cash Benefits*, edited by Jerry L. Mashaw et al. Kalamazoo, Mich.: W. E. Upjohn Institute for Employment Research, 1996.

Burkhauser, Richard V., Andrew J. Houtenville, and Nigar Nargis. "Economic Outcomes of Working-Age People over the Business Cycle: An Examination of the 1980s and 1990s." Federal Reserve Bank of San Francisco (March 2001).

Kruse, Douglas. "Persons with Disabilities: Demographic, Income, and Health Care Characteristics." *Monthly Labor Review* 121 (September 1998): 8–15.

Louis Harris and Associates. *2000 N.O.D./Harris Survey of Americans with Disabilities.* New York: Louis Harris and Associates, 2000.

McNeil, John. "Employment, Earnings, and Disability." US Bureau of the Census, Washington, D.C., 2000.

Putnam, Robert. *Bowling Alone: The Collapse and Revival of American Community.* New York: Simon and Schuster, 2000.

Schlozman, Kay L., Nancy Burns, and Sidney Verba. "'What Happened at Work Today?': A Multistage Model of Gender, Employment, and Political Participation." *Journal of Politics* 61 (February 1999): 29–53.

Schur, Lisa. "Do Jobs Create Active Citizens? Employment and Political Participation." Draft, Department of Labor Studies and Employment Relations, Rutgers University, 2001.

Schur, Lisa, and Douglas Kruse. *Non-standard Work and Disability Income.* Report to the Disability Research Institute, School of Management and Labor Relations, Rutgers University, October 2001.

Schur, Lisa, Todd G. Shields, Douglas L. Kruse, Kay Schriner. "Enabling Democracy: Voter Turnout and People with Disabilities." *Political Research Quarterly* 55 (March 2002): 167–190.

US Commission on Civil Rights. *Accommodating the Spectrum of Individual Abilities.* Washington, D.C.: US Commission on Civil Rights, 1983.

Yuker, Harold E., ed. *Attitudes Toward Persons with Disabilities.* New York: Springer Publishing, 1988.

---

*Lisa Schur is an assistant professor in the department of labor studies and employment relations at Rutgers University. This paper was presented at the Association for Evolutionary Economies annual meeting in Atlanta, Georgia, January 4–6, 2002.

Schur, Lisa. "The Difference a Job Makes: The Effects of Employment among People with Disabilities." *Journal of Economic Issues* 36, no. 2 (2002): 339–348.

Reprinted from the *Journal of Economic Issues* by special permission of the copyright holder, the Association for Evolutionary Economics.

Overview—Supreme Court Ruling in *Alabama v. Garrett*

*By the National Association of Protection and Advocacy Systems**

Feb. 21, 2001—Today's decision is a blow to the rights of people with disabilities. By the narrowest of margins (5–4), the Supreme Court ruled that state employees can no longer sue their employers for money damages under the ADA.

The decision continues this Supreme Court's trend of chipping away at federal civil rights protections in the name of states' rights.

In doing so, the Court virtually ignored the extensive record of discrimination by states against people with disabilities. As Justice Breyer so aptly noted in his dissenting opinion, "the legislative record bears out Congress' finding that the adverse treatment of person with disabilities was often arbitrary or invidious. . ." "It is difficult to see how the Court can find the legislative record here inadequate. . . the record indicates that state governments subjected those with disabilities to seriously adverse, disparate treatment. . ."

Indeed, the ADA was the result of strong bi-partisan efforts in Congress, and was signed into law by former President Bush (who also filed a brief in the Garrett case in support of the ADA). Disability advocates hope that the current Bush administration will continue to strongly support and enforce the ADA.

While today's decision rolls back the protections afforded by Congress, it is imperative to note that this decision affects only the ability of people with disabilities to sue state employers in federal court for money damages in employment discrimination cases.

The ruling does not prevent individual suits against a state employer for injunctive relief, nor does it bar suits initiated by the federal government for money damages.

The ruling likewise does not bar suits for money damages against private employers or local governments.

Perhaps most importantly, the Court explicitly declined to rule on the constitutionality of Title II of the ADA, which applies to state and local government programs. As a result, the *Olmstead* decision and other similar decisions are unaffected by today's ruling.

The Garrett case involved two state employees with disabilities in Alabama—Patricia Garrett, a registered nurse with breast cancer, and Milton Ash, a corrections officer with severe asthma. Both suffered job discrimination because of their disabilities.

---

*National Association of Protection and Advocacy Systems** provides advocacy services to individuals with disabilities. he Association is now known as the National Disability Rights Network.

National Association of Protection and Advocacy Systems, "Overview—Supreme Court Ruling in *Alabama v. Garrett*." Press release, February 21, 2001. http://www.accessiblesociety.org/topics/ada/garrettoverview.htm.

Used by permission.

The Applicability of the ADA to Personal Assistance Services in the Workplace

*By Robert Silverstein**

BACKGROUND AND STATEMENT OF THE ISSUE

Congress has stated that it is the policy of the United States to provide assistance to individuals with disabilities to lead productive work lives.[1] Congress has also found that Americans with significant disabilities often are unable to obtain health care insurance that provides coverage of the services and supports that enable them to live independently and enter or rejoin the workforce.[2]

Personal assistance services (such as attendant services, personal assistance with transportation to and from work, reader services, job coaches, and related assistance) may remove many of the barriers between significant disability and work. Coverage for such services is a powerful and proven tool for individuals with significant disabilities to obtain and retain employment.[3]

For individuals with disabilities, the fear of losing health care and related services is one of the greatest barriers keeping individuals from maximizing their employment, earnings potential, and independence. Recognizing these realities, on December 17, 1999 President Clinton signed into law the Ticket to Work and Work Incentives Improvement Act (TWWIIA).[4] One purpose of TWWIIA is to encourage states to adopt the option of allowing individuals with disabilities to purchase Medicaid coverage that is necessary to enable such individuals to maintain employment (Medicaid Buy-In programs).[5] A second purpose of TWWIIA is to establish the Ticket to Work and Self-Sufficiency Program that will allow individuals with disabilities to seek the services necessary to obtain and retain employment and reduce their dependency on cash benefit programs.[6]

Many states are currently analyzing whether and the extent to which personal assistance services (PAS) should be provided to individuals with disabilities in the workplace under the Medicaid program either as a benefit under the State plan or as a service provided under a waiver. Similar analyses are being undertaken by state agencies regarding the operation of the state vocational rehabilitation program under Title I of the Rehabilitation Act[7] and by state and local workforce investment boards and One-Stop career centers under Title I of the Workforce Investment Act.[8]

Policy deliberations under these federal/state partnership programs require an understanding of the obligations of employers to provide PAS under the Americans with Disabilities Act. The purpose of this policy brief is to explore the responsibilities of employers to provide PAS in the workplace. More specifically, the policy brief addresses the following issue: whether, and if so, under what circumstances the provision of PAS in the workplace is a reasonable accommodation as defined in the ADA?

Summary

Some people with disabilities have functional limitations that may create barriers to employment. For example, a quadriplegic may have the requisite education, experience and expertise to perform the essential functions of a job, but may be unable to perform non-essential job functions (e.g., turning pages) without assistance.

Title I of the ADA is a federal civil rights statute that requires employers to assist qualified individuals with disabilities overcome particular impediments/barriers to employment resulting from their functional limitations. More specifically, when a disabled person's functional limitations become barriers to employment, the ADA requires employers to consider whether reasonable accommodation will remove the barrier, thereby providing genuine, effective, and meaningful employment opportunities for qualified individuals with disabilities.[9]

In general, personal assistance services (PAS) is a form of assistance used by persons with disabilities to perform tasks that the person would perform for himself or herself if he or she did not have a disability. Personal assistance services include assistance in performing tasks that range from assistance in reading, communication, and performing manual tasks (e.g., turning pages) to assistance in bathing, eating, toileting, personal hygiene, and dressing.

The issue analyzed in this paper is whether, and if so, under what circumstances the provision of PAS in the workplace is a reasonable accommodation as defined in the ADA? In a nutshell, the ADA requires employers to provide personal assistance services to an applicant or employee with a disability so long as the services are job-related and are not primarily for the personal benefit of the individual with a disability. Job-related assistance in the performance of such tasks as reading, communication, the performance of nonessential manual tasks, and business-related travel may be considered reasonable accommodations. Assistance in performing such tasks as eating, toileting, dressing and personal hygiene are primarily personal in nature and generally will not be considered reasonable accommodations.[10]

Set out in the following pages is a more detailed analysis of the issue, starting with a brief recitation of definitions of key terms.

DEFINITIONS OF PERSONAL ASSISTANCE SERVICES

Under the Ticket to Work and Work Incentives Improvement Act[11] and the Rehabilitation Act,[12] the term " personal assistance services" generally means:

> A range of services provided by one or more persons designed to assist an individual with a disability to perform daily living activities on or off the job that the individual would typically perform if the individual did not have a disability. Such services shall be designed to increase the individual's control in life and ability to perform everyday activities on or off the job.

The State Medicaid Manual[13] defines the scope of personal care services (also known in States by other names such as personal assistance services, personal attendant services, etc) as:

> A range of human assistance provided to persons with disabilities and chronic conditions of all ages, which enables them to accomplish tasks they would normally do for themselves if they did not have a disability. Assistance may be in the form of hands-on assistance (actually performing a task for an individual) or cueing so that the person performs the task by him/herself. Such assistance most often relates to performance of activities of daily living (ADLs) and instrumental activities of daily living (IADLs). [footnote 11 at page 47 in Primer] Medicaid Manual section 4480]
>
> ADLs include eating, bathing, dressing, toileting, transferring, and maintaining continence.
>
> IADLs capture more complex life activities and include personal hygiene, light housework, laundry, meal preparation, transportation, grocery shopping, using the telephone, medication management, and money management.

TITLE I OF THE ADA

A reasonable accommodation under the ADA is a modification or adjustment to a job, the work environment, or the way things usually are done that enables a qualified individual with a disability to enjoy equal employment opportunity. An equal opportunity means an opportunity to attain the same level of performance or to enjoy equal benefits and privileges of employment as are available to an average similarly- situated applicant or employee without a disability.[14] Thus, if an adjustment or modification is job-related, e.g., specifically assists the individual in performing the duties of a particular job, it will be considered a type of reasonable accommodation.[15]

Under the ADA, an employer with 15 or more employees must make reasonable accommodation to the known physical or mental limitations of an otherwise qualified applicant or employee unless the employer can demonstrate that the accommodation would impose an undue hardship on the operation of the business.[16] A qualified person with a disability is a person with a disability who meets the skill, experience, education and other job-related requirements of a position held or desired and who, with or without reasonable accommodation, can perform the essential functions of a job.[17]

In general, an employer may not make pre-employment inquiries about whether a person has a disability. Thus, for example, an employer generally may not ask an applicant "will you need reasonable accommodation related to your disability to perform the job?" However, an employer may ask an applicant whether he or she needs reasonable accommodation and what type of accommodation is needed to perform the functions of the job if the employer reasonably believes the applicant will need reasonable accommodation because of an obvious disability or when the applicant voluntarily discloses the need for reasonable accommodation.[18]

The process of identifying whether, and to what extent a reasonable accommodation is required should be flexible and involve both the employer and the individual with a disability in an interactive process. The determination of whether a particular accommodation is reasonable and required under the ADA must be made on a case-by-case basis.[19]

The statute and EEOC regulations provide examples of common types of reasonable accommodation that an employer may be required to provide.[20] This list is illustrative, not exhaustive.[21]

ANALYSIS OF THE ISSUE

The following "personal assistance services" may be considered "reasonable accommodation" under the ADA because they are job-related. This list is derived from a review of the statute, regulations and policy interpretations issued by EEOC and the Department of Labor.

- Qualified readers or interpreters[22]
- A personal assistant that acts as a page turner for an employee with no hands[23] or an individual who aids a person that uses a wheelchair file to retrieve work materials that are out of reach,[24] or a person that assists an individual with physical limitations resulting from a stroke transport materials from one place to another[25]
- A travel attendant that acts as a sighted guide to assist an employee who is blind on occasional business trips[26] or who assists an employee with a mobility impairment on business trips[27]
- A security guide that opens the entry or exit doors for an individual who is a paraplegic[28]
- A temporary job coach to assist in the training of a qualified individual with a cognitive disability[29]

On the other hand, the obligation to provide a reasonable accommodation does not extend to the provision of adjustments or modifications that are primarily for the personal benefit of the individual with a disability. If an adjustment or modification assists the individual throughout his or her daily activities, on and off the job, generally it will be considered a personal item that the employer is not required to provide.[30]

Accordingly, an employer would generally not be required to provide an employee with a disability with a prosthetic limb, wheelchair or eyeglasses. Nor would an employer have to provide as an accommodation any amenity or convenience that is not job-related, such as a private hot plate, or refrigerator that is not provided to employees without disabilities (See Senate Report at 31; House Labor Report at page 62).[31]

It should be noted, however, that the provision of such items might be required as reasonable accommodations if they are specifically designed or required to meet job-related rather than personal needs. An employer, for example, may have to provide an individual with a disabling visual impairment with eyeglasses specially designed to enable the individual to use the office computer monitors, but that are not otherwise needed by the individual outside the office.[32]

The regulations issued by the Department of Justice implementing Title III of the ADA (public accommodations) are more explicit with regard to whether the obligation to make reasonable modifications and provide auxiliary aids and services, and communication accessibility extends to services of a personal nature. The regulations state:

> This part does **not** require a public accommodation to provide its customers, clients, or participants with personal devices, such as wheelchairs; individually prescribed devices, such as prescription eyeglasses or hearing aids; or **services of a personal nature including assistance in eating, toileting, or dressing.**[33]

The Department of Justice prepared a manual explaining the provisions of Title III of the ADA—The Americans with Disabilities Act: Title III Technical Assistance Manual Covering Public Accommodations and Commercial Facilities (November 1993). The DOJ ADA Technical Assistance Manual explains that the phrase "services of a personal nature" is not to be interpreted as referring to minor assistance provided to individuals with disabilities. For example, measures taken as alternatives to barrier removal, such as retrieving items from shelves or actions required as modifications in policies, practices, and procedures such as a bank filling out a deposit slip, would not be considered "services of a personal nature."

Also if a public accommodation customarily provides its clients with what might otherwise be considered services of a personal nature, it must provide the same services for individuals with disabilities.[34]

In addition to specifying whether a particular personal assistance service is or is not a reasonable accommodation under the ADA, the regulations also specify that it would be a reasonable accommodation to permit an individual with a disability the opportunity to provide or use services that an employer is not required to provide as a reasonable accommodation.[35] For example, an employer could not prohibit an individual from using a personal attendant providing assistance in toileting paid under the Medicaid program or a job coach paid by a public or private social service agency.[36]

Further, there is nothing in the ADA that prohibits an employer from providing an accommodation beyond those required by the ADA.[37]

NOTES

1. 42 USC 1320b-19 note.

2. Id.

3. Id.

4. Public Law 106-170.

5. Section 201(a)(1) of Public Law 106-170 adds a new section 1902(a)(10)(A)(ii)(XV) to the Social Security Act.

6. 42 USC 1320b-19 note, Section 2(b)(3). See also 42 USC 1329b-19.

7. 29 USC 720–751.

8. 29 USC 2801–2945.

9. See Interpretative Guidance on Title I of the ADA issued by the Equal Employment Opportunity Commission (EEOC) at 56 FR 35739 (July 26, 1991).

10. This conclusion is based on a thorough review of the ADA statute, regulations, and policy interpretations and guidance issued by The Equal Employment Opportunity Commission (EEOC), the Department of Justice (DOJ), and the Department of Labor (DOL). A review of the case law provided no additional guidance.

11. 42 USC 1320b-22(b)(2)(B)(ii); 34 CFR 361.5 (39).

12. 34 CFR 361.5(39).

13. Section 4480 of the State Medicaid Manual, Personal Care Services.

14. A Technical Assistance Manual on the Employment Provisions of the Americans with Disabilities Act (January 1992) at 3.3 (page III–2).

15. EEOC Interpretative Guidance at 56 FR 35747 (July 26, 1991). See also EEOC Technical Assistance Manual 3.4 (page III–4).

16. 29 CFR 1630.9(a).

17. 29 CFR 1630.2(m).

18. ADA Enforcement Guidance: Pre-employment Disability-Related Questions and Medical Examinations at page 6-7 (October 10, 1995).

19. EEOC Interpretative Guidance at 56 FR 35739 and 35748 (July 26, 1991).

20. See 42 USC 12111(9) and 29 CFR 1630.2 (o) (2). See also EEOC Technical Assistance Manual , 3.5 at page III–6.

21. 56 FR 35744 (July 26, 1991).

22. 29 CFR 1630.2(o)(2)(ii).

23. EEOC Interpretative Guidance 56 FR 35744 (July 26, 1991). See also EEOC Technical Assistance Manual 10 (page III–33).

24. Personal Assistance Services in the Workplace (Department of Labor, ODEP Education Kit 1997).

25. Id.

26. EEOC Interpretative Guidance 56 FR 35744 (July 26, 1991). See also EEOC Technical Assistance Manual, 10 (page III–33).

27. DOL/ODEP PAS In the Workplace Education Kit.

28. DOL/ODEP PAS in the Workplace Education Kit.

29. EEOC Interpretative Guidance, 56 FR 35747 (July 26, 1991). The EEOC Interpretative Guidance also explains that an employer would not, however, be required to restructure the essential functions of a position to fit the skills of an individual with a disability who is not otherwise qualified to perform the position, as is done in certain supported employment programs.

30. EEOC Interpretative Guidance 56 FR 35747 (July 26, 1991). See also EEOC Technical Assistance Manual 3.4 (page III–5).

31. EEOC Interpretative Guidance 56 FR 35747 July 26, 1991). See also EEOC ADA Technical Assistance Manual 3.4 (at page III–5).

32. Id.

33. 28 CFR 36.306. See also regulations implementing Section 188 (nondiscrimination) of the Workforce Investment Act [29 CFR 37.7(n)] which specify that: "This part does not require a recipient to provide any of the following to individuals with disabilities: (1) Personal devices, such as wheelchairs; (2) individually prescribed eyeglasses or hearing aids; (3) readers for personal use or study; or (4) services of a personal nature, including assistance in eating, toileting, or dressing."

34. DOJ Technical Assistance Manual at page 26.

35. EEOC Interpretative Guidance 56 FR 35744 (July 26, 1991). See also page 56 FR 35745.

36. EEOC Interpretative Guidance 56 FR 35744 (July 26, 1991).

37. EEOC Interpretative Guidance 56 FR 35744 (July 26, 1991). See also EEOC Technical Assistance Manual 3.4 (at page III-5).

*Robert Silverstein is the director of the Center for the Study and Advancement of Disability Policy.

Silverstein, Robert. "The Applicability of the ADA to Personal Assistance Services in the Workplace." *Institute for Community Inclusion*, Policy Brief Issue 10, 2003.

Used by permission.

DISCUSSION QUESTIONS

1. How does employment affect the lives of people with disabilities?

2. Discuss the implications of the U.S. Supreme Court's trend of chipping away at federal civil rights protections in the name of states' rights as it applies to the employment of individuals with disabilities.

3. Discuss the following issue: whether, and if so, under what circumstances the provision of personal assistance services in the workplace is a reasonable accommodation as defined in the Americans with Disabilities Act.

CHAPTER 10:

Ensuring Self-Determination

This chapter describes the knowledge and skills that individuals with disabilities will need to have to participate in self-determination activities. Self-determination is the freedom to live as one chooses or to act or decide without consulting another or others. Self-determination enables individuals with disabilities learn to define and achieve goals important to them. Self-determination for students with disabilities focuses on several major areas including: identifying strengths, weaknesses, needs and preferences; decision-making skills; rights and responsibilities; goal setting; anticipating consequences; creativity; communication skills; accessing resources and support; negotiation skills; and experiencing and learning from outcomes.

The first article, "Self-Determination: Position Statement," advocates for people with disabilities to enjoy and exercise the same rights afforded to all people. The disability organizations are committed to ensuring that people with disabilities are able to exercise control over their life choices and to engage in self-advocacy for their own benefit.

The second and third articles, "Self-Determination and the Education of Students with Disabilities" and "Promoting the Self-Determination of Students with Severe Disabilities," focus on the importance of teaching self-determination skills to students with disabilities. Research shows postsecondary benefits to students who can use self-determination skills while looking for employment or to gain access to further training or education. Evidence is also available that students benefit from participating in self-determination activities while in school. In addition, the third article identifies barriers to and solutions for promoting self-determination in students with severe disabilities.

The fourth article, "Leadership by People with Disabilities in Self-Determination Systems Change," discusses the importance of participation by individuals with disabilities in self-directed activities to become more independent within their communities. Also discussed is the influence that individuals with disabilities in leadership positions have in NGOs, associations, and organizations, especially in the crafting of policies and systems related to persons with disabilities. Surveys done on the participation of individuals with disabilities in leadership roles in the organizations revealed barriers that prohibited full participation and effective outcomes for both the individuals and the organizations. The article concludes by identifying policy and practice principles of self-determination from a variety of disability-related organizations.

Efforts to bring about increased self-determination must be aligned with other disability advocacy and reform efforts. If people with disabilities are to achieve full citizenship as outlined by the Convention on the Rights of Persons with Disabilities, their challenges must become the challenges of the communities in which they live.

Self-Determination: Position Statement

By The Arc and the American Association of Intellectual and Developmental Disabilities

People with intellectual and/or developmental disabilities[1] have the same right to self-determination as all people. They must have opportunities and experiences that enable them to exert control in their lives and to advocate on their own behalf.

ISSUE

Many of our constituents have not had the opportunity or the support to control choices and decisions about important aspects of their lives. Instead, they are often overprotected and involuntarily segregated. Many of these people have not had opportunities to learn the skills and have the experiences that would enable them to take more personal control and make choices. The lack of such learning opportunities and experiences has impeded the right of people with these disabilities to become participating, valued, and respected members of their communities. Furthermore, state monitoring and licensure policies and practices may be contrary to the principles of self-determination.

POSITION

Our constituents, as Self-Advocates, have the same right to self-determination as all people and must have the freedom, authority, and support to exercise control over their lives. To this end, they:

+ Must have the opportunity to advocate for themselves with the knowledge that their desires will be heard and respected.

- Must have opportunities to acquire skills and develop beliefs that enable them to take greater personal control.
- Must be active participants in decision-making about their lives.
- Must be supported, assisted, and empowered to vote and to become active members and leaders on community boards, committees, and agencies.
- Must have the primary leadership role in setting the policy direction for the self-determination movement.
- Must have the option to direct their own care and allocate available resources.
- Must be able to hire, train, manage, and fire their personal assistants.
- Must have the opportunity to be involved in governmental decisions that have an impact on their lives.

Additionally, in working with our constituents:
- Families and substitute decision-makers should be supported to understand the concept and implementation of self-determination, including the limits on their powers.
- Disability organizations should make self-determination a priority and include this important concept in their conferences, publications, advocacy, training, services, policies, and research.
- Governments should regularly review and revise laws, regulations, policies, and funding systems to promote self-determination. The affected individuals must be involved in these reviews and revisions.

NOTE

1. "People with intellectual and/or developmental disabilities" refers to those defined by AAIDD classification and DSM IV. In everyday language they are frequently referred to as people with cognitive, intellectual and/or developmental disabilities although the professional and legal definitions of those terms both include others and exclude some defined by DSM IV.

*The Arc is the world's largest community based organization devoted to promoting and improving supports and services for all people with intellectual and developmental disabilities.

American Association on Intellectual and Developmental Disabilities is the oldest and largest interdisciplinary organization of professionals and citizens concerned about intellectual and developmental disabilities.

The Arc and American Association on Intellectual and Developmental Disabilities. "Self-Determination," 2008. http://www.thearc.org/NetCommunity/Page.aspx?pid=1363.

Used by permission.

Self-Determination and the Education of Students with Disabilities

By Michael Wehmeyer*

Promoting self-determination has been recognized as best practice in the education of adolescents with disabilities since the early 1990s, when the Individuals with Disabilities Education Act (IDEA) mandated increased student involvement in transition planning. Promoting self-determination involves addressing the knowledge, skills, and attitudes students will need to take more control over and responsibility for their lives.

Students with disabilities who are self-determined are more likely to succeed as adults, and efforts to build self-determination skills are integrated into the practices of schools that provide high-quality transition programs. However, promoting self-determination should not begin in high school. Students in elementary and middle school need to receive such instruction as well.

WHAT IS SELF-DETERMINATION?

Although the self-determination construct has been used in various disciplines for centuries, its application in special education has been relatively recent. Field, Martin, Miller, Ward, and Wehmeyer (1998) defined self-determination as

> a combination of skills, knowledge, and beliefs that enable a person to engage in goal-directed, self-regulated, autonomous behavior. An understanding of one's strengths and limitations, together with a belief of oneself as capable and effective are essential to self-determination. When acting on the basis of these skills and attitudes, individuals have greater ability to take control of their lives and assume the role of successful adults in our society (p. 2).

Martin and Marshall (1995) described self-determined people as individuals who

> know how to choose—know what they want and how to get it. From an awareness of personal needs, self-determined individuals choose goals, then doggedly pursue them. This involves asserting an individual's presence, making his or her needs known, evaluating progress toward meeting goals, adjusting performance, and creating unique approaches to solve problems (p. 147).

Self-determined people are causal agents; they make things happen in their lives. They are goal oriented and apply problem-solving and decision-making skills to guide their actions. They know what they do well and where they need assistance. Self-determined people are actors in their own lives instead of being acted upon by others.

Why Is Self-Determination Important for Students with Disabilities?

Self-determination is important for all people, including students with disabilities. The skills leading to enhanced self-determination, like goal setting, problem solving, and decision making, enable students to assume greater responsibility and control. Moreover, when students with disabilities show they can make things happen and take responsibility for planning and decision-making, others change how they view them and what they expect from them. People with disabilities have emphasized that having control over their lives, instead of having someone else make decisions for and about them, is important to their self-esteem and self-worth (Ward, 1996).

Special education research has shown that students with disabilities who left school more self-determined were more than twice as likely as their peers who were not as self-determined to be employed one year after graduation, and they earned significantly more. Three years after graduation, they were more likely to have obtained jobs that provided benefits like health coverage and vacation and were more likely to be living somewhere other than the family home (Wehmeyer & Palmer, in press; Wehmeyer & Schwartz, 1997).

What Can Educators Do to Promote Student Self-Determination?

The educational planning and decision-making process is an ideal situation in which to teach goal setting, problem solving and decision making for all students (Powers, et al., 1996; Wehmeyer, Agran, & Hughes, 1998).

Teach the skills and knowledge students need to become self-determined. The educational programs of all students should promote the skills needed to

+ Set personal goals
+ Solve problems that act as barriers to achieving these goals
+ Make appropriate choices based on personal preferences and interests
+ Participate in decisions that impact the quality of their lives
+ Advocate for themselves
+ Create action plans to achieve goals
+ Self-regulate and self-manage day-to-day actions

These are not only independent living and self-management skills, they also involve students with disabilities in the general curriculum as required by the IDEA. Most state and district standards include standards pertaining to goal setting, decision making, and problem solving. For example, the Texas Essential Knowledge and Skills (TEKS) 6th grade social studies standards require students to use problem-solving and decision-making skills and to work independently and with others in a variety of settings. Students are expected to

- Use a problem-solving process to identify a problem, gather information, list and consider options, consider advantages and disadvantages, choose and implement a solution, and evaluate the effectiveness of the solution.
- Use a decision-making process to identify a situation that requires a decision, gather information, identify options, predict consequences, and take action to implement a decision (Texas Education Agency, 1997).

Instruction promoting components of self-determination should be infused throughout the curriculum. Doll, Sands, Wehmeyer, and Palmer (1996) identified age-appropriate activities addressing many of these components:

Early Elementary
- Provide opportunities for students to make choices, teaching them that they can exert control and that most choices have limited options from which to select.
- Promote early problem-solving skills by encouraging students to think aloud as they address simple problems. Teachers should model their own problem-solving processes.
- Provide feedback regarding the outcomes of their choices to begin to teach students to link choices and consequences.
- Teach students to evaluate their work in comparison to a standard ("Does your paper look like this?") to lay the foundation for later self-management skills.

Late Elementary and Middle School
- Teach students to systematically analyze potential options with related benefits and disadvantages in order to participate in simple decisions, and to examine past decisions to determine if the consequences were anticipated or desired.

+ Coach them in setting and committing to personal and academic goals, including identifying steps to achieve goals and obtaining support to monitor progress.
+ Encourage them to evaluate task performance and reflect on ways to improve and enhance performance.

Junior High and High School
+ Encourage students to make decisions that affect their day-to-day activities, including academic goals, post-school outcomes, schedules, and others.
+ Emphasize the link between goals that students set and the daily decisions and choices they make, and teach them to break long-term goals into short-term objectives.

Promote active involvement in educational planning and decision-making. The IDEA requires that from 14 years onward, transition needs and services be addressed on a student's IEP and goals related to these services be based on student needs, interests, and preferences. Transition planning provides a powerful context in which to both teach and practice skills like goal setting, problem solving, effective communication and listening skills, assertiveness and self-advocacy, and decision-making. Younger students (in elementary and middle school) should be involved in planning activities as well.

Teach students to direct their own learning. Research has shown conclusively that students with disabilities can learn and use strategies like self-instruction, self-monitoring, and self-evaluation, and antecedent cue regulation to learn academic content such as reading or math skills or to improve performance in such areas as vocational education and independent living skills. Teaching students to self-direct learning promotes self-determination and autonomy.

Communicate high expectations and emphasize student strengths and uniqueness. One simple yet powerful activity that can promote student self-determination is to have high expectations for students and communicate those expectations to students often. Students with disabilities are often all too aware of what they cannot do, and they often are not as aware of their unique strengths and abilities.

Create a learning community that promotes active problem solving and choice opportunities. Students who learn to solve problems do so in classrooms that value diversity in opinion and expression and create a 'safe' place for students to provide answers that might be incorrect, knowing that they will be provided the support to learn from mistakes and, eventually, solve problems successfully. Such learning communities often emphasize collaborative efforts, including classroom rule setting, and enable students to make choices about when, where, and how they learn what they need to achieve (Sands, Kozleski, & French, 1999).

Create partnerships with parents and students to ensure meaningful involvement. A focus on self-determination is not a license to exclude parents and family from decision-making and educational planning. While much can be done at school to promote self-determination, unless parallel activities occur at home, these efforts will not be sufficient. Parents are a student's first and longest lasting teachers, and it is important that from elementary school on, teachers work to ensure the meaningful involvement of parents, family, and students in educational planning and decision making.

REFERENCES

Doll, E., Sands, D., Wehmeyer, M. L., & Palmer, S. (1996). Promoting the development and acquisition of self-determined behavior. In D. J. Sands & M. L. Wehmeyer (Eds.), *Self-determination across the life span: Independence and choice for people with disabilities* (pp. 65–90). Baltimore: Paul H. Brookes.

Field, S., Martin, J., Miller, R., Ward, M., & Wehmeyer, M. (1998). *A practical guide for teaching self-determination*. Reston, VA: Council for Exceptional Children.

Martin, J. E., & Marshall, L. H. (1995). ChoiceMaker: A comprehensive self-determination transition program. *Intervention in School and Clinic, 30,* 147–156.

Powers, L., Wilson, R., Matuszewski, J., Phillips, A., Rein, C., Schumacher, D., & Gensert, J. (1996). Facilitating adolescent self-determination: What does it take? In D.J. Sands & M.L. Wehmeyer (Eds.), *Self-determination across the life span: Independence and choice for people with disabilities* (pp. 257–284). Baltimore: Paul H. Brookes.

Sands, D.J., Kozleski, E., & French, N. (1999). *Inclusive education in the 21st Century.* Belmont, CA: Wadsworth.

Texas Education Agency. (1997). *Texas Essential Knowledge and Skills.* Austin, TX: Author.

Ward, M.J. (1996). Coming of age in the age of self-determination: A historical and personal perspective. In D.J. Sands & M.L. Wehmeyer (Eds.), *Self-determination across the life span: Independence and choice for people with disabilities* (pp. 1–16). Baltimore: Paul H. Brookes.

Wehmeyer, M. L., Agran, M., & Hughes, C. (1998). *Teaching self-determination to students with disabilities: Basic skills for successful transition.* Baltimore: Paul H. Brookes.

Wehmeyer, M.L., & Palmer, S. (in press). Adult outcomes for students with cognitive disabilities three years after high school: The impact of self-determination. *Education and Training in Mental Retardation and Developmental Disabilities.*

Wehmeyer, M. L., & Schwartz, M. (1997). Self-determination and positive adult outcomes: A follow-up study of youth with mental retardation or learning disabilities. *Exceptional Children, 63,* 245–255.

---

*Michael Wehmeyer, Ph.D.,** is associate professor, Department of Special Education, and associate director, Beach Center on Disability at the University of Kansas.

Wehmeyer, Michael. "Self-Determination and the Education of Students with Disabilities." Council for Exceptional Children (September 2002). http://www.cec.sped.org/AM/Template.cfm?Section=Home&TEMPLATE=/CM/ContentDisplay.cfm&CONTENTID=2337.

Used by permission.

Promoting the Self-Determination of Students with Severe Disabilities

By Michael Wehmeyer*

Promoting the self-determination of students with disabilities has become best practice in special education, particularly in promoting more positive transitions from school to post-school life. Promoting self-determination means addressing skills, knowledge, and attitudes students will need to take more control over and responsibility for their lives.

While efforts to promote self-determination are in place, most of the methods, materials, and strategies they use do not adequately address the instructional needs of students with severe disabilities (Wehmeyer, 1998).

Wehmeyer, Agran, and Hughes (2000) surveyed 1,200 teachers of students with severe disabilities about their beliefs concerning self-determination and the barriers to providing instruction to promote this outcome. Some of barriers they identified are:

+ Lack of student benefit from instruction in self-determination (42%)
+ Insufficient training or information on promoting self-determination (41%)
+ Lack of authority to provide instruction in this area (32%)
+ More urgent need for instruction in other areas (29%)
+ Lack of teacher knowledge of curricular/assessment materials and strategies (17%)

This digest addresses several issues raised by this list of barriers to promoting the self-determination of students with severe disabilities.

Can Students with Severe Disabilities Benefit from Instruction to Promote Self-Determination?

The most frequently identified barrier was that teachers did not believe students would benefit from such instruction. This reason is at the heart of a perception that people with severe disabilities cannot be self-determined because of the nature or extent of their impairment (Wehmeyer, 1998). However, such perceptions are based on misperceptions of self-determination as equivalent to being completely independent or autonomous and in absolute control of one's life.

Many students with severe disabilities will not be able to learn all the skills and knowledge needed to solve difficult problems. However, this is equally true for most areas in which students with severe disabilities receive instruction, a situation that has been dealt with by the principle of partial participation (Baumgart et al., 1982). This principle states that even if a student cannot do all steps in a task or activity, he or she can likely learn at least one step and maximize his or her participation.

There are portions of even complex tasks such as decision-making or problem-solving in which students with severe disabilities can participate, thus making them more self-determined. For example, the expression of a preference is an important part of decision-making and all people, independent of the severity of their disability, can express preferences and make choices.

There is also research to support that using self-directed learning strategies enhances students' autonomy and independence (Agran, 1997). Promoting skills that enable students with severe disabilities to become more independent, even if they are not fully independent, can improve quality of life (Wehmeyer & Schwartz, 1998). Students with severe disabilities can become more self-determined, even if they won't become fully autonomous.

Strategies to Promote Self-Determination

Assess Interests and Preferences and Promote Choice Making.

Promoting active choice making is the primary way teachers address self-determination for students with severe disabilities. Making a choice involves the identification and communication of a preference. For students with severe disabilities, there are multiple barriers to making choices. Because many such students have too few opportunities, they do not know how to make choices and need targeted, direct instruction in this skill. Other students with severe disabilities do not express their preferences though conventional means and teachers must use alternative means to assess personal preferences.

Hughes, Pitkin, and Lorden (1998) reviewed the literature on strategies to determine preferences of students with severe disabilities. Strategies they identified included:

- Infer preferences from a student's behavior when a student responds to situations in which choices are presented.
- Use computer and micro-switch technology to enable students to indicate preferences.
- Observe whether students approach an object when it is presented as a choice.
- Consider a wide range of verbal, gestural, and other communicative efforts as a means to determine preference.
- Record the amount of free time a student spends engaged in particular activities.

Additionally, a student's family will have considerable knowledge regarding a student's preferences, and teachers should take advantage of this resource.

Student Participation in Educational Goal Setting and Educational Planning.

Self-determined behavior is goal directed. Students with severe disabilities can, and should, participate in goal setting. Agran, Blanchard, and Wehmeyer (2000) taught teachers of 19 students with severe disabilities to teach their students to set and reach transition-related goals. They provided supports to enable students to answer four questions leading to setting an educational goal: What do I want to learn? What do I know about it now? What must change for me to learn what I don't know? What can I do to make this happen? Although many students could not articulate direct responses to each question, teachers used the questions as focal points for planning activities that promoted active student involvement in goal setting.

For example, when addressing the question "What do I want to learn?" teachers helped students identify personal preferences in transition (work, living, recreation). Students became active partners in goal setting, and teachers and students worked diligently to ensure that goals were linked to student preferences, interests, and abilities. Teachers then taught students self-directed learning strategies (discussed below) that enabled them to participate in the instructional process as well. Students were successful in achieving their goals.

A process commonly used to involve students with severe disabilities in educational planning is person-centered planning. Compared to typical planning processes, person-centered planning emphasizes identifying the dreams and visions of the student and his or her family; creating teams of stakeholders that include the student, family members, and educators as well as other people who are important in the student's life (neighbors, employer); and generating educational plans that emphasize the student's abilities and preferences and identifying supports in the community to achieve goals related to these plans. Such efforts are ideal for actively involving students in goal setting, as well as in educational problem solving and decision-making.

Involvement in Problem Solving and Decision Making.

Solving problems and making decisions often require complex cognitive skills. However, each of these tasks can be divided into smaller steps, and students with severe disabilities can learn skills that enable them to complete each step more independently and, thus, enhance their involvement in the more complex task.

The decision-making process involves identifying options; identifying consequences from each option; assessing the risk associated with each consequence; examining how each option coincides with personal preferences, interests, and needs; and making a judgment about which option is optimal. Many students with severe disabilities can be taught, through role modeling and other strategies, to contribute to the process of generating options and can increase their knowledge about consequences associated with options through personal experiences and instruction. All students have preferences, and all students can become more involved in comparing decision-options with personal preferences. Decision-making ends with making a choice, and students with severe disabilities can be involved in that step.

Student-Directed Learning Strategies.

Student-directed learning strategies, alternatively referred to as self-regulated learning or self-management strategies, involve teaching students to modify and regulate their own behavior. Such strategies enable students to regulate their own behavior, without external control and allow students to become active participants in their own learning. There is considerable research evidence that many students with severe disabilities can learn and use self-directed learning strategies to promote independence and improved task performance (Agran, 1997). There are many such strategies, but the primary ones include teaching students to:

+ Independently perform a task by following a set of pictures or other visual or auditory cues (antecedent cue regulation).
+ Make task-specific statements out loud prior to performing a task (self-instruction).

- Observe and record own performance of a target behavior or action (self-monitoring).
- Compare the behavior being monitored with own desired goal (self-evaluation).
- Provide reinforcement upon successful completion of a task (self-reinforcement).

These strategies are typically used in combination. For example, a student with severe disabilities could be taught to perform a vocational task more independently through a simple self-instruction strategy such as the "Did-Next-Now" strategy, in which the student learns how to complete a task sequence by stating what response he or she just completed, what needs to be done next, and then directing himself or herself to perform the response. Then, the student could be taught to make a checkmark on a graph sheet next to a picture of the task (self-monitoring) when the task is finished. After three weeks the student can be taught to count total checkmarks (self-evaluation) and, if they total a predetermined amount, to engage in a reinforcing activity such as computer free time (self-reinforcement). The variations on these scenarios are limitless. For example, you could substitute teaching a student to perform a task by looking at a picture sequence (antecedent cue regulation) in the previous sequence if the student cannot adequately self-instruct. If counting check marks on a graph page is too complex, students can put a marble in a glass jar until it reaches a certain line as the self-evaluation component.

It is also important to consider technology's potential to promote independence and self-regulated learning for students with severe disabilities. Available technologies such as handheld personal computers are being used to promote independent performance and to decrease student reliance on others to perform tasks, thus enhancing self-determination (Davies, Stock, & Wehmeyer, 2002).

REFERENCES

Agran, M. (1997). Student-directed learning: Teaching self-determination skills. Pacific Grove, CA: Brooks/Cole.

Agran, M., Blanchard, C., & Wehmeyer, M.L. (2000). Promoting transition goals and self-determination through student-directed learning: The Self-Determined Learning Model of Instruction. Education and Training in Mental Retardation and Developmental Disabilities, 35, 351–364.

Baumgart, D., Brown, L., Pumpian, I., Nisbet, J., Ford, A., Sweet, M. Messina, R., & Schroeder, J. (1982). Principle of partial participation and individualized adaptations in educational programs for severely handicapped students. Journal of the Association for Persons with Severe Disabilities, 7, 17–27.

Davies, D.M., Stock, S., & Wehmeyer, M.L. (2002). Enhancing independent time management and personal scheduling for individuals with mental retardation through use of a palmtop visual and audio prompting system. Mental Retardation, 40, 358–365.

Hughes, C., Pitkin, S., & Lorden, S. (1998). Assessing preferences and choices of persons with severe and profound mental retardation. Education and Training in Mental Retardation and Developmental Disabilities, 33, 299–316.

Wehmeyer, M.L. (1998). Self-determination and individuals with significant disabilities: Examining meanings and misinterpretations. Journal of the Association for Persons with Severe Handicaps, 23, 5–16.

Wehmeyer, M.L., Agran, M., & Hughes, C. (2000). A national survey of teachers' promotion of self-determination and student-directed learning. Journal of Special Education, 34, 58–68.

Wehmeyer, M. L. & Schwartz, M. (1998). The relationship between self-determination, quality of life, and life satisfaction for adults with mental retardation. Education and Training in Mental Retardation and Developmental Disabilities, 33, 3–12.

*Michael Wehmeyer, Ph.D., is associate professor, Department of Special Education, and associate director, Beach Center on Disability at the University of Kansas.

Wehmeyer, Michael. "Promoting the Self-Determination of Students with Severe Disabilities." *Council for Exceptional Children,* September 2002. http://www.cec.sped.org/AM/Template.cfm?Section=CEC_Today1&TEMPLATE=/CM/ContentDisplay.cfm&CONTENTID=2228.

Used by permission.

Leadership by People with Disabilities in Self-Determination Systems Change

By Laurie E. Powers, Nancy Ward, Lisa Ferris, Tia Nelis, Michael Ward, Colleen Wieck, and Tamar Heller*

People with disabilities have been in the forefront of advancing self-determination services and policies. This article discusses the involvement of individuals in person-directed services and the roles of individual leaders with disabilities and disability organizations led by people with disabilities in shaping policies and systems. Findings from 3 surveys of the involvement of individuals with disabilities in disability organizations and agencies are presented. Cross-disability principles for self-determination and recommendations for promoting disability leadership are discussed. Advancing leadership requires supporting the development of individual leaders with disabilities, building the capacities of organizations led by people with disabilities, and encouraging cross-disability partnerships.

National trends in supporting people with disabilities have increasingly shifted toward person-directed of services (Powers, Sowers, & Singer, in press). Likewise, at the collective level, leaders with disabilities have performed critical roles in shaping policy and systems improvements (Shapiro, 1993). Clearly, leadership by persons with disabilities has been essential for the evolution of services and policies. This article examines the involvement of individuals with disabilities in person-directed services and in organizations and systems that shape disability services and policies. Included is a discussion of principles and action steps for advancing self-determination and leadership among persons with disabilities as well as current trends in cross-disability leadership.

Involvement of Individuals in Person-Directed Services

The philosophy of person direction recognizes the capacity of individuals to "assess their own needs, determine how and by whom these needs should be met, and monitor the quality of services they receive" (National Institute on Consumer-Directed Long-Term Services, 1996, p. 4). The importance of personal control is highlighted by research showing a positive association between perceptions of control and quality of life for individuals with disabilities and elders (Hofland, 1988; Nosek, Fuhre, & Potter, 1995; Rodin, 1986).

Common features of person-directed services include

1. the authority and accountability of the service user;
2. individualized, person-directed support planning;
3. user selection, training, and supervision of support providers;
4. limited oversight by professionals;
5. flexible benefits needed to maintain the person's health and quality of life in the community;
6. individualized funding of support plans and user authorization of payment; and
7. user monitoring of care quality (DeJong, Batavia, & McKnew, 1992; Fenton et al., 1997; Kane, 1996; Scala & Mayberry, 1997).

Preliminary findings on the effectiveness of person-directed services have generally pointed to positive outcomes, including enhanced control over life and services, satisfaction with services, availability of services, productivity, and employment (Beatty, Richmond, Tepper, & DeJong, 1998; Benjamin, 1998; Conroy & Yuskauskas, 1996; Grana and Yamashiro, 1987; Richmond, Beatty, Tepper, & DeJong, 1997).

The development of person-directed services can be traced to a variety of sources, including the Housebound and Aid and

Attendance Programs, operated by the Veteran's Administration for over 40 years (Cameron, 1993); the independent living movement, which over the past 30 years has promoted the development of personal assistance services for persons with physical disabilities (DeJong, Batavia, & McKnew, 1992); self-determination-based systems change efforts in developmental disabilities, which have gained momentum during the last decade (Moseley, 2001); and empowerment service models in psychiatric disability, which include "peer-run" services and person-directed services (Fisher, 1998). For example, as early as 1983, the Minnesota Governor's Council on Developmental Disabilities began differentiating between a consumer-powered system and one driven by resources and providers. Demonstration grants by several Developmental Disabilities Councils tested the feasibility of direct control of funding for services and supports. In Minnesota, project participants reported receiving more supports at a lower cost and with greater satisfaction as a result of directly controlling the resources (Patten, 1991).

Typically, the language used to describe person-directed services varies across the disability community. Many younger persons from the independent living movement emphasize *consumer control* and associate it with the management of personal assistance or attendant services. Regarding developmental disabilities, consumer-directed services are most often referred to as *self-determined or self-directed services*. Among elders, the person-direction language is not as well defined and may be referenced to *autonomy or consumer-directed services*. Terms used in the mental health and psychiatric survivor community include *empowerment, liberation, peer-run services*, and *self-determination*.

The emergence of person-directed models reflects a public policy shift from social benevolence toward people with disabilities to a growing acknowledgment of, and respect for, their capabilities, autonomy, and personal rights (Powers, 1996). Attention has been redirected from a relatively one-dimensional focus on reducing impairment to recognizing the importance of factors such as equal access, reasonable accommodation, and individual control of supports.

The growing emphasis on community-based, long-term services has enhanced opportunities for adults of all ages with disabilities to participate in life and to assume greater control over their supports. For example, as a result of changes in philosophy, advocacy, laws, and funding regulations, the number of institutionalized individuals with developmental disabilities has dramatically decreased over the past two decades (Braddock, Hemp, Parish, Westrich, & Park, 1998; Nirje, 1969; Smith, 1996). Similar shifts have begun to occur, although more slowly, for individuals with psychiatric disabilities and for older adults. Increased access to community-based services for individuals with disabilities has also been facilitated by the Supreme Court ruling on *L.C. v. Olmstead* (1999) related to the right of individuals with disabilities to be supported in the "the most integrated setting" as required by the Americans with Disabilities Act (ADA). Department of Justice regulations implementing this provision required that "a public entity shall administer services, programs, and activities in the most integrated setting appropriate to the needs of qualified individuals with disabilities" 28C.F.R. 35.130(d).

These policy and attitudinal advancements have laid the foundation for unprecedented opportunities for self-determination and the expression of full citizenship by people with disabilities. However, person-directed services currently are accessible to only a small portion of those persons who desire to direct their supports. Increasing the number and scope of consumer-directed service models will likely require further validation of their benefits, policy, and system improvements to address the barriers to consumer-directed services, ongoing consumer advocacy, and the strengthening of political will necessary to divert increased funds toward community-based, person-controlled services. Accomplishing these steps will necessitate the involvement of leaders with disabilities in collective efforts for systems improvement.

Involvement of Individuals with Disabilities at the Systems Level

The preceding discussion of person-directed services highlights the essential and expanding roles that customers may have in the design, implementation, and evaluation of their long-term services. Likewise, activists with disabilities have spearheaded the passage of key legislation, such as the Americans with Disabilities Act and the Rehabilitation Act; the development of federal requirements for state rehabilitation agencies to establish consumer advisory boards; and federal Medicaid waivers for community-based services and personal care programs (Covert, Macintosh, & Shumway, 1994; Powers, 1996; Ragged Edge, 1997). Hundreds of national, local, and state advocacy organizations are active in monitoring and shaping the direction of long-term services for elders and persons with disabilities (Dybwad & Bersani, 1996; Estes & Swan, 1993; Shapiro, 1993). Growing advocacy in the psychiatric disability community is focused on initiatives such as ending forced treatment and adapting personal assistance services for individuals with psychiatric disabilities (Lefley, 1996; Pita, Ellison, & Kantor, 1999).

Although impressive, much of the information available on the involvement of leaders with disabilities in moving these initiatives forward refers to the influence of advocates and advocacy groups that are outside of a service system. In contrast, very little is known about the level of involvement and leadership of people with disabilities within systems and agencies focused on disability. This is important to understand because system development typically occurs as a result of the interplay of internal and external forces. Furthermore, understanding the roles assumed by persons with disabilities within systems may contribute to our understanding of opportunities and barriers associated with their involvement.

Involvement of Individuals with Disabilities in Leadership Roles

To explore this question, the National Center for Self-Determination and 21st Century Leadership (see Note) conducted surveys of University Affiliated Programs (UAPs; currently referred to as University Centers of Excellence in Developmental Disabilities) and Developmental Disabilities Councils (DDCs), to examine the participation by individuals with disabilities and strategies DDCs and UAPs used to involve individuals with disabilities in their organizations (Powers et al., 1999). Information was also collected on barriers that hinder the participation of individuals with disabilities as well as ideas to overcome them.

Surveys were mailed to the directors of 50 state DDCs and 64 UAPs. A cover letter encouraging their participation was sent by the American Association of University Affiliated Programs and the National Association of Developmental Disabilities Councils or the Consortium of Developmental Disabilities Councils. A second survey was sent to organizations that did not respond to the first mailing. The response rate was 38% for UAPs and 54% for DDCs.

Among the 30 DDCs that responded, 193 individuals with disabilities were reported to be directly involved in DDC activities. Twenty-four percent of involved individuals with disabilities were identified as being in leadership roles through which they were able to influence key policies and practices of their organization. Eleven percent of individuals with disabilities were paid staff members, representing 12% of total DDC staff members. Eighty-seven percent of the individuals with disabilities participated as council members. This is consistent with federal requirements for individuals with disabilities to participate on DDCs. One percent were consultants and .5% had some other type of involvement. With regard to compensation, 76% of individuals with disabilities were volunteers, 12% were salaried, 9% received stipends, and 3% were hourly employees.

Among the 24 UAPs that responded, 236 individuals with disabilities were reported to be actively involved: 42% were in advisory roles; 28% were in staff positions, representing 4% of the total UAP staff members; 18% were consultants; 3% were trainees; and 9% performed other roles. Seventeen percent of individuals were identified as being in leadership roles through which they could influence policies and practices. With regard to compensation, 36% of individuals with disabilities were volunteers, 28% were hourly employees, 20% were salaried employees with benefits, and 16% received stipends.

Nine percent of the individuals with disabilities in both organizations were identified as ethnically or culturally diverse. Many respondents said that recruiting ethnically and culturally diverse staff members and participants was difficult. However, they identified a variety of strategies to increase the involvement of diverse individuals, including providing materials in Spanish, creating community partnerships with minority advocates, using cultural diversity as a resource, and including minority recruitment in mission statements.

One hundred percent of UAP and DDC respondents indicated that they somehow collaborated with self-advocacy groups. This collaboration included donating office space, helping disseminate information, providing training, and coordinating statewide networking. When asked about barriers that impede collaboration with self-advocacy groups, lack of funding, transportation, and self-advocate group infrastructure were the top responses. Other barriers that were identified included lacks of (a) staff and resources, (b) common goals, (c) trust among advocates and professionals, (d) leadership skills and training, and (e) staff members who were eager to work with individuals with developmental disabilities.

UAPs and DDCs identified a number of barriers to involving individuals with disabilities in leadership roles, including the following:

+ difficulty recruiting ethnically and culturally diverse staff members and participants,
+ language and communication barriers,
+ difficulty providing supports to individuals and a lack of support providers,
+ lack of leadership opportunities and difficulty recruiting individuals for leadership roles,
+ limited knowledge of leadership training approaches or resources,
+ lack of funding,
+ lack of transportation,
+ difficulty assessing individual support needs and providing accommodations, and
+ administrative or policy barriers (e.g., hiring constraints).

A number of strategies were identified by the respondents to increase leadership by individuals with disabilities in their organizations. These included

1. expanding outreach to include increased numbers of participants with disabilities, particularly those who are ethnically and culturally diverse;
2. expanding training opportunities;
3. increasing the effectiveness of advisory councils as leadership bodies;
4. hiring more staff members with disabilities;
5. involving individuals with disabilities more directly in training, planning, and policy development;
6. improving accessibility; and
7. collaborating with other state agencies and groups.

We recommend using caution when generalizing these findings to all DDCs and UAPs because of the low response rates and potential respondent bias. Given these limitations, the findings indicated that a notable minority of individuals with disabilities involved in these organizations were identified as being in leadership roles (17% and 24%). Higher percentages of individuals, including those who were ethnically or culturally diverse, were involved in unpaid advisory roles than in paid staff positions. Considered as a whole, the findings suggest that there is opportunity to increase the participation of people with disabilities in paid staff positions and in leadership roles in these organizations.

The findings also suggest that some DDCs and UAPs had difficulty recruiting, placing, and supporting individuals with disabilities in leadership roles. Furthermore, many of those who were in advisory capacities were not perceived as functioning in leadership roles. Further study is needed to determine whether this is because these individuals lacked skills or knowledge, their voices were not being heard, there was confusion about the definition of a leadership role, or they were not viewed as leaders. The identification of strategies to avoid the tokenism of advisory members, staff members, and consultants with disabilities also may be an important next step.

Furthermore, although all of the respondents indicated that their organizations collaborated with self-advocacy organizations, most of their activities involved DDCs or UAPs performing functions for self-advocacy organizations. The extent to which these organizations genuinely collaborated on joint activities with self-advocacy leaders was unclear. Major barriers to collaboration that were cited included lacks of resources, trust, common goals, and training, suggesting that partnerships between these organizations and self-advocacy groups could be strengthened. Increasing the number of staff members with disabilities and others in leadership roles may create additional opportunities to involve leaders from self-advocacy organizations.

Issues such as transportation, minority recruitment, compensation, training, and support must be addressed to pave the way for the increased meaningful participation of individuals with disabilities. Most important, increasing leadership opportunities for individuals with disabilities must be perceived as a priority. It is clear that many opportunities and strategies have already been identified to increase the opportunity for leadership by persons with disabilities in DDCs and UAPs. Our challenge remains to mobilize the commitment and channel the resources required to make leadership by individuals with disabilities a stronger reality.

Collaboration with Self-Advocacy Organizations

We conducted a related survey of the directors of state developmental disabilities services agencies to examine the extent to which these agencies provided support to state self-advocacy organizations (Ward, Ward, Ferris, & Powers, 2000). Survey questions asked how much direct funding states provided to self-advocacy organizations, which activities were supported, what barriers were inhibiting funding, and how these could be overcome. Surveys and cover letters were mailed to developmental disabilities agencies in the 58 U.S. states, districts, and territories. Additional surveys and reminder notices were faxed to the directors who did not initially respond. The final survey response rate was 57% (33 agencies responded).

Forty-two percent (14) of the agencies that responded to the survey indicated they provided in-kind or direct financial support to self-advocacy organizations. Fifty-eight percent (19) of the agencies that responded reported they did not currently provide such support. All but one agency indicated they would consider providing support to self-advocacy organizations in their states. The most commonly supported activities included educating policymakers, service providers, and the public about self-determination or self-advocacy (11 agencies); funding state conferences and transportation (10 agencies); and providing administrative support (8 agencies). Six agencies reported that they provided other types of support, such as local self-advocacy chapter development, staff advisors, office space, and technical assistance. The average amount of in-kind support and direct funding for self-advocacy organizations reported by the respondents was $84,000 annually (range of $10,000 to $400,000).

Obstacles to supporting self-advocacy organizations that were identified by state respondents included difficulty navigating state purchasing and contracting rules; difficulty addressing the potential conflict of interest related to funding an organization that may advocate for issues affecting the state; and lack of awareness of self-advocacy organizations and their activities. Several strategies for supporting self-advocacy organizations were identified by state respondents. They emphasized the importance of building long-term relationships with self-advocacy organizations and individual leaders that increase information sharing and the identification of activities that could be supported. Strategies to address funding obstacles included earmarking funds in state budgets, developing contracts with a specific scope of work, and directing funds to a third-party organization that could function as a fiscal agent for a self-advocacy organization that was not yet incorporated. Respondents also emphasized the importance of providing funding to self-advocacy organizations that would enable them to hire their own support staff.

Principles and Action Steps for Advancing Self-Determination and Leadership

Based on these findings and the input solicited from numerous cross-disability disability leaders, the National Center for Self-Determination and 21st Century Leadership and the Alliance for Self-Determination developed a series of principles, recommendations, and action steps for increasing the leadership of people with disabilities at the individual and systems level.

Principles for Self-Determination

The following principles for self-determination build on those initially developed by leaders in developmental disabilities (Nerney & Shumway, 1996). They were revised to address cross-disability perspectives on self-determination as an outcome of the 1999 National Summit on Self-Determination, Consumer-Direction and Control. The Summit brought together 120 leaders of self-determination initiatives focused on developmental and psychiatric disability, independent living, aging, and youth. Cross-disability definitions of self-determination, obstacles to expressing self-determination, and recommendations for enhancing the self-determination agenda were discussed (Alliance for Self-Determination, 1999). Following the Summit, a cross-disability work group developed draft principles for self-determination, which were disseminated to over 20,000 people with diverse disabilities. Further revisions of the principles were completed in response to the feedback received (Alliance for Self-Determination, 2001). This living document is as follows:

Preamble. The self-determination movement has its roots in the broader human and civil rights movements. The principles of self-determination must be broad enough to include all individuals with disabilities and concrete enough to guide policies and practices. The following principles go to the heart of self-determination:

Freedom. Freedom for Americans with disabilities is no different than it is for other Americans: Taking advantage of any of life's opportunities and exercising all rights guaranteed under our Constitution (e.g., deciding where, how, and with whom one lives, works, plays). People with disabilities must determine for themselves what important things they do with their lives, what relationships they establish, how they will contribute to their communities, and which supports or services they use. They do not have to accept predetermined programs or actions imposed based on a label of disability, such as segregated schooling, institutional placement, service slots, or forced treatment of any kind.

Authority. Americans have the authority to determine and direct their lives, including controlling their money, voting, and entering into contracts (such as for buying a home or getting married). Americans with disabilities must have that same authority, including deciding how funds available for their support will be used. Support funds must be assigned to individuals rather than slots, based on agreements developed by individuals and funders. People must be allowed to use funds to purchase the supports they require, personally selecting and directing people to provide that support.

Support. People with disabilities may use support to care for themselves and to meaningfully participate in their communities. Each individual can determine the unique supports that work for him or her. Individuals may rely on trusted others to assist in identifying life goals and supports, and to develop and manage plans and budgets. Those who assist will focus on providing people with support and access to life opportunities at the highest potential. Independent brokers must also be available to assist people in designing, setting up, and managing their supports; fiscal intermediaries must be available to assist with employment paperwork and bill paying. Both must work at the direction of the person with a disability and be free from conflicts of interest.

Responsibility. People with disabilities have the responsibility to fulfill the ordinary obligations of citizenship (e.g., voting, obeying laws, directing their own lives, participating in community life) by using supports in ways that are wise, fiscally responsible, and life affirming. Policy barriers, for example to accessing health insurance or personal assistance services, must be removed when they prevent people who earn money from receiving needed supports.

The application of these principles is essential if people with disabilities are to exercise their basic rights and to access resources that truly support their capacities to direct their lives and to fully participate in their communities.

Action Steps for Promoting Leadership Opportunities

Concurrent with the development of principles for self-determination, action steps for promoting leadership by people with disabilities were identified at two gatherings of cross-disability leaders sponsored by the National Center for Self-Determination and 21st Century Leadership (2000). Many of these recommendations were subsequently incorporated into the Developmental Disabilities Assistance Act of 2000 (P.L. 106-402). These action steps follow:

1. Support opportunities for current leaders with disabilities to provide leadership education and mentoring for individuals with disabilities who desire to become leaders.

    + Involve individuals with disabilities in training others to review grants.
    + Provide all trainers and trainees with the support and accommodations they need—before, during, and after activities.
    + Encourage networking between established grassroots organizations that have received grant awards and with other organizations applying for funds.
    + Expand the opportunities for current leaders with disabilities to provide leadership training to new leaders with disabilities.
    + Give opportunities for people to have mentors and be mentors.
    + Expand training and opportunities for people with disabilities to serve on boards, committees, and other leadership positions, and to hold political office.
    + After people leave leadership positions, assist them in identifying and getting involved in new opportunities.
    + Ensure that people with disabilities are the primary training force for educating the agencies that serve them.

2. Establish or strengthen the direct funding of organizations led by individuals with disabilities.

    + Ask leaders with disabilities about the goals that are important to them, the projects to fund, and who should be making funding decisions.

- Include as staff members leaders with disabilities who connect with and provide technical assistance to disability organizations.
- Ensure that requests for grant proposals are accessible to all in easy-to-read language and do not put disability groups at a disadvantage in the application process.
- Explain the rules related to how funding works (for example, lobbying and reporting requirements).
- Target funding for specific areas: Be aware of limits of funding and don't ask disability organizations to do everything.
- Give funding to disability groups for grant writers and provide free technical assistance related to hiring grant writers, writing grants, and managing grants.
- Involve individuals with disabilities in making funding decisions by including them as participants on review panels.
- Know the disability groups in your area, including their focus and relationships. Provide opportunities for them to work together and allow them to compete for funding.
- Expand opportunities for collaboration among independent living centers, self-advocacy groups, psychiatric survivor groups, and other organizations to accomplish common goals: Fund people working together.
- Give funding to help disability groups become private, nonprofit organizations if that is what they want to do. Temporarily fund groups that are not private nonprofits through other organizations that are selected by the group and that agree to function as fiscal agents for the group.
- Provide disability groups with opportunities and funding for a variety of projects such as employment, community education, transportation, leadership development, and coalition building. Fund activities that benefit your organization and disability groups.
- Have the same accountability expectations for different disability groups and provide proper support (for example, ask

for reports, pay for or offer technical assistance, fund an annual audit).

3. Support and expand participation of individuals with disabilities in cross-disability and culturally diverse leadership coalitions.

   + Ensure that materials and activities are accessible to all people. Accessibility means that people can participate, understand, and contribute.
   + Support leaders' working together to share resources and knowledge. Be truly cross-disability and culturally diverse.
   + Ensure that people of all abilities and cultures are included at the proposal or planning stages of an activity, not as an afterthought.
   + Provide funding for projects that identify and promote leaders from all geographic and diverse backgrounds, including inner city, rural, and tribal reservations.

These action steps include key elements for supporting the development of individual leaders with disabilities, building the capacities of organizations led by people with disabilities, and encouraging cross-disability partnerships. They signal the emergence of increasing momentum in acknowledging the essential roles that leaders with disabilities play in informing, influencing, and creating life opportunities for all people, including those with disabilities.

TRENDS IN CROSS-DISABILITY LEADERSHIP

We conclude this article by highlighting the shift toward cross-disability organizing and action that is underway. Historically, disability groups have been separated by lack of awareness, misperception, and discrete funding streams that have encouraged separation and competition. However, legislation such as ADA, which has fostered the awareness of common issues across groups, and increasing opportunities for groups to work together are fostering increasing collaboration and partnership. An example of this shift is the following Statement of Solidarity that has been agreed on by the American Disabled for Attendant Program Today (ADAPT), the National Council of Independent Living Centers, and Self Advocates Becoming Empowered:

STATEMENT OF SOLIDARITY

As we enter the new millennium, organizations advocating for disability rights and services need to reaffirm their commitment to the philosophy of independent living, self-determination, self-advocacy and cross-disability cooperation. ADAPT, National Council on Independent Living (NCIL) and Self Advocates Becoming Empowered (SABE) recognize the need for and the power of organizations that are composed of and run by people with disabilities. ADAPT, NCIL and SABE make a pledge of solidarity to work cooperatively to bring about the societal changes that will lead to the integration and empowerment of all people with disabilities. Integration means having enforced civil rights, a quality education, real jobs, real home life, access to needed resources, real choices and knowing what these choices are. ADAPT, NCIL and SABE advocating together, independently and with other organizations work on issues of concern to our members that include but are not limited to:

+ the protection and enforcement of the Americans with Disabilities Act (ADA) and all other disability rights laws;
+ reform of the institutionally biased Medicaid/Medicare systems so that no person with a disability is forced into a nursing home, group home or any congregate living situation because of the lack of appropriate community services and supports;
+ access to and development of accessible, affordable integrated housing;
+ access to supported living services coordinated with but separate from housing;
+ accessible and affordable transportation, including voluntary training about how to use public transportation;

- access to and development of competitive or supported integrated employment;
- quality integrated educational opportunities, including continuing education for adults;
- access to independent living skills training.

ADAPT, NCIL and SABE recognize there is power in numbers and change will occur when people with disabilities come together and take direct action (May, 2001).

CONCLUSIONS

The preceding discussion examined the involvement of individuals with disabilities in person-directed services and in organizations and systems that shape disability services and policies. Caution is required in the interpretation of the survey findings presented because of a variety of factors, such as limited response rate, potential respondent bias, and the subjective nature of some of the questions (e.g., "Is this person in a position of leadership?"). However, given these limitations, the findings suggest that although individuals with disabilities are involved in disability organizations and partnerships exist among consumer leaders and agencies, there is considerable room for enhancement in these areas. Some of the most noteworthy barriers are those related to leadership, such as lack of awareness of self-advocacy organizations and training and support strategies, which may be addressable without significant system reform. Other barriers, such as institutional operating policies and wage and benefits issues, are more complex and may represent institutionalized practices reflecting a historical decreased value for the contributions of leaders with disabilities. Still, the momentum for leadership by people with disabilities at the individual and collective level seems quite strong and there are many chances to apply the principles and action steps presented to enhance opportunities for leadership and the capacity of systems to benefit from that leadership.

Clearly, people with disabilities are increasingly asserting their rights and responsibilities as citizens, service users, and leaders. An assumption underlying this article is that the design and delivery of person-directed, self-determination-based supports is promoted by the active involvement of individuals with disabilities at the individual and systems level. This assumption is supported by numerous examples of personal and collective activities by people with disabilities that have stimulated improvements in systems and services. Promoting self-determination and leadership requires building the capacities of individuals with disabilities and organizations led by people with disabilities, as well as encouraging cross-disability partnerships.

The critical role of leadership by people with disabilities is gaining recognition beyond the bounds of the advocacy or service community. Participation and leadership by individuals with disabilities is extending to research, training, politics, law, and business; the historic net of limitation that has held people with disabilities in dependent, recipient roles is being lifted.

This evolution in the rights and opportunities available to people with disabilities does not come easily. It requires personal, systemic, and societal change. Although improvements are gradually occurring, we have a long way to go before people with disabilities will access the same opportunities as others in employment, housing, medical care, and virtually every other life area. Major obstacles remain in services and systems that prevent people with disabilities from expressing their citizenship. Maintaining the momentum for systems improvement will require the active involvement of individuals with disabilities and disability organizations led by individuals in various roles inside and outside of service systems. People with disabilities are the stewards of the self-determination and disability movement, and their leadership must be bolstered and respected.

AUTHORS' NOTE

This article was funded in part by the Administration on Developmental Disabilities. The views stated in this article do not necessary reflect those of the funders.

NOTE

The National Center for Self-Determination and 21st Century Leadership is a collaboration of the Center on Self-Determination at Oregon Health & Science University, Oklahoma People First, the Rehabilitation Research and Training Center on Aging and Developmental Disability at the University of Illinois at Chicago, and the Minnesota Governor's Council on Developmental Disabilities.

REFERENCES

Alliance for Self-Determination. (1999). *Proceedings From the National Leadership Summit on Self-Determination and Consumer-Direction and Control.* Retrieved February 26, 2002, from www.ohsu.edu/selfdetermination/ summit2.html

Alliance for Self-Determination. (2001). *Principles for self-determination.* Retrieved March 27, 2002, from www.ohsu.edu/selfdetermination/principles.html

Americans with Disabilities Act of 1990, 42 U.S.C. § 12101 et *seq.*

Beatty, P. W., Richmond, G. W., Tepper, S., & DeJong, G. (1998). Personal assistance for people with physical disabilities: Consumer-direction and satisfaction with services. *Archives of Physical Medicine and Rehabilitation, 79,* 674–677.

Benjamin, A. E. (1998). *Comparing client-directed and agency models for providing supportive services at home.* Los Angeles: University of California.

Braddock, D., Hemp, R., Parish, S., Westrich, J., & Park, H. (1998). *The state of the states in developmental disabilities* (5th ed.). Washington, DC: AAMR.

Cameron, K. A. (1993). *International and domestic programs using "cash and counseling" strategies to pay for long-term care.* Washington, DC: United Seniors Health Cooperative.

Conroy, J., & Yuskauskas, A. (1996). *Independent evaluation of the Monadnock Self-Determination Project.* Ardmore, PA: The Center for Outcome Analysis.

Covert, S. B., Macintosh, J. D., & Shumway, D. L. (1994). Closing the Laconia State School and Training Center: A case study in systems change. In V. J. Bradley, J. W. Ashbaugh, & B. C. Blaney (Eds.), *Creating individual supports for people with developmental disabilities: A mandate for change at many levels* (pp. 197–212). Baltimore: Brookes.

DeJong, G., Batavia, A. I., & McKnew, L. B. (1992, Winter). The independent living model of personal assistance in national long-term-care policy. *Aging and Disability,* 89–95.

Developmental Disabilities Assistance and Bill of Rights Act of 2000. P.L. 106-402.

Dybwad, G., & Bersani, H. A. (1996). *New voices: Self-advocacy by people with disabilities.* Cambridge, MA: Brookline Publishers.

Estes, C. L., & Swan, J. H. (1993). *The long term care crisis: Elders trapped in the no-care zone.* Beverly Hills, CA: Sage.

Fenton, M., Entrikin, T., Morrill, S., Marburg, G., Shumway, D., & Nerney, T. (1997). *Beyond managed care: An owner's manual for self-determination.* Concord, NH: Self-Determination for Persons with Developmental Disabilities.

Fisher, D. (1998, June). Recovery: The behavioral healthcare guideline of tomorrow. *Behavioral Healthcare Tomorrow.*

Grana, J. M., & Yamashiro, S. M. (1987). *An evaluation of the Veterans Administration Housebound and Aid and Attendant Allowance Program, Project HOPE.* Washington, DC: Department of Health and Human Services.

Hofland, B. F. (1988). Autonomy in long term care: Background issues and programmatic response. *The Gerontologist, 28,* 3–9.

Kane, R. (1996, August). The quality conundrum in home care. *Aging Today,* 7–8.

L. C. v. Olmstead, 119 S. Ct. 2181 (1999).

Lefley, H. (1996). *Family caregiving in mental illness.* Thousand Oaks, CA: Sage.

Minnesota Governor's Council on Developmental Disabilities. (1983). *Developmental disabilities and public policy.* St. Paul: Author.

Moseley, C. (2001). *Self-determination for persons with developmental disability: Final and summative program report.* Durham: Institute on Disability, University of New Hampshire.

Mount, B., & Zwernik, K. (1988). *It's never too early, it's never too late. A booklet about personal futures planning.* Minneapolis, MN: Metropolitan Council.

National Center for Self-Determination and 21st Century Leadership. (2000). *Recommendations and action steps for promoting leadership development.* Portland: Center on Self-Determination, Oregon Health & Science University.

National Institute on Consumer-Directed Long-Term Services. (1996). *Principles of consumer-directed home and community-based services.* Washington, DC: The National Council on the Aging.

Nerney, T., & Shumway, D. (1996). *Beyond managed care: Self-determination for people with developmental disabilities.* Concord: Institute on Disability, University of New Hampshire.

Nirje, B. (1969). The normalization principle and its management implications. In R. Kugel and W. Wolfensberger (Eds.), *Changing patterns in residential services for the mentally retarded* (pp. 51–57). Washington, DC: U.S. Government Printing Office.

Nosek, M., Fuhre, M., & Potter, C. (1995). Life satisfaction of people with physical disabilities: Relationship to personal assistance, disability status, and handicap. *Rehabilitation Psychology, 40*(3), 192–202.

Patten, S. (1991). *An evaluation of grants awarded for October 1989 to September 1990.* St. Paul: Minnesota Governor's Council on Developmental Disabilities.

Pita, D. D., Ellison, M. L., & Kantor, E. (1999). *Psychiatric personal assistance services: A new service strategy.* Unpublished data available from the Center for Psychiatric Rehabilitation, Boston University.

Powers, L. E. (1996). Family and consumer autism in disability policy. In G. H. S. Singer, L. E. Powers, & A. L. Olson (Eds.), *Redefining family support: Innovations in public-private partnerships* (pp. 413–433). Baltimore: Brookes.

Powers, L. E., Sowers, J. A., & Singer, G. H. S. (in press). A cross-disability analysis of consumer-directed long-term services. *American Rehabilitation.*

Powers, L. E., Ward, M., Ferris, L., Ward, N., Nelis, T., Wieck, C., & Heller, T. (1999). *Surveys of the involvement of people with disabilities in university affiliated programs and developmental disabilities councils.* Portland: Oregon Health & Science University, National Center for Self-Determination and 21st Century Leadership.

Ragged Edge. (1997, July/August). How Kansas got "consumer control" into the law. *Ragged Edge,* 21–25.

Richmond, G. W., Beatty, P., Tepper, S., & Delong, G. (1997). The effect of consumer-directed personal assistance services on the productivity outcomes of people with disabilities. *Journal of Rehabilitation Outcomes Measurement, 1* (4), 48–51.

Rodin, J. (1986). Aging and health: Effects of the sense of control. *Science, 233,* 1271–1275.

Scala, M. A., & Mayberry, P. S. (1997, July). *Consumer-directed home services: Issues and models.* Oxford: Ohio Long-Term Care Research Project, Miami University.

Shapiro, J. P. (1993). *No pity: People with disabilities forging a new civil rights movement.* New York: Times Books.

Smith, G. A. (1996). The HCB Waiver Program: The fading of Medicaid's "Institutional Bias." *Mental Retardation, 34*(4), 226–238.

Ward, N., Ward, M., Ferris, L., & Powers, L. E. (2000). *Survey of support for self-advocacy organizations by developmental disabilities agencies.* Portland: Oregon Health & Science University, National Center for Self-Determination and 21st Century Leadership.

---

*Laurie E. Powers, PhD, is an associate professor of pediatrics, public health, and psychiatry and co-director of the Center on Self-Determination at Oregon Health & Science University.

Nancy Ward is a national self-advocacy leader who supports Oklahoma People First.

Lisa Ferris, MA, is a research associate at the Center on Self-Determination at Oregon Health & Science University.

Tia Nelis is a national self-advocacy leader from the Rehabilitation Research and Training Center on Aging and Developmental Disabilities at the University of Illinois at Chicago.

Michael Ward, PhD, is director of the Arizona Council on Developmental Disabilities.

Colleen Wieck, PhD, is director of the Minnesota Governor's Council on Developmental Disabilities.

Tamar Heller, PhD, is acting director of the Department of Disability and Human Development and director of the Rehabilitation Research and Training Center on Aging and Developmental Disabilities at the University of Illinois at Chicago.

Powers, Laurie E., Nancy Ward, Lisa Ferris, Tia Nelis, Michael Ward, Colleen Wieck, and Tamar Heller. "Leadership by People with Disabilities in Self-Determination Systems Change." *Journal of Disability Policy Studies* 13 (2002): 126–134. Reprinted by permission of SAGE Publications, Inc.

DISCUSSION QUESTIONS

1. What are the benefits of self-determination to the individual with a disability and to society?

2. Should individuals with severe disabilities be given the opportunity to be self-determined?

3. Why should people with disabilities play critical roles in shaping policy and systems improvements in implementing the Convention on the Rights of Persons with Disabilities (CRPD)?

4. Why is it important to promote cross-disability organizing and action as it relates to self-determination and the implementation of the CRPD?

Convention on the Rights of Persons with Disabilities

Preamble

The States Parties to the present Convention,

(a) *Recalling* the principles proclaimed in the Charter of the United Nations which recognize the inherent dignity and worth and the equal and inalienable rights of all members of the human family as the foundation of freedom, justice and peace in the world,

(b) *Recognizing* that the United Nations, in the Universal Declaration of Human Rights and in the International Covenants on Human Rights, has proclaimed and agreed that everyone is entitled to all the rights and freedoms set forth therein, without distinction of any kind,

(c) *Reaffirming* the universality, indivisibility, interdependence and inter-relatedness of all human rights and fundamental freedoms and the need for persons with disabilities to be guaranteed their full enjoyment without discrimination,

(d) *Recalling* the International Covenant on Economic, Social and Cultural Rights, the International Covenant on Civil and Political Rights, the International Convention on the Elimination of All Forms of Racial Discrimination, the Convention on the Elimination of All Forms of Discrimination against Women, the Convention against Torture and Other Cruel, Inhuman or Degrading Treatment or Punishment, the Convention on the Rights of the Child, and the International Convention on the Protection of the Rights of All Migrant Workers and Members of Their Families,

(e) *Recognizing* that disability is an evolving concept and that disability results from the interaction between persons with impairments and attitudinal and environmental barriers that hinders their full and effective participation in society on an equal basis with others,

(f) *Recognizing* the importance of the principles and policy guidelines contained in the World Programme of Action concerning Disabled Persons and in the Standard Rules on the Equalization of Opportunities for Persons with Disabilities in influencing the promotion, formulation and evaluation of the policies, plans, programmes and actions at the national, regional and international levels to further equalize opportunities for persons with disabilities,

(g) *Emphasizing* the importance of mainstreaming disability issues as an integral part of relevant strategies of sustainable development,

(h) *Recognizing also* that discrimination against any person on the basis of disability is a violation of the inherent dignity and worth of the human person,

(i) *Recognizing further* the diversity of persons with disabilities,

(j) *Recognizing* the need to promote and protect the human rights of all persons with disabilities, including those who require more intensive support,

(k) *Concerned* that, despite these various instruments and undertakings, persons with disabilities continue to face barriers in their participation as equal members of society and violations of their human rights in all parts of the world,

(l) *Recognizing* the importance of international cooperation for improving the living conditions of persons with disabilities in every country, particularly in developing countries,

(m) *Recognizing* the valued existing and potential contributions made by persons with disabilities to the overall well-being and diversity of their communities, and that the promotion of the full enjoyment by persons with disabilities of their human rights and fundamental freedoms and of full participation by persons with disabilities will result in their enhanced sense of belonging and in significant advances in the human, social and economic development of society and the eradication of poverty,

(n) *Recognizing* the importance for persons with disabilities of their individual autonomy and independence, including the freedom to make their own choices,

(o) *Considering* that persons with disabilities should have the opportunity to be actively involved in decision-making processes about policies and programmes, including those directly concerning them,

(p) *Concerned* about the difficult conditions faced by persons with disabilities who are subject to multiple or aggravated forms of discrimination on the basis of race, colour, sex, language, religion, political or other opinion, national, ethnic, indigenous or social origin, property, birth, age or other status,

(q) *Recognizing* that women and girls with disabilities are often at greater risk, both within and outside the home, of violence, injury or abuse, neglect or negligent treatment, maltreatment or exploitation,

(r) *Recognizing* that children with disabilities should have full enjoyment of all human rights and fundamental freedoms on an equal basis with other children, and recalling obligations to that end undertaken by States Parties to the Convention on the Rights of the Child,

(s) *Emphasizing* the need to incorporate a gender perspective in all efforts to promote the full enjoyment of human rights and fundamental freedoms by persons with disabilities,

(t) *Highlighting* the fact that the majority of persons with disabilities live in conditions of poverty, and in this regard recognizing the critical need to address the negative impact of poverty on persons with disabilities,

(u) *Bearing in mind* that conditions of peace and security based on full respect for the purposes and principles contained in the Charter of the United Nations and observance of applicable human rights instruments are indispensable for the full protection of persons with disabilities, in particular during armed conflicts and foreign occupation,

(v) *Recognizing* the importance of accessibility to the physical, social, economic and cultural environment, to health and education and to information and communication, in enabling persons with disabilities to fully enjoy all human rights and fundamental freedoms,

(w) *Realizing* that the individual, having duties to other individuals and to the community to which he or she belongs, is under a responsibility to strive for the promotion and observance of the rights recognized in the International Bill of Human Rights,

(x) *Convinced* that the family is the natural and fundamental group unit of society and is entitled to protection by society and the State, and that persons with disabilities and their family members should receive the necessary protection and assistance to enable families to contribute towards the full and equal enjoyment of the rights of persons with disabilities,

(y) *Convinced* that a comprehensive and integral international convention to promote and protect the rights and dignity of persons with disabilities will make a significant contribution to redressing the profound social disadvantage of persons with disabilities and promote their participation in the civil, political, economic, social and cultural spheres with equal opportunities, in both developing and developed countries,

Have agreed as follows:

ARTICLE 1—PURPOSE

The purpose of the present Convention is to promote, protect and ensure the full and equal enjoyment of all human rights and fundamental freedoms by all persons with disabilities, and to promote respect for their inherent dignity.

Persons with disabilities include those who have long-term physical, mental, intellectual or sensory impairments which in interaction with various barriers may hinder their full and effective participation in society on an equal basis with others.

ARTICLE 2—DEFINITIONS

For the purposes of the present Convention:

"Communication" includes languages, display of text, Braille, tactile communication, large print, accessible multimedia as well as written, audio, plain-language, human-reader and augmentative and alternative modes, means and formats of communication, including accessible information and communication technology;

"Language" includes spoken and signed languages and other forms of non spoken languages;

"Discrimination on the basis of disability" means any distinction, exclusion or restriction on the basis of disability which has the purpose or effect of impairing or nullifying the recognition, enjoyment or exercise, on an equal basis with others, of all human rights and fundamental freedoms in the political, economic, social, cultural, civil or any other field. It includes all forms of discrimination, including denial of reasonable accommodation;

"Reasonable accommodation" means necessary and appropriate modification and adjustments not imposing a disproportionate or undue burden, where needed in a particular case, to ensure to persons with disabilities the enjoyment or exercise on an equal basis with others of all human rights and fundamental freedoms;

"Universal design" means the design of products, environments, programmes and services to be usable by all people, to the greatest extent possible, without the need for adaptation or specialized design. "Universal design" shall not exclude assistive devices for particular groups of persons with disabilities where this is needed.

ARTICLE 3—GENERAL PRINCIPLES

The principles of the present Convention shall be:

(a) Respect for inherent dignity, individual autonomy including the freedom to make one's own choices, and independence of persons;

(b) Non-discrimination;

(c) Full and effective participation and inclusion in society;

(d) Respect for difference and acceptance of persons with disabilities as part of human diversity and humanity;

(e) Equality of opportunity;

(f) Accessibility;

(g) Equality between men and women;

(h) Respect for the evolving capacities of children with disabilities and respect for the right of children with disabilities to preserve their identities.

ARTICLE 4—GENERAL OBLIGATIONS

1. States Parties undertake to ensure and promote the full realization of all human rights and fundamental freedoms for all persons with disabilities

without discrimination of any kind on the basis of disability. To this end, States Parties undertake:

(a) To adopt all appropriate legislative, administrative and other measures for the implementation of the rights recognized in the present Convention;

(b) To take all appropriate measures, including legislation, to modify or abolish existing laws, regulations, customs and practices that constitute discrimination against persons with disabilities;

(c) To take into account the protection and promotion of the human rights of persons with disabilities in all policies and programmes;

(d) To refrain from engaging in any act or practice that is inconsistent with the present Convention and to ensure that public authorities and institutions act in conformity with the present Convention;

(e) To take all appropriate measures to eliminate discrimination on the basis of disability by any person, organization or private enterprise;

(f) To undertake or promote research and development of universally designed goods, services, equipment and facilities, as defined in article 2 of the present Convention, which should require the minimum possible adaptation and the least cost to meet the specific needs of a person with disabilities, to promote their availability and use, and to promote universal design in the development of standards and guidelines;

(g) To undertake or promote research and development of, and to promote the availability and use of new technologies, including information and communications technologies, mobility aids, devices and assistive technologies, suitable for persons with disabilities, giving priority to technologies at an affordable cost;

(h) To provide accessible information to persons with disabilities about mobility aids, devices and assistive technologies, including new technologies, as well as other forms of assistance, support services and facilities;

(i) To promote the training of professionals and staff working with persons with disabilities in the rights recognized in the present Convention so as to better provide the assistance and services guaranteed by those rights.

2. With regard to economic, social and cultural rights, each State Party undertakes to take measures to the maximum of its available resources and, where needed, within the framework of international cooperation, with a view to achieving progressively the full realization of these rights, without prejudice to those obligations contained in the present Convention that are immediately applicable according to international law.

3. In the development and implementation of legislation and policies to implement the present Convention, and in other decision-making processes concerning issues relating to persons with disabilities, States Parties shall closely consult with and actively involve persons with disabilities, including children with disabilities, through their representative organizations.

4. Nothing in the present Convention shall affect any provisions which are more conducive to the realization of the rights of persons with disabilities and which may be contained in the law of a State Party or international law in force for that State. There shall be no restriction upon or derogation from any of the human rights and fundamental freedoms recognized or existing in any State Party to the present Convention pursuant to law, conventions, regulation or custom on the pretext that the present Convention does not recognize such rights or freedoms or that it recognizes them to a lesser extent.

5. The provisions of the present Convention shall extend to all parts of federal States without any limitations or exceptions.

ARTICLE 5—EQUALITY AND NON-DISCRIMINATION

1. States Parties recognize that all persons are equal before and under the law and are entitled without any discrimination to the equal protection and equal benefit of the law.

2. States Parties shall prohibit all discrimination on the basis of disability and guarantee to persons with disabilities equal and effective legal protection against discrimination on all grounds.

3. In order to promote equality and eliminate discrimination, States Parties shall take all appropriate steps to ensure that reasonable accommodation is provided.

4. Specific measures which are necessary to accelerate or achieve de facto equality of persons with disabilities shall not be considered discrimination under the terms of the present Convention.

ARTICLE 6—WOMEN WITH DISABILITIES

1. States Parties recognize that women and girls with disabilities are subject to multiple discrimination, and in this regard shall take measures to ensure the full and equal enjoyment by them of all human rights and fundamental freedoms.

2. States Parties shall take all appropriate measures to ensure the full development, advancement and empowerment of women, for the purpose of guaranteeing them the exercise and enjoyment of the human rights and fundamental freedoms set out in the present Convention.

ARTICLE 7—CHILDREN WITH DISABILITIES

1. States Parties shall take all necessary measures to ensure the full enjoyment by children with disabilities of all human rights and fundamental freedoms on an equal basis with other children.

2. In all actions concerning children with disabilities, the best interests of the child shall be a primary consideration.

3. States Parties shall ensure that children with disabilities have the right to express their views freely on all matters affecting them, their views being given due weight in accordance with their age and maturity, on an equal basis with other children, and to be provided with disability and age-appropriate assistance to realize that right.

ARTICLE 8—AWARENESS-RAISING

1. States Parties undertake to adopt immediate, effective and appropriate measures:

(a) To raise awareness throughout society, including at the family level, regarding persons with disabilities, and to foster respect for the rights and dignity of persons with disabilities;

(b) To combat stereotypes, prejudices and harmful practices relating to persons with disabilities, including those based on sex and age, in all areas of life;

(c) To promote awareness of the capabilities and contributions of persons with disabilities.

2. Measures to this end include:

(a) Initiating and maintaining effective public awareness campaigns designed:

(i) To nurture receptiveness to the rights of persons with disabilities;

(ii) To promote positive perceptions and greater social awareness towards persons with disabilities;

(iii) To promote recognition of the skills, merits and abilities of persons with disabilities, and of their contributions to the workplace and the labour market;

(b) Fostering at all levels of the education system, including in all children from an early age, an attitude of respect for the rights of persons with disabilities;

(c) Encouraging all organs of the media to portray persons with disabilities in a manner consistent with the purpose of the present Convention;

(d) Promoting awareness-training programmes regarding persons with disabilities and the rights of persons with disabilities.

ARTICLE 9—ACCESSIBILITY

1. To enable persons with disabilities to live independently and participate fully in all aspects of life, States Parties shall take appropriate measures to ensure to persons with disabilities access, on an equal basis with others, to the physical environment, to transportation, to information and communications, including information and communications technologies and systems, and to other facilities and services open or provided to the public, both in urban and in rural areas. These measures, which shall include the

identification and elimination of obstacles and barriers to accessibility, shall apply to, inter alia:

(a) Buildings, roads, transportation and other indoor and outdoor facilities, including schools, housing, medical facilities and workplaces;

(b) Information, communications and other services, including electronic services and emergency services.

2. States Parties shall also take appropriate measures:

(a) To develop, promulgate and monitor the implementation of minimum standards and guidelines for the accessibility of facilities and services open or provided to the public;

(b) To ensure that private entities that offer facilities and services which are open or provided to the public take into account all aspects of accessibility for persons with disabilities;

(c) To provide training for stakeholders on accessibility issues facing persons with disabilities;

(d) To provide in buildings and other facilities open to the public signage in Braille and in easy to read and understand forms;

(e) To provide forms of live assistance and intermediaries, including guides, readers and professional sign language interpreters, to facilitate accessibility to buildings and other facilities open to the public;

(f) To promote other appropriate forms of assistance and support to persons with disabilities to ensure their access to information;

(g) To promote access for persons with disabilities to new information and communications technologies and systems, including the Internet;

(h) To promote the design, development, production and distribution of accessible information and communications technologies and systems at an early stage, so that these technologies and systems become accessible at minimum cost.

Article 10—Right to life

States Parties reaffirm that every human being has the inherent right to life and shall take all necessary measures to ensure its effective enjoyment by persons with disabilities on an equal basis with others.

Article 11—Situations of risk and humanitarian emergencies

States Parties shall take, in accordance with their obligations under international law, including international humanitarian law and international human rights law, all necessary measures to ensure the protection and safety of persons with disabilities in situations of risk, including situations of armed conflict, humanitarian emergencies and the occurrence of natural disasters.

ARTICLE 12—EQUAL RECOGNITION BEFORE THE LAW

1. States Parties reaffirm that persons with disabilities have the right to recognition everywhere as persons before the law.

2. States Parties shall recognize that persons with disabilities enjoy legal capacity on an equal basis with others in all aspects of life.

3. States Parties shall take appropriate measures to provide access by persons with disabilities to the support they may require in exercising their legal capacity.

4. States Parties shall ensure that all measures that relate to the exercise of legal capacity provide for appropriate and effective safeguards to prevent abuse in accordance with international human rights law. Such safeguards shall ensure that measures relating to the exercise of legal capacity respect the rights, will and preferences of the person, are free of conflict of interest and undue influence, are proportional and tailored to the person's circumstances, apply for the shortest time possible and are subject to regular review by a competent, independent and impartial authority or judicial body. The safeguards shall be proportional to the degree to which such measures affect the person's rights and interests.

5. Subject to the provisions of this article, States Parties shall take all appropriate and effective measures to ensure the equal right of persons with disabilities to own or inherit property, to control their own financial affairs and to have equal access to bank loans, mortgages and other forms of financial credit, and shall ensure that persons with disabilities are not arbitrarily deprived of their property.

ARTICLE 13—ACCESS TO JUSTICE

1. States Parties shall ensure effective access to justice for persons with disabilities on an equal basis with others, including through the provision of procedural and age-appropriate accommodations, in order to facilitate their effective role as direct and indirect participants, including as witnesses, in all legal proceedings, including at investigative and other preliminary stages.

2. In order to help to ensure effective access to justice for persons with disabilities, States Parties shall promote appropriate training for those working in the field of administration of justice, including police and prison staff.

ARTICLE 14—LIBERTY AND SECURITY OF PERSON

1. States Parties shall ensure that persons with disabilities, on an equal basis with others:

(a) Enjoy the right to liberty and security of person;

(b) Are not deprived of their liberty unlawfully or arbitrarily, and that any deprivation of liberty is in conformity with the law, and that the existence of a disability shall in no case justify a deprivation of liberty.

2. States Parties shall ensure that if persons with disabilities are deprived of their liberty through any process, they are, on an equal basis with others,

entitled to guarantees in accordance with international human rights law and shall be treated in compliance with the objectives and principles of the present Convention, including by provision of reasonable accommodation.

Article 15—Freedom from torture or cruel, inhuman or degrading treatment or punishment

1. No one shall be subjected to torture or to cruel, inhuman or degrading treatment or punishment. In particular, no one shall be subjected without his or her free consent to medical or scientific experimentation.

2. States Parties shall take all effective legislative, administrative, judicial or other measures to prevent persons with disabilities, on an equal basis with others, from being subjected to torture or cruel, inhuman or degrading treatment or punishment.

Article 16—Freedom from exploitation, violence and abuse

1. States Parties shall take all appropriate legislative, administrative, social, educational and other measures to protect persons with disabilities, both within and outside the home, from all forms of exploitation, violence and abuse, including their gender-based aspects.

2. States Parties shall also take all appropriate measures to prevent all forms of exploitation, violence and abuse by ensuring, inter alia, appropriate forms of gender- and age-sensitive assistance and support for persons with disabilities and their families and caregivers, including through the provision of information and education on how to avoid, recognize and report instances of exploitation, violence and abuse. States Parties shall ensure that protection services are age-, gender- and disability-sensitive.

3. In order to prevent the occurrence of all forms of exploitation, violence and abuse, States Parties shall ensure that all facilities and programmes designed to serve persons with disabilities are effectively monitored by independent authorities.

4. States Parties shall take all appropriate measures to promote the physical, cognitive and psychological recovery, rehabilitation and social reintegration of persons with disabilities who become victims of any form of exploitation, violence or abuse, including through the provision of protection services. Such recovery and reintegration shall take place in an environment that fosters the health, welfare, self-respect, dignity and autonomy of the person and takes into account gender- and age-specific needs.

5. States Parties shall put in place effective legislation and policies, including women- and child-focused legislation and policies, to ensure that instances of exploitation, violence and abuse against persons with disabilities are identified, investigated and, where appropriate, prosecuted.

ARTICLE 17—PROTECTING THE INTEGRITY OF THE PERSON

Every person with disabilities has a right to respect for his or her physical and mental integrity on an equal basis with others.

ARTICLE 18—LIBERTY OF MOVEMENT AND NATIONALITY

1. States Parties shall recognize the rights of persons with disabilities to liberty of movement, to freedom to choose their residence and to a nationality, on an equal basis with others, including by ensuring that persons with disabilities:

(a) Have the right to acquire and change a nationality and are not deprived of their nationality arbitrarily or on the basis of disability;

(b) Are not deprived, on the basis of disability, of their ability to obtain, possess and utilize documentation of their nationality or other documentation of identification, or to utilize relevant processes such as immigration proceedings, that may be needed to facilitate exercise of the right to liberty of movement;

(c) Are free to leave any country, including their own;

(d) Are not deprived, arbitrarily or on the basis of disability, of the right to enter their own country.

2. Children with disabilities shall be registered immediately after birth and shall have the right from birth to a name, the right to acquire a nationality and, as far as possible, the right to know and be cared for by their parents.

ARTICLE 19—LIVING INDEPENDENTLY AND BEING INCLUDED IN THE COMMUNITY

States Parties to the present Convention recognize the equal right of all persons with disabilities to live in the community, with choices equal to others, and shall take effective and appropriate measures to facilitate full enjoyment by persons with disabilities of this right and their full inclusion and participation in the community, including by ensuring that:

(a) Persons with disabilities have the opportunity to choose their place of residence and where and with whom they live on an equal basis with others and are not obliged to live in a particular living arrangement;

(b) Persons with disabilities have access to a range of in-home, residential and other community support services, including personal assistance necessary to support living and inclusion in the community, and to prevent isolation or segregation from the community;

(c) Community services and facilities for the general population are available on an equal basis to persons with disabilities and are responsive to their needs.

ARTICLE 20—PERSONAL MOBILITY

States Parties shall take effective measures to ensure personal mobility with the greatest possible independence for persons with disabilities, including by:

(a) Facilitating the personal mobility of persons with disabilities in the manner and at the time of their choice, and at affordable cost;

(b) Facilitating access by persons with disabilities to quality mobility aids, devices, assistive technologies and forms of live assistance and intermediaries, including by making them available at affordable cost;

(c) Providing training in mobility skills to persons with disabilities and to specialist staff working with persons with disabilities;

(d) Encouraging entities that produce mobility aids, devices and assistive technologies to take into account all aspects of mobility for persons with disabilities.

ARTICLE 21—FREEDOM OF EXPRESSION AND OPINION, AND ACCESS TO INFORMATION

States Parties shall take all appropriate measures to ensure that persons with disabilities can exercise the right to freedom of expression and opinion, including the freedom to seek, receive and impart information and ideas on an equal basis with others and through all forms of communication of their choice, as defined in article 2 of the present Convention, including by:

(a) Providing information intended for the general public to persons with disabilities in accessible formats and technologies appropriate to different kinds of disabilities in a timely manner and without additional cost;

(b) Accepting and facilitating the use of sign languages, Braille, augmentative and alternative communication, and all other accessible means, modes and formats of communication of their choice by persons with disabilities in official interactions;

(c) Urging private entities that provide services to the general public, including through the Internet, to provide information and services in accessible and usable formats for persons with disabilities;

(d) Encouraging the mass media, including providers of information through the Internet, to make their services accessible to persons with disabilities;

(e) Recognizing and promoting the use of sign languages.

ARTICLE 22—RESPECT FOR PRIVACY

1. No person with disabilities, regardless of place of residence or living arrangements, shall be subjected to arbitrary or unlawful interference with his or her privacy, family, home or correspondence or other types of communication or to unlawful attacks on his or her honour and reputation. Persons

with disabilities have the right to the protection of the law against such interference or attacks.

2. States Parties shall protect the privacy of personal, health and rehabilitation information of persons with disabilities on an equal basis with others.

ARTICLE 23—RESPECT FOR HOME AND THE FAMILY

1. States Parties shall take effective and appropriate measures to eliminate discrimination against persons with disabilities in all matters relating to marriage, family, parenthood and relationships, on an equal basis with others, so as to ensure that:

(a) The right of all persons with disabilities who are of marriageable age to marry and to found a family on the basis of free and full consent of the intending spouses is recognized;

(b) The rights of persons with disabilities to decide freely and responsibly on the number and spacing of their children and to have access to age-appropriate information, reproductive and family planning education are recognized, and the means necessary to enable them to exercise these rights are provided;

(c) Persons with disabilities, including children, retain their fertility on an equal basis with others.

2. States Parties shall ensure the rights and responsibilities of persons with disabilities, with regard to guardianship, wardship, trusteeship, adoption of children or similar institutions, where these concepts exist in national legislation; in all cases the best interests of the child shall be paramount. States Parties shall render appropriate assistance to persons with disabilities in the performance of their child-rearing responsibilities.

3. States Parties shall ensure that children with disabilities have equal rights with respect to family life. With a view to realizing these rights, and to prevent concealment, abandonment, neglect and segregation of children with disabilities, States Parties shall undertake to provide early and comprehensive information, services and support to children with disabilities and their families.

4. States Parties shall ensure that a child shall not be separated from his or her parents against their will, except when competent authorities subject to judicial review determine, in accordance with applicable law and procedures, that such separation is necessary for the best interests of the child. In no case shall a child be separated from parents on the basis of a disability of either the child or one or both of the parents.

5. States Parties shall, where the immediate family is unable to care for a child with disabilities, undertake every effort to provide alternative care within the wider family, and failing that, within the community in a family setting.

Article 24—Education

1. States Parties recognize the right of persons with disabilities to education. With a view to realizing this right without discrimination and on the basis of equal opportunity, States Parties shall ensure an inclusive education system at all levels and lifelong learning directed to:

(a) The full development of human potential and sense of dignity and self-worth, and the strengthening of respect for human rights, fundamental freedoms and human diversity;

(b) The development by persons with disabilities of their personality, talents and creativity, as well as their mental and physical abilities, to their fullest potential;

(c) Enabling persons with disabilities to participate effectively in a free society.

2. In realizing this right, States Parties shall ensure that:

(a) Persons with disabilities are not excluded from the general education system on the basis of disability, and that children with disabilities are not excluded from free and compulsory primary education, or from secondary education, on the basis of disability;

(b) Persons with disabilities can access an inclusive, quality and free primary education and secondary education on an equal basis with others in the communities in which they live;

(c) Reasonable accommodation of the individual's requirements is provided;

(d) Persons with disabilities receive the support required, within the general education system, to facilitate their effective education;

(e) Effective individualized support measures are provided in environments that maximize academic and social development, consistent with the goal of full inclusion.

3. States Parties shall enable persons with disabilities to learn life and social development skills to facilitate their full and equal participation in education and as members of the community. To this end, States Parties shall take appropriate measures, including:

(a) Facilitating the learning of Braille, alternative script, augmentative and alternative modes, means and formats of communication and orientation and mobility skills, and facilitating peer support and mentoring;

(b) Facilitating the learning of sign language and the promotion of the linguistic identity of the deaf community;

(c) Ensuring that the education of persons, and in particular children, who are blind, deaf or deafblind, is delivered in the most appropriate languages and modes and means of communication for the individual, and in environments which maximize academic and social development.

4. In order to help ensure the realization of this right, States Parties shall take appropriate measures to employ teachers, including teachers with

disabilities, who are qualified in sign language and/or Braille, and to train professionals and staff who work at all levels of education. Such training shall incorporate disability awareness and the use of appropriate augmentative and alternative modes, means and formats of communication, educational techniques and materials to support persons with disabilities.

5. States Parties shall ensure that persons with disabilities are able to access general tertiary education, vocational training, adult education and lifelong learning without discrimination and on an equal basis with others. To this end, States Parties shall ensure that reasonable accommodation is provided to persons with disabilities.

ARTICLE 25—HEALTH

States Parties recognize that persons with disabilities have the right to the enjoyment of the highest attainable standard of health without discrimination on the basis of disability. States Parties shall take all appropriate measures to ensure access for persons with disabilities to health services that are gender-sensitive, including health-related rehabilitation. In particular, States Parties shall:

(a) Provide persons with disabilities with the same range, quality and standard of free or affordable health care and programmes as provided to other persons, including in the area of sexual and reproductive health and population-based public health programmes;

(b) Provide those health services needed by persons with disabilities specifically because of their disabilities, including early identification and intervention as appropriate, and services designed to minimize and prevent further disabilities, including among children and older persons;

(c) Provide these health services as close as possible to people's own communities, including in rural areas;

(d) Require health professionals to provide care of the same quality to persons with disabilities as to others, including on the basis of free and informed consent by, inter alia, raising awareness of the human rights, dignity, autonomy and needs of persons with disabilities through training and the promulgation of ethical standards for public and private health care;

(e) Prohibit discrimination against persons with disabilities in the provision of health insurance, and life insurance where such insurance is permitted by national law, which shall be provided in a fair and reasonable manner;

(f) Prevent discriminatory denial of health care or health services or food and fluids on the basis of disability.

ARTICLE 26—HABILITATION AND REHABILITATION

1. States Parties shall take effective and appropriate measures, including through peer support, to enable persons with disabilities to attain and maintain maximum independence, full physical, mental, social and vocational

ability, and full inclusion and participation in all aspects of life. To that end, States Parties shall organize, strengthen and extend comprehensive habilitation and rehabilitation services and programmes, particularly in the areas of health, employment, education and social services, in such a way that these services and programmes:

(a) Begin at the earliest possible stage, and are based on the multidisciplinary assessment of individual needs and strengths;

(b) Support participation and inclusion in the community and all aspects of society, are voluntary, and are available to persons with disabilities as close as possible to their own communities, including in rural areas.

2. States Parties shall promote the development of initial and continuing training for professionals and staff working in habilitation and rehabilitation services.

3. States Parties shall promote the availability, knowledge and use of assistive devices and technologies, designed for persons with disabilities, as they relate to habilitation and rehabilitation.

ARTICLE 27—WORK AND EMPLOYMENT

1. States Parties recognize the right of persons with disabilities to work, on an equal basis with others; this includes the right to the opportunity to gain a living by work freely chosen or accepted in a labour market and work environment that is open, inclusive and accessible to persons with disabilities. States Parties shall safeguard and promote the realization of the right to work, including for those who acquire a disability during the course of employment, by taking appropriate steps, including through legislation, to, inter alia:

(a) Prohibit discrimination on the basis of disability with regard to all matters concerning all forms of employment, including conditions of recruitment, hiring and employment, continuance of employment, career advancement and safe and healthy working conditions;

(b) Protect the rights of persons with disabilities, on an equal basis with others, to just and favourable conditions of work, including equal opportunities and equal remuneration for work of equal value, safe and healthy working conditions, including protection from harassment, and the redress of grievances;

(c) Ensure that persons with disabilities are able to exercise their labour and trade union rights on an equal basis with others;

(d) Enable persons with disabilities to have effective access to general technical and vocational guidance programmes, placement services and vocational and continuing training;

(e) Promote employment opportunities and career advancement for persons with disabilities in the labour market, as well as assistance in finding, obtaining, maintaining and returning to employment;

(f) Promote opportunities for self-employment, entrepreneurship, the development of cooperatives and starting one's own business;

(g) Employ persons with disabilities in the public sector;

(h) Promote the employment of persons with disabilities in the private sector through appropriate policies and measures, which may include affirmative action programmes, incentives and other measures;

(i) Ensure that reasonable accommodation is provided to persons with disabilities in the workplace;

(j) Promote the acquisition by persons with disabilities of work experience in the open labour market;

(k) Promote vocational and professional rehabilitation, job retention and return-to-work programmes for persons with disabilities.

2. States Parties shall ensure that persons with disabilities are not held in slavery or in servitude, and are protected, on an equal basis with others, from forced or compulsory labour.

Article 28—Adequate standard of living and social protection

1. States Parties recognize the right of persons with disabilities to an adequate standard of living for themselves and their families, including adequate food, clothing and housing, and to the continuous improvement of living conditions, and shall take appropriate steps to safeguard and promote the realization of this right without discrimination on the basis of disability.

2. States Parties recognize the right of persons with disabilities to social protection and to the enjoyment of that right without discrimination on the basis of disability, and shall take appropriate steps to safeguard and promote the realization of this right, including measures:

(a) To ensure equal access by persons with disabilities to clean water services, and to ensure access to appropriate and affordable services, devices and other assistance for disability-related needs;

(b) To ensure access by persons with disabilities, in particular women and girls with disabilities and older persons with disabilities, to social protection programmes and poverty reduction programmes;

(c) To ensure access by persons with disabilities and their families living in situations of poverty to assistance from the State with disability-related expenses, including adequate training, counselling, financial assistance and respite care;

(d) To ensure access by persons with disabilities to public housing programmes;

(e) To ensure equal access by persons with disabilities to retirement benefits and programmes.

Article 29—Participation in political and public life

States Parties shall guarantee to persons with disabilities political rights and the opportunity to enjoy them on an equal basis with others, and shall undertake:

(a) To ensure that persons with disabilities can effectively and fully participate in political and public life on an equal basis with others, directly or through freely chosen representatives, including the right and opportunity for persons with disabilities to vote and be elected, inter alia, by:

(i) Ensuring that voting procedures, facilities and materials are appropriate, accessible and easy to understand and use;

(ii) Protecting the right of persons with disabilities to vote by secret ballot in elections and public referendums without intimidation, and to stand for elections, to effectively hold office and perform all public functions at all levels of government, facilitating the use of assistive and new technologies where appropriate;

(iii) Guaranteeing the free expression of the will of persons with disabilities as electors and to this end, where necessary, at their request, allowing assistance in voting by a person of their own choice;

(b) To promote actively an environment in which persons with disabilities can effectively and fully participate in the conduct of public affairs, without discrimination and on an equal basis with others, and encourage their participation in public affairs, including:

(i) Participation in non-governmental organizations and associations concerned with the public and political life of the country, and in the activities and administration of political parties;

(ii) Forming and joining organizations of persons with disabilities to represent persons with disabilities at international, national, regional and local levels.

Article 30—Participation in cultural life, recreation, leisure and sport

1. States Parties recognize the right of persons with disabilities to take part on an equal basis with others in cultural life, and shall take all appropriate measures to ensure that persons with disabilities:

(a) Enjoy access to cultural materials in accessible formats;

(b) Enjoy access to television programmes, films, theatre and other cultural activities, in accessible formats;

(c) Enjoy access to places for cultural performances or services, such as the-atres, museums, cinemas, libraries and tourism services, and, as far as pos-sible, enjoy access to monuments and sites of national cultural importance.

2. States Parties shall take appropriate measures to enable persons with dis-abilities to have the opportunity to develop and utilize their creative, artistic and intellectual potential, not only for their own benefit, but also for the enrichment of society.

3. States Parties shall take all appropriate steps, in accordance with interna-tional law, to ensure that laws protecting intellectual property rights do not constitute an unreasonable or discriminatory barrier to access by persons with disabilities to cultural materials.

4. Persons with disabilities shall be entitled, on an equal basis with others, to recognition and support of their specific cultural and linguistic identity, including sign languages and deaf culture.

5. With a view to enabling persons with disabilities to participate on an equal basis with others in recreational, leisure and sporting activities, States Parties shall take appropriate measures:

(a) To encourage and promote the participation, to the fullest extent possible, of persons with disabilities in mainstream sporting activities at all levels;

(b) To ensure that persons with disabilities have an opportunity to organize, develop and participate in disability-specific sporting and recreational activi-ties and, to this end, encourage the provision, on an equal basis with others, of appropriate instruction, training and resources;

(c) To ensure that persons with disabilities have access to sporting, recre-ational and tourism venues;

(d) To ensure that children with disabilities have equal access with other children to participation in play, recreation and leisure and sporting activities, including those activities in the school system;

(e) To ensure that persons with disabilities have access to services from those involved in the organization of recreational, tourism, leisure and sporting activities.

ARTICLE 31—STATISTICS AND DATA COLLECTION

1. States Parties undertake to collect appropriate information, including statistical and research data, to enable them to formulate and implement policies to give effect to the present Convention. The process of collecting and maintaining this information shall:

(a) Comply with legally established safeguards, including legislation on data protection, to ensure confidentiality and respect for the privacy of persons with disabilities;

(b) Comply with internationally accepted norms to protect human rights and fundamental freedoms and ethical principles in the collection and use of statistics.

2. The information collected in accordance with this article shall be disaggregated, as appropriate, and used to help assess the implementation of States Parties' obligations under the present Convention and to identify and address the barriers faced by persons with disabilities in exercising their rights.

3. States Parties shall assume responsibility for the dissemination of these statistics and ensure their accessibility to persons with disabilities and others.

ARTICLE 32—INTERNATIONAL COOPERATION

1. States Parties recognize the importance of international cooperation and its promotion, in support of national efforts for the realization of the purpose and objectives of the present Convention, and will undertake appropriate and effective measures in this regard, between and among States and, as appropriate, in partnership with relevant international and regional organizations and civil society, in particular organizations of persons with disabilities. Such measures could include, inter alia:

(a) Ensuring that international cooperation, including international development programmes, is inclusive of and accessible to persons with disabilities;

(b) Facilitating and supporting capacity-building, including through the exchange and sharing of information, experiences, training programmes and best practices;

(c) Facilitating cooperation in research and access to scientific and technical knowledge;

(d) Providing, as appropriate, technical and economic assistance, including by facilitating access to and sharing of accessible and assistive technologies, and through the transfer of technologies.

2. The provisions of this article are without prejudice to the obligations of each State Party to fulfil its obligations under the present Convention.

ARTICLE 33—NATIONAL IMPLEMENTATION AND MONITORING

1. States Parties, in accordance with their system of organization, shall designate one or more focal points within government for matters relating to the implementation of the present Convention, and shall give due consideration to the establishment or designation of a coordination mechanism within government to facilitate related action in different sectors and at different levels.

2. States Parties shall, in accordance with their legal and administrative systems, maintain, strengthen, designate or establish within the State Party, a framework, including one or more independent mechanisms, as appropriate, to promote, protect and monitor implementation of the present Convention.

When designating or establishing such a mechanism, States Parties shall take into account the principles relating to the status and functioning of national institutions for protection and promotion of human rights.

3. Civil society, in particular persons with disabilities and their representative organizations, shall be involved and participate fully in the monitoring process.

ARTICLE 34—COMMITTEE ON THE RIGHTS OF PERSONS WITH DISABILITIES

1. There shall be established a Committee on the Rights of Persons with Disabilities (hereafter referred to as "the Committee"), which shall carry out the functions hereinafter provided.

2. The Committee shall consist, at the time of entry into force of the present Convention, of twelve experts. After an additional sixty ratifications or accessions to the Convention, the membership of the Committee shall increase by six members, attaining a maximum number of eighteen members.

3. The members of the Committee shall serve in their personal capacity and shall be of high moral standing and recognized competence and experience in the field covered by the present Convention. When nominating their candidates, States Parties are invited to give due consideration to the provision set out in article 4, paragraph 3, of the present Convention.

4. The members of the Committee shall be elected by States Parties, consideration being given to equitable geographical distribution, representation of the different forms of civilization and of the principal legal systems, balanced gender representation and participation of experts with disabilities.

5. The members of the Committee shall be elected by secret ballot from a list of persons nominated by the States Parties from among their nationals at meetings of the Conference of States Parties. At those meetings, for which two thirds of States Parties shall constitute a quorum, the persons elected to the Committee shall be those who obtain the largest number of votes and an absolute majority of the votes of the representatives of States Parties present and voting.

6. The initial election shall be held no later than six months after the date of entry into force of the present Convention. At least four months before the date of each election, the Secretary-General of the United Nations shall address a letter to the States Parties inviting them to submit the nominations within two months. The Secretary-General shall subsequently prepare a list in alphabetical order of all persons thus nominated, indicating the State Parties which have nominated them, and shall submit it to the States Parties to the present Convention.

7. The members of the Committee shall be elected for a term of four years. They shall be eligible for re-election once. However, the term of six of the

members elected at the first election shall expire at the end of two years; immediately after the first election, the names of these six members shall be chosen by lot by the chairperson of the meeting referred to in paragraph 5 of this article.

8. The election of the six additional members of the Committee shall be held on the occasion of regular elections, in accordance with the relevant provisions of this article.

9. If a member of the Committee dies or resigns or declares that for any other cause she or he can no longer perform her or his duties, the State Party which nominated the member shall appoint another expert possessing the qualifications and meeting the requirements set out in the relevant provisions of this article, to serve for the remainder of the term.

10. The Committee shall establish its own rules of procedure.

11. The Secretary-General of the United Nations shall provide the necessary staff and facilities for the effective performance of the functions of the Committee under the present Convention, and shall convene its initial meeting.

12. With the approval of the General Assembly of the United Nations, the members of the Committee established under the present Convention shall receive emoluments from United Nations resources on such terms and conditions as the Assembly may decide, having regard to the importance of the Committee's responsibilities.

13. The members of the Committee shall be entitled to the facilities, privileges and immunities of experts on mission for the United Nations as laid down in the relevant sections of the Convention on the Privileges and Immunities of the United Nations.

Article 35—Reports by States Parties

1. Each State Party shall submit to the Committee, through the Secretary-General of the United Nations, a comprehensive report on measures taken to give effect to its obligations under the present Convention and on the progress made in that regard, within two years after the entry into force of the present Convention for the State Party concerned.

2. Thereafter, States Parties shall submit subsequent reports at least every four years and further whenever the Committee so requests.

3. The Committee shall decide any guidelines applicable to the content of the reports.

4. A State Party which has submitted a comprehensive initial report to the Committee need not, in its subsequent reports, repeat information previously provided. When preparing reports to the Committee, States Parties are invited to consider doing so in an open and transparent process and to give due consideration to the provision set out in article 4.3 of the present Convention.

5. Reports may indicate factors and difficulties affecting the degree of fulfilment of obligations under the present Convention.

ARTICLE 36—CONSIDERATION OF REPORTS

1. Each report shall be considered by the Committee, which shall make such suggestions and general recommendations on the report as it may consider appropriate and shall forward these to the State Party concerned. The State Party may respond with any information it chooses to the Committee. The Committee may request further information from States Parties relevant to the implementation of the present Convention.

2. If a State Party is significantly overdue in the submission of a report, the Committee may notify the State Party concerned of the need to examine the implementation of the present Convention in that State Party, on the basis of reliable information available to the Committee, if the relevant report is not submitted within three months following the notification. The Committee shall invite the State Party concerned to participate in such examination. Should the State Party respond by submitting the relevant report, the provisions of paragraph 1 of this article will apply.

3. The Secretary-General of the United Nations shall make available the reports to all States Parties.

4. States Parties shall make their reports widely available to the public in their own countries and facilitate access to the suggestions and general recommendations relating to these reports.

5. The Committee shall transmit, as it may consider appropriate, to the specialized agencies, funds and programmes of the United Nations, and other competent bodies, reports from States Parties in order to address a request or indication of a need for technical advice or assistance contained therein, along with the Committee's observations and recommendations, if any, on these requests or indications.

ARTICLE 37—COOPERATION BETWEEN STATES PARTIES AND THE COMMITTEE

1. Each State Party shall cooperate with the Committee and assist its members in the fulfilment of their mandate.

2. In its relationship with States Parties, the Committee shall give due consideration to ways and means of enhancing national capacities for the implementation of the present Convention, including through international cooperation.

ARTICLE 38—RELATIONSHIP OF THE COMMITTEE WITH OTHER BODIES

In order to foster the effective implementation of the present Convention and to encourage international cooperation in the field covered by the present Convention:

(a) The specialized agencies and other United Nations organs shall be entitled to be represented at the consideration of the implementation of such provisions of the present Convention as fall within the scope of their mandate. The Committee may invite the specialized agencies and other competent bodies as it may consider appropriate to provide expert advice on the implementation of the Convention in areas falling within the scope of their respective mandates. The Committee may invite specialized agencies and other United Nations organs to submit reports on the implementation of the Convention in areas falling within the scope of their activities;

(b) The Committee, as it discharges its mandate, shall consult, as appropriate, other relevant bodies instituted by international human rights treaties, with a view to ensuring the consistency of their respective reporting guidelines, suggestions and general recommendations, and avoiding duplication and overlap in the performance of their functions.

ARTICLE 39—REPORT OF THE COMMITTEE

The Committee shall report every two years to the General Assembly and to the Economic and Social Council on its activities, and may make suggestions and general recommendations based on the examination of reports and information received from the States Parties. Such suggestions and general recommendations shall be included in the report of the Committee together with comments, if any, from States Parties.

ARTICLE 40—CONFERENCE OF STATES PARTIES

1. The States Parties shall meet regularly in a Conference of States Parties in order to consider any matter with regard to the implementation of the present Convention.

2. No later than six months after the entry into force of the present Convention, the Conference of States Parties shall be convened by the Secretary-General of the United Nations. The subsequent meetings shall be convened by the Secretary-General biennially or upon the decision of the Conference of States Parties.

ARTICLE 41—DEPOSITARY

The Secretary-General of the United Nations shall be the depositary of the present Convention.

ARTICLE 42—SIGNATURE

The present Convention shall be open for signature by all States and by regional integration organizations at United Nations Headquarters in New York as of 30 March 2007.

ARTICLE 43—CONSENT TO BE BOUND

The present Convention shall be subject to ratification by signatory States and to formal confirmation by signatory regional integration organizations.

It shall be open for accession by any State or regional integration organization which has not signed the Convention.

ARTICLE 44—REGIONAL INTEGRATION ORGANIZATIONS

1."Regional integration organization" shall mean an organization constituted by sovereign States of a given region, to which its member States have transferred competence in respect of matters governed by the present Convention. Such organizations shall declare, in their instruments of formal confirmation or accession, the extent of their competence with respect to matters governed by the present Convention. Subsequently, they shall inform the depositary of any substantial modification in the extent of their competence.

2. References to "States Parties" in the present Convention shall apply to such organizations within the limits of their competence.

3. For the purposes of article 45, paragraph 1, and article 47, paragraphs 2 and 3, of the present Convention, any instrument deposited by a regional integration organization shall not be counted.

4. Regional integration organizations, in matters within their competence, may exercise their right to vote in the Conference of States Parties, with a number of votes equal to the number of their member States that are Parties to the present Convention. Such an organization shall not exercise its right to vote if any of its member States exercises its right, and vice versa.

ARTICLE 45—ENTRY INTO FORCE

1. The present Convention shall enter into force on the thirtieth day after the deposit of the twentieth instrument of ratification or accession.

2. For each State or regional integration organization ratifying, formally confirming or acceding to the present Convention after the deposit of the twentieth such instrument, the Convention shall enter into force on the thirtieth day after the deposit of its own such instrument.

ARTICLE 46—RESERVATIONS

1. Reservations incompatible with the object and purpose of the present Convention shall not be permitted.

2. Reservations may be withdrawn at any time.

ARTICLE 47—AMENDMENTS

1. Any State Party may propose an amendment to the present Convention and submit it to the Secretary-General of the United Nations. The Secretary-General shall communicate any proposed amendments to States Parties, with a request to be notified whether they favour a conference of States Parties for the purpose of considering and deciding upon the proposals. In the event that, within four months from the date of such communication, at least one third of the States Parties favour such a conference, the

Secretary-General shall convene the conference under the auspices of the United Nations. Any amendment adopted by a majority of two thirds of the States Parties present and voting shall be submitted by the Secretary-General to the General Assembly of the United Nations for approval and thereafter to all States Parties for acceptance.

2. An amendment adopted and approved in accordance with paragraph 1 of this article shall enter into force on the thirtieth day after the number of instruments of acceptance deposited reaches two thirds of the number of States Parties at the date of adoption of the amendment. Thereafter, the amendment shall enter into force for any State Party on the thirtieth day following the deposit of its own instrument of acceptance. An amendment shall be binding only on those States Parties which have accepted it.

3. If so decided by the Conference of States Parties by consensus, an amendment adopted and approved in accordance with paragraph 1 of this article which relates exclusively to articles 34, 38, 39 and 40 shall enter into force for all States Parties on the thirtieth day after the number of instruments of acceptance deposited reaches two thirds of the number of States Parties at the date of adoption of the amendment.

ARTICLE 48—DENUNCIATION

A State Party may denounce the present Convention by written notification to the Secretary-General of the United Nations. The denunciation shall become effective one year after the date of receipt of the notification by the Secretary-General.

ARTICLE 49—ACCESSIBLE FORMAT

The text of the present Convention shall be made available in accessible formats.

ARTICLE 50—AUTHENTIC TEXTS

The Arabic, Chinese, English, French, Russian and Spanish texts of the present Convention shall be equally authentic.

IN WITNESS THEREOF the undersigned plenipotentiaries, being duly authorized thereto by their respective Governments, have signed the present Convention.

Source: Annex 1, Final report of the Ad Hoc Committee on a Comprehensive and Integral International Convention on the Protection and Promotion of the Rights and Dignity of Persons with Disabilities [A/61/611 - PDF, 117KB]